1/06

ALSO BY LEAH HAGER COHEN

Nonfiction

Train Go Sorry: Inside a Deaf World

Glass, Paper, Beans:
Revelations on the Nature and Value of Ordinary Things

The Stuff of Dreams:
Behind the Scenes of an American Community Theater

Fiction

Heat Lightning

Heart, You Bully, You Punk

RANDOM HOUSE   NEW YORK

WITHOUT APOLOGY

GIRLS, WOMEN, AND THE DESIRE TO FIGHT

LEAH HAGER COHEN

LIBRARY OF CONGRESS CATALOGING-IN-PUBLICATION DATA

Cohen, Leah Hager.
Without apology: girls, women, and the desire to fight / Leah Hager Cohen.
p.   cm.
ISBN 1-4000-6157-1
1. Teenage girls—United States.   2. Aggressiveness in adolescence—United States.
3. Boxing—United States.   4. Women boxers—United States.   I. Title.
HQ798.C5644 2005
302.5'4'083520973—dc22   2004050314

Printed in the United States of America on acid-free paper

Random House website address: www.atrandom.com

987654321

First Edition

Book design by Jo Anne Metsch

To Lori Lyn Taylor

and to the strong memory of Elizabeth Bradspies Gallant,
1946–1990

CONTENTS

AUTHOR'S NOTE

For all of the young boxers in this book and their family members, I have used pseudonyms—although they would have preferred to appear in these pages under their real names. After all that we risked together, I decided to err on the side of protectiveness. Vinny Busa is also a pseudonym. No other details have been changed.

In the fall of 2001 a photographer friend invited me to accompany her to a boxing club where she'd heard a group of girls was training with a female coach. The girls were young adolescents who lived in public housing, and the gym was in the tougher part of Somerville, a working-class city across the river from Boston. She was interested in taking some pictures and suggested I might like to take some notes. More because I admired her work than because I was drawn to the subject, I agreed to meet her there. I wound up spending much of the next year with the four girl boxers, ages ten to fifteen, and their trainer. What follows is the story of our time together, in and around the boxing gym.

But this is not strictly a book about boxing. Any girl who boxes challenges, wittingly or not, the idea of what it means to be a girl in our culture. Through the prism of what she does with her fists, she sheds a fiercely contrarian light on our most fundamental notions about femininity and power and appetite and shame and desire. I didn't fully grasp this when I began reporting. And I didn't fully grasp it through the stories of the girls and their trainer. Instead, the more time I spent around their world, the more I craved admittance to it.

This was strange, because I had never liked boxing. When I thought about it at all, it had always been with a light, barely considered disgust. As a child I encountered boxing very rarely, and then by accident: a flash of torso and trunks on television as I passed through a room, a glimpse of bare, clenched bodies awkwardly circling. The grotesque intimacy of the boxers' embrace, the purity of their intention to harm, all in the absence of reason or feeling: These things rendered the sport unfathomable and the boxers unreachable. I never looked longer than a few seconds before hastily exiting, leaving the room to the male viewers, who were supposed to want to watch. Such appetites, I understood, lay beyond me.

Aggression itself was a stranger to me. I can't remember any time I claimed it for myself or claimed even to be familiar with it. I don't mean I was thorough in my *disavowal* of aggression; I mean I really believed aggression was absent in me. On Valentine's Day, when I was nine, my parents, thinking it might do me good, gave me a cap gun. I fired it once, blocking both ears, one with shoulder, one with palm, before giving it away to my little brother.

I remember it still, the gun—its white plastic butt with an enormous "ruby" glued to its side, its silver-painted hammer and trigger, which were hard to pull and threatened to pinch, and the tight roll of red paper with its peppery dots, which made such a sudden noise and smelled of real smoke. Didn't we all know I would give it away? Weren't we all secretly reassured when I did?

When, so many years later, I found myself drawn toward the world of these girl boxers, I was astonished. They were not. They made room for me in their circle, their ring, and what I found there changed me, changed how I understood myself as a woman in the world, and how I understood girls' passages into womanhood. And so what follows is also that story: how, through boxing, I became more whole.

It's partly a mystery story, since the idea that something as brutal as boxing could contain the possibility of healing presents a puzzle. But it is first and foremost a story of tangibles, begun not in intellectual musings but in insistent cues from the body: heart rate, muscle tension, chemical shifts. It springs from twin impulses, aggression and desire, which are intertwined at their root. The etymology of aggression is usually given as the Latin *aggredi*, which means to attack, or to step toward, but the more basic root, through the Sanskrit *griddhra*, greedy, is the Aryan *gardh*, to desire. Aggression, in its marrow, is about desire.

This discovery, that aggression and desire are inseparable, turns out to be the first clue. For they are forbidden to girls in equal measure, and they are also in equal measure requisite for life.

PART 1

SPEED BAG

My first impulse was to dismiss her. Whatever my idea of how a boxing coach should look, it was nothing like this woman standing above me on the ring apron, elbows on the ropes, calling out to her boxer in the ring. She wore a pink tank top, red shorts, white socks, and black boxing shoes, and her hair, wavy and fine and light brown, was held back with a pink scrunchie, and her limbs looked tender and ungainly and very white. She was little, Raphaëlla Johnson, five-four and not much over a hundred pounds. But it wasn't just her physical size, it was her voice, too, a girl's voice, indelibly gentle and light.

"You're dropping your hands!" she yelled. "Jab! Keep firing the jab! *Work!*"

In the ring, a teenage Latina girl was sparring with a white man in his thirties. The girl wore red headgear and gloves, and a thick white mouth-guard that made it look as if she couldn't suppress a smile. Her tank top said DON'T EVEN DON'T EVEN DON'T EVEN DON'T EVEN DON'T EVEN DON'T EVEN THINK ABOUT IT. Her sparring partner, broadly muscular, wore black headgear and gloves. His bare torso was a gallery of sweat-glazed tattoos, the most magnificent of which—an American flag in the shape of the United States, with portraits of a woman and three children set inside the borders—rippled across his trapezius muscles and caught the light as he danced. Whenever the girl seemed to tire, the man would yell at her, provoke her, hit her in the face.

"C'mon, *move!*" yelled the coach. "Thirty seconds!" Clustered around her on the ring apron, variously standing or kneeling, were three other girls and a woman, all drinking in the spectacle with unchecked merriment, erupting in bursts of excited laughter, hoots of encouragement, and sharp exhortations that echoed those of the coach. Their obvious pleasure in the event seemed to me incongruous and complicated. But no more so than the sheer physical presence of the coach, to whom my gaze kept returning, even as the action in the ring commanded my attention. She was thirty-two, I would later learn, but she looked half that. She was so small, that was the thing. She was the size of me.

I'd never before been in a boxing gym. It was late October, late in the day, when I first pulled up, just a few minutes earlier, in the shabby lot behind the building. Through the windshield I could see a feeble growth of weeds, then cement steps leading to a wide metal door, with a sign forbidding its use. ONLY ENTRANCE TO BOXING CLUB GYM, it said, above a long arrow pointing off to the left. Below that a second sign read NO PARKING AT ALL OUT BACK. Beside me, a couple of other cars and a pickup truck had been left on the chewed-up asphalt in apparent disregard of the warning. It had begun to drizzle. I considered the other vehicles for a long moment, and turned off my engine.

The windows had been boarded up and painted over, and save for the two rather stern signs, the whole side of the building was featureless. From the other side of the concrete exterior came a sort of pumping sound, impressively rhythmic, like machinery operating beyond a factory wall. I'd followed the arrow to an unmarked door, yanked it open. Smells of leather and sweat, a short flight up, then into a musty, unpopulated office with an open door at the other end, and I'd found myself quickening my steps toward the noise beyond that door, my timorousness overtaken by a building curiosity until I stood where I was now, astonished by what I was seeing.

I had come prepared to meet this woman boxer and the girls she coached, but I was expecting to find them—I don't know, doing drills, stretching, throwing punches in the air, maybe, not actually sparring in the ring, battling, getting hit in the face, pounding their own gloved fists against another sweating body. When the time clock blared three times, signaling the end of the round, the girl fell to the floor for comic effect, and when her headgear and mouthguard were removed, she was grinning. But the next girl who climbed through the ropes and sparred with the man had something wild about her. She was frightening to watch, and at the same time I felt frightened for her; her pupils were dilated, and the force of her blows seemed fueled by something uncontrolled. Her gloves crashed against the man's headgear with a wrecking sound. When her headgear came off at the end of sparring, it seemed the coach had to speak with her for a minute, touch her hair and make eye contact, rub her shoulders and hug her, before the girl resurfaced, like a small child returning to waking life by degrees from a night terror.

With the sparring finished, for the first time I took a look around the room beyond the ring. Everyone else in the gym was male. A handful of men and not-really-yet-men worked out in pairs or solo along the periphery of the gym, signaling with their inattention the relative normality of what had just happened in the ring. But it had my heart pounding, my breath shallow. I knew I had entered a foreign land.

The Somerville Boxing Club had been around for over twenty years, but on that first evening it had been in its current location, the back of a large stone church built in 1917, for only two weeks. Filling the rear sanctuary of what had most recently housed a Brazilian evangelical ministry, it looked more lived-in than that. The space projected a heady confusion of functions, a few sheets of plywood having transformed the altar into locker rooms of unequal size, one for each gender, with a weight-lifting area sandwiched between them. Three flags—Irish, Puerto Rican, and Italian—provided vertical drapes above the dais and evoked a certain theatricality. A couple of old pews, covered in blue velvet and leaking stuffing out the back, bordered, respectively, the weight area and the bloodstained ring, behind which hung a huge American flag and a dozen fight posters. The rest was equipment: heavy bags and speed bags, a double-end bag, a hook for jump ropes; some mats, medicine balls, cracked mirrors for shadow boxing propped against the walls; Vaseline, paper towels, water bottles; a greenish doctor's-office scale; spit buckets rigged with plastic funnels and tubing and duct tape. The time clock beeped at clear, dispassionate intervals, and skin and leather connected soundly, beating out their own, more complex counterpoint. The boom box played salsa or hip-hop or techno or pop, or static when the dial slipped between stations and no one bothered to go tune it for a while. When I got there that evening, it was playing, of all things, "Calling All Angels."

Now the coach was squirting water into the white girl's mouth, which was tipped open in the manner of a baby bird's beak. The girl's hands, still gloved, hung limp at her sides. The coach spoke to her, too softly for me to hear the words, but in a tone that was tender and intimate. The girl, looking down, listened with all her being, nodding occasionally, panting a little. Their heads were almost touching. I got a better look at the coach's face, which—even though what I had witnessed her boxers doing made it impossible to be dismissive—only completed my idea of an unboxerly persona: open, guileless, undefended. Raphaëlla's features don't seem set or sleek; there is a haphazard quality to them, an artlessness, which is her beauty. When she smiles at you, the smile floods her face, every muscle giving itself over to the action, and you feel yourself the recipient of something tangible, an actual object with heft.

Later I would learn that she was the first female New England Golden Gloves champion, that she was a painter as well as a fighter, that she was working toward a master's degree in education, not with the intent of getting a teaching job but for the sole purpose of becoming a better coach, that she'd been to five funerals in the past year, that she had been harmed, that she believed everyone who made his or her way into the gym was in some way broken inside. That night it seemed all I knew was her size, and the knowledge was profound.

I was impatient to meet her and the four girls with whom she was obviously so intensely engaged. But even as the tattooed man stepped out of the ring (a former pro boxer, I later learned, he sometimes sparred with the girls as a personal favor to Raphaëlla), one of the younger girls stepped into the ring to work one-on-one with her coach. The other three girls moved onto the mats for push-ups and sit-ups. So I bided my time, waiting for them to finish.

As the dinner hour ended, more bodies came through the gym doors, from wiry boys to grizzled men, and outside the heavy fire door, which was eventually propped open in defiance of a handwritten sign taped on it, a wedge of sky showed blue-black, throwing into high relief the light, the heat, the fleshly congregation within. Everybody, as he entered, fell wordlessly into the shifting landscape of activity. A boy with an orange bandanna around his head, one foot up on a velvet pew, wrapped his hands. A tall white man worked the speed bag, shifting his weight from one hip to the other with unlikely grace. A barrel-chested man in glasses, arms folded across his formidable girth, scrutinized a lithesome kid on the double-end bag. A couple of brothers jumped rope with the finesse and footwork of circus acrobats. Someone fed the boom box a techno CD and cranked the volume. A trainer greased up a guy's face with fine, utilitarian speed: the nose, the chin, the cheek, the cheek. None of them betrayed the slightest interest in the presence of the girls training among them.

I turned 360 degrees, reading the motivational slogans tacked to the walls: VICTORY GOES TO THOSE WILLING TO PAY THE PRICE; THE WILL TO WIN IS NOT NEARLY IMPORTANT AS THE WILL TO PREPARE TO WIN! I tried to eavesdrop on the bits of conversation between trainers and boxers, but the room was too loud. I cut wide swaths around the multiplying num-bers of men working out on the main floor of the gym, so as not to get slapped by anyone's jump rope. It was plain to me that I didn't belong, yet the boxers' attitude toward me seemed one of easy indifference.

At last the girls finished their workout and came tumbling down like cubs from the ring and the free-weight area. I met them then: Jacinta and Josefina and Candida Rodriguez, three sisters, ages fifteen, twelve, and ten, respectively; Nikki Silvano, also fifteen and Jacinta's best friend; and Maria, mother to the Rodriguezes. Five people, and they seemed like a dozen that night, talking in bursts, reaching out to slap or pinch or muss one another even as they chatted with me. Maria talked to me as though well accustomed to speaking with reporters, which she was not, but she was roundly and assertively expressive, an agent for her daughters at all times. We were standing over by one of the speed bags, the one by the door to the parking lot, and she and some of the girls took turns swatting at it. Josefina, the middle daughter (known as Sefina), swung herself up on the recently erected wooden supports from which the gym equipment hung, and Maria interrupted herself to snap at the girl to get her butt *down*. She was telling me the story of the Women's Nationals that August, how Raphaëlla had taken the two big girls down to Augusta, Georgia, and how Jacinta had come home with a silver medal and left her opponent a bloody nose and two black eyes.

Candida—Candi—at ten the littlest, and too short to hit the speed bag even at its lowest adjustment without standing on something, burst out, "I want to hit a boy!" She'd been training with Raphaëlla for eight months and hadn't even had a proper sparring session yet: tough to find anyone her size.

Maria regarded her with proud amusement. "You want to fight a boy?"

"Hit. I said hit. Hit is different than fight."

Jacinta calmly grabbed her little sister and turned her upside down. Candi, her knees hooked at Jacinta's middle, her hands folded behind her head, began to do sit-ups from that vertical position.

"A moth!" cried Sefina. It fluttered on the floor. "Kill it! Step on it!"

"Don't kill it," said Maria, sucking her teeth derisively.

Sefina got down on her knees and poked at the quivering body.

Nikki told me she'd come home from Augusta with a bronze, that her legs were wobbling in the ring because she hadn't been training that long, that the ref stopped her fight and gave it to the other girl, and that she'd been mad. She explained that she and Jacinta had known each other since attending the same day-care program as little kids, and that Maria had given them matching cornrows for their bouts in Augusta. "I'm five things," said Nikki, ticking them off for me on her fingers: "Irish, Italian, Dutch, Cherokee, French." She had a lightness of presentation and demeanor that made her seem deceptively uncomplicated.

Sefina came over, bawling hoarsely. Jacinta had given her a fat lip, playing. Maria rolled her eyes. "This one cries a lot," she said.

"Sorry," said Jacinta, laughter quivering all about her dark eyes and dimples.

"Shut up!" Sefina lunged for the older girl, who yelped in mock fright and darted out of range. *"Mira, mira, Mami!"* Gingerly she lifted back the injured lip.

"Callete," shushed Maria, pretending to slap her with the back of her hand. Then, to me, "This one's better at gymnastics. She can do flips and everything. Go, show her a cartwheel." But Sefina had drifted over to one of the full-length mirrors propped against the wall to examine her wound.

Someone had switched the music from Top Forty to hip-hop, something with a lot of *fuck you, bitch* in it and a solid, galvanizing bass line, and the outside air sifted chilly and pinpricked with rain through the doorway, and inside the sweat ran and ran and the time clock rode on, insistent, above everything else, dictating intervals of work and rest. Jacinta hit Nikki in the back with a medicine ball, and Nikki pretended, halfheartedly, to be mad. I tried to keep up with Maria's amiable, expansive narration of her own childhood, in Puerto Rico and Boston, and her own adolescent wish to fight, to box, to work out with the boys. Around us, the girls fought and played and finally retreated to the locker room to change.

Raphaëlla emerged in jeans and a jacket, a gym bag slung over her shoulder, car keys out. I'd been eager to shake her hand and introduce myself properly. I asked whether I could be in touch for an interview. She asked how long it would take, and recited her number at work. She was not impolite. But her manner contrasted sharply with the easy accessibility offered by Maria and the girls. I felt chastened by her aloofness, all the more so because it felt deserved.

The unsettled feeling I'd had out in the parking lot earlier, the anxiety I'd needed to stuff aside in order to make myself go into the building, had not been based on anything so literal as the fear of coming to harm from the boxers within. It wasn't that I was intimidated by the thought of mingling with people who inflict pain for sport. I think it was the product of my own barely acknowledged scorn for the idea of boxing and for those who choose to identify themselves with it. I was about to enter a club whose members I had never met but whom I secretly held in a measure of contempt. How fitting, then, that I had felt nervous about coming inside. And now it was as though Raphaëlla had seen through me.

I had come expecting to find something alien, and found instead, in the person before me, an eerie and shocking resemblance. We might have been sisters, this woman and I. I watched her bid the others farewell with all the warmth and openness she'd kept from her contact with me, and then she was gone, out the side door into the wedge of darkness. The girls left soon after, but I stayed awhile. I was reeling, embarrassed at all that I was feeling.

What *was* this place? I prowled around a bit, unable to go home just yet. The church's main sanctuary was locked up tight, but its lights were on. Peeking through the crack between the doors, I could catch stained-glass slivers of high, arched windows: This was where the Masons, who owned the building, convened. The basement held a social hall with a large adjacent kitchen that smelled of age and damp. That was all, really.

Some bathrooms, a boiler room. And the great incongruity of its upstairs tenant, the boxing club.

Going back through the office, I found a man sitting behind the desk. He was short and stocky, with a cleft chin and a toothpick in his mouth and a backward baseball cap. He had dark pebble eyes that didn't hold my gaze. A grandmotherly woman in a green suit sat on the other side of the desk, on which had been laid wads of hundred-dollar bills. Her name was Ann Cooper, and she was recently back from Las Vegas, where the gym's star fighter had just relocated. Her hand was soft and cool, and she smelled like face powder. She seemed something like a den mother, but when I tried to get her actual title, she waved her hand modestly. "Oh, we're all just volunteers. Aren't we, Vinny?" The man with the pebble eyes shrugged and worked his toothpick to the other side of his mouth.

The money, apparently, had come from the boxer in Las Vegas, John "The Quiet Man" Ruiz, who had won the World Boxing Association heavyweight title from Evander Holyfield some seven months earlier— the first Latino ever to hold a world heavyweight title. His portrait hung, several times over, around the shabby little room. (Later I would learn that Raphaëlla had contributed one; she often painted portraits of the boxers she loved.) Ann Cooper's eyes teared up when she talked about John Ruiz. " 'Cause we've struggled, you know," she said. "Everybody always said we'd never have a world champion out of our club. Not that that's the most important thing—we're here for the kids, first. But it doesn't hurt." She touched a wad of bills with her long polished fingernails. Rent. Gym fees were twenty-five dollars a month for kids who could afford to pay. As it happened, almost none of them could.

The warmth of this woman, and the sorrow shimmering about her, intrigued me. As did the gross unease of the toothpick man. And the man who emerged pink-skinned from the gym's single bathroom, wearing a little white towel around his waist and concern for no one's gaze as he trod past us on his way to the locker room. And the noble-warrior image of the Quiet Man in the pictures, somber-eyed, naked to the waist, girded by a championship belt of almost burdensome dimensions. And the live-fuse beat of the music inside the gym, and the sharp percussion of fists at their own nonmusical purpose. The idea of all these young boxers bent on being here because they loved—what? Fighting? Hitting? Survival? The odd—*absurd*—impression of wholesomeness about the club, of something nurturing, nourishing, as though this were still a sanctuary, a place of healing instead of hurting. And above all: the fact that girls and women had dug out a place here.

I went back inside the gym proper, sat on a pew, and watched the men. What I am used to, when I report on a story, is disappearing inside it. I could feel that happening now, but only imperfectly. Something unfamiliar was getting in the way, asserting itself amid the rhythms and sweat and brewing questions. This unfamiliar thing was my awareness of *me*. It was as though I'd had ten cups of coffee before coming, as though I'd swallowed some sort of radioactive dye that made my physical presence irrefutable. It was as though, on some cellular level, my body knew what was to come, that this would not be a place where I could lose myself inside the story. That the opposite would prove true.

I sat there, watching the boxers, and floated in the din and the kinesthetic swirl. After a while I became aware of something specific leaping and burning within me, and when I went to put a name to it, it was jealousy.

In her 1987 book, *On Boxing,* Joyce Carol Oates famously wrote, "Boxing is a purely masculine activity and it inhabits a purely masculine world." Of the female spectator, she has a "characteristic repugnance for boxing" and is "likely to identify with the losing, or hurt, boxer." Of the female boxer: "[She] cannot be taken seriously—she is parody, she is cartoon, she is monstrous."

Seven years after these words were published, United States Amateur Boxing, responding to a lawsuit filed by a sixteen-year-old girl in Washington State and backed by the American Civil Liberties Union, officially lifted its ban on female bouts. Anomalous boxing matches between women had taken place in this country since at least the late eighteen hundreds, and in England at least a hundred years before that. But the first legally sanctioned bout between two women on American soil took place in October 1993. A year later the Amateur International Boxing Association (AIBA), adopted similar regulations recognizing women's boxing. A year after that, on an October afternoon in Massachusetts, Raphaëlla Johnson biked seven miles through the pouring rain from her apartment in Brighton to the Somerville Boxing Club.

She was twenty-four when she pushed through the doors, bicycle seat in one hand, rainwater trickling from her hair into her eyes, and looked around for somebody to confront. She had not heard of the lawsuit in Washington State; she hadn't heard of USA Boxing, nor of AIBA. All she'd heard, when she asked the instructor of the cardio-boxing class she had begun taking at Beacon Hill Athletic Club if he would train her to fight, was derisive laughter and his declaration that women would never box in the state of Massachusetts. This spurred her as nothing else; she'd gone home and flung open the Yellow Pages, found the Somerville club, and pedaled straight over.

There she found Frank Murphy and Ralph Palmacci, Sr., both in their seventies, both sitting on a couple of folding chairs. Later, Franky would tell people she arrived "with a mean look in her eye," but they regarded her mildly, and without—this was the first breakthrough—amusement. She demanded to know whether anybody at this place would train her. Franky's left hand was occupied with a long brown cigarette. He held up his right and told her to hit it. Raphaëlla socked him as hard as she could. Franky shrugged. "Okay," he said. "I guess *so*."

Four months later she and Franky were driving over icy roads in his battered Cadillac with the broken windows and the reek of stale cigarette smoke, bound for Lowell Memorial Auditorium, where she would compete in her first bout. Before a crowd of two thousand largely disbelieving spectators, she boxed and won, becoming New England's first ever female Golden Gloves champion. Even then, it was hard getting sanctioned bouts—promoters shied away from putting women on the fight cards, and there were so few female opponents around. Still, for two years Raphi got in as many fights as she could, and when the first Women's National Championships were held in 1997, in Augusta, Georgia, she was there for that bit of history, too. She came home with a silver medal and a broken nose, and hung up her gloves in order to coach, her sights set now on bringing girls to the Olympics.

Women's boxing is not yet an Olympic sport. It is the fervent wish of many that it will never be one. But the International Olympic Committee, having committed itself to gender equity in future Olympic Games, plans to drastically reduce or eliminate all-male sports, so for boxing to remain in the Olympics at all, a women's event may have to be accepted. In any case, the foundation for eventual inclusion is being well laid. The first Women's World Championships were held in 2001, in Scranton,

Pennsylvania. The same year, France hosted the first all-European women's boxing championships; Egypt hosted the first all-African event; and Thailand, the first all-Asian. Recognized female boxing programs exist in more than forty countries, on every continent except Antarctica. Whether or not the Olympics ever admits them, female boxers have, over the past decade, staked out an impressive and growing territory.

What, then, of Oates? Can her words be dismissed as plainly out-dated, patently wrong? The power of the truths they contain has hardly been unseated since she wrote her treatise. She gives it on her authority that women identify with the boxer who is losing, the boxer who is hurt, but what makes the idea so troubling is that for all one might like to ob-ject, one feels she is right. The issue is given only a sentence in her book, which is, after all, concerned almost exclusively with men; but it hints at something of groaning weight, something bitter and bilious and dismaying.

If this is true, if women do automatically identify with the hurt, the losing, party, it becomes necessary to wonder why this should be so. Does it begin before or after our birth? Is it in our nature, or has it been learned? I think of those rare occasions when I would pass through a room: the pale violet flicker of the TV, a man's legitimate engagement with the combat in the box, and me, not lingering, not looking long, though of course, of *course,* if there was anyone to feel empathy for, it was the one receiving the blow, never the one dealing—who was he? No one you could empathize with, emptied of humanity—and then me, pass-ing from the room, passing a test, the test of not looking, of not wanting to look.

Oates calls the female boxer "monstrous." This we know well, too. For men and boys, no matter how much polite society may hold boxing in disfavor, the activity remains a heightened or extreme expression of qualities thought to be natural and of value. But the idea that a woman should want to box, feel a *need* to box, flies in the face of what we think we understand about women. Women's arms, women's hands, are for giving succor, not dealing blows. Yet women and girls have found their way into this world of their own volition. Currently 2,153 girls and women are registered with USA Boxing, and thousands more are boxing in other countries. In light of the considerable taboo against female ag-gression, the drive of these women and girls to box is extraordinary.

The jealousy I experienced that first night at the club had to do with recognizing a kind of freedom I hadn't known existed. There ought to have been something scary about the sight of Jacinta and Nikki in the penlike confines of the ring, encumbered by headgear, mouthguards, and the fat, shiny fingerless gloves. But the young women I saw sparring that night were so plainly, dizzyingly free. Free in their choice to be there in the first place, and free from the responsibility to take care of the other person. But above all free to *want,* in public and without apology—to want to remain on their feet, to want to have and use power, to want to test their bodies and their mettle and take pleasure in the experience.

You cannot box without committing yourself to being awake in your body; you cannot box without committing yourself to caring. There is nothing nihilistic about boxing. It is the opposite of cool. There is no room for charade, no time for equivocation. Boxing is a graphic confession of the desire to remain present and to persevere.

A long time ago I'd made a wrong turn and linked up freedom with abnegating the body. Not such an unusual mistake, not for women, not for girls. I'd had great hope in it, actually. If only I could undo the knot binding self to flesh. I'd had some success loosening it. I just hadn't quite figured out how to take that further step when I walked into the boxing gym, more or less by accident, and, not having words for anything yet, not understanding anything yet, I responded in a way that would force me to question all I thought I knew about being a woman.

It was like falling in love with the last possible person on earth you thought you could be attracted to. It was like coming upon a great thuggish figure in an alley and having him turn around only to smile an angel's greeting. But which aspect was real—the oily coat and foul breath, or the benevolence in the eyes?

To hear them tell it, the girls came by boxing casually. They all lived in Charlestown, a neighborhood of Boston that lies across the Charles River, cut off from the rest of the city, and just east of Somerville. They'd grown up in and around the cluster of housing projects huddled between the Tobin Bridge and the public high school. ("Dum-Dum High," the kids called it. "Somebody pulls the fire alarm every single day.") The

Police Athletic League and Charlestown Against Drugs cosponsored free sports programs at the school, and more than anything else, it was this coincidence of geography—the fact that it was happening right across the street—that drew the girls into boxing.

It was Jacinta, then a tenth-grader, who wandered alone into the gym one spring afternoon through a door left open. She found a boxing class going on, all boys, with cops coaching them, and a heap of madly enticing stuff: gloves, mitts, freestanding heavy bags. She couldn't keep her hands off it. Three times somebody told her not to touch the equipment. Finally she sat down against the wall to watch the boys training.

The coach, Desmond Tyler, a patrolman and sometimes-preacher, noticed her there, aged fourteen, dark-eyed, dimpled, regarding the action coolly. He'd seen her before, playing football with the boys, running them all over the field, in fact, and he'd thought, Why not, let's see if she can box. He put her in the ring—only a makeshift ring, mats laid out on the floor—against his third best fighter, whom he instructed to hold back. No need. She hit him fearlessly, and hard, and within the round he was wobbling, nose bleeding. Desi, as everybody called the coach, had to rush the boy out into the hallway to spare him the embarrassment of the others seeing him cry.

Jacinta, and sometimes her little sisters, too, began to work out with the boys when they could. Desi had never heard of the female trainer who worked with girls over in Somerville, but his partner had, and eventually they got around to putting in a call. The first time Raphi came down to the Charlestown High gym, Desi thought it was a joke: this little wispy thing, a boxing coach? But he introduced her to Jacinta. "My prize pupil," he called her, in front of them both. "She needs a workout with the girls." Raphi got out the mitts, which are what the trainer wears and the boxer hits during practice, and as Desi tells it, within five minutes she was doing more with Jacinta than Desi had done in all their hours together.

There was Desi, all big and impressive, cornrows hanging to his collar, with his cop's air of authority, his Bible teacher's serenity, and twenty years of boxing experience under his belt. His jaw just dropped. And there were his boys, the Charlestown kids, all rangy and tough, who stopped what they were doing and watched. Because in front of them stood Raphi and Jacinta, sizing each other up for the first time, hands held high, encased, respectively, in trainer's mitts and gloves: the one barking terse commands with unguessed-at authority, and the other responding, smacking her fists against the mitts like lightning, each blow sounding a gorgeous report. I have seen them do this dozens of times, and it remains enthralling. The well-matched power of each, a marvelous thing. And joyful, full of the purely physical joy that leaves them, at the end, both panting, both with a flush in their cheeks and sweat dampening their hair.

That was the year the Somerville Boxing Club was homeless, having lost its lease to the space above Anthony's function hall (ANTHONY'S IS SECOND TO NONE IN SERVICE & FOOD—JUSTICE OF THE PEACE AVAILABLE), a blue-awninged building on Highland Avenue, two blocks away from the old church where it would find its new quarters. A lot of Somerville felt cramped and struggling, and this particular part of the city, known as Winter Hill, was no exception. Along the narrow, hilly avenue, the properties seemed to go church, church, funeral home, bar. Down along all the even narrower side streets, three-family houses on lots hardly big enough for their lawn-Madonnas vied for space.

Winter Hill, with its unpretty air of defiant survival, seemed a fitting setting for a boxing club, but this was still half a year before the club would relocate. So Jacinta and her sisters, and a week later, her best friend, Nikki Silvano, joined Raphi that spring and summer, nomadically traipsing with her from the Charlestown High gym to World Gym in Assembly Square, from City Gym in Boston to the Chelsea warehouse that the heavyweight champ John Ruiz had rented to train for his upcoming fight. They showed up wherever someone would let them in to train for free. Something about the girls' willingness to migrate, to adapt to changes at the last minute, to enter, over and over, unfamiliar territory, where they were admitted by the grace of whoever was in charge, went a long way toward explaining how they came to box in the first place. None of them, by her own assessment, felt afraid to box or to enter these gyms. It was a safer version of what they'd already witnessed, and what they themselves had engaged in all their lives.

For Nikki, the girl who'd sparred with such ferocity on my first night at the gym, one of her earliest memories was of her own violence. She was five, playing outside the projects. A boy her age or a little older sailed her paper airplane into a Dumpster. And then, "I was slamming his head into the Dumpster until blood came out and he wasn't moving."

Nikki lived in the nicer section of the projects with her mother, her younger brother, and her mother's boyfriend. They had two floors and a slab of lawn in front of their brick row house. Her mother, Maureen, was one of ten children by six different fathers. She had been thrown out of the house by *her* mother when she was fifteen, and spent the next year and a half homeless, sleeping in cellars and on roofs, and stealing from stores to survive, until she moved in with the man who would become Nikki's father. Maureen was home-disabled, a term she employed to encompass a variety of ailments including endometriosis, asthma, depression, and what she referred to as a deteriorating disease in her spine. This woman who was turned out on the street as a teenager now rarely left her house.

She had made her living room a shrine to Elvis. Memorabilia, decorated mirrors, album covers, paintings on black velvet, and homemade pencil sketches of the King surrounded her as she lit a cigarette and related, in her sandpapery voice, one of her own early memories of Nikki. In this memory, too, Nikki was about five, on the playground, climbing up a rope ladder. Her cousin, a boy one year older, was in her way. When he wouldn't move, Nikki started pounding him, yanking and shaking him, screaming, "You fucker! You fucker!" Maureen watched from a bench, frozen with awe and, she told me, somewhat wonderingly, as if bemused by her own lack of pity, engulfed with pride.

More striking than Nikki's violence in these anecdotes is the quasi-heroic quality it is assigned in the retelling. Within this environment, specifically the Charlestown projects but more generally any neighborhood where the threat of physical harm is high and constant, violent impulses can be a source of real comfort and pride. Maria and the girls told similar stories about themselves, always with a mixture of boastfulness and something else: a desire to shock, as if only in the reaction of an outsider could fear or horror be registered. The fact that perpetrators of the kind of daily violence that was part of the girls' lives were rarely censured, were in fact frequently given increased respect, was a further act of harm, perhaps as damaging to the perpetrators as to their victims.

Nikki's eyes are green, real pale sea green, but she was contemplating colored contacts to do something about this. Her hair is brown, dyed an unlikely auburn, and she wore it slicked back in a single ponytail or two fat round pom-poms, shiny and smooth as a doll's acrylic locks. She might have been called willowy if she weren't so strong. She favored baggy pants and sweatshirts, loose tomboy clothes, but now and then experimented with a clingy stretch T-shirt, some low-rider jeans, what the kids referred to matter-of-factly as hootchie-mama gear, and it was thrilling and unsettling to her how differently people treated her then. Her skin was milky and turned red in one second, to her eternal chagrin, but she had a strategy for dealing with this, and with her nostrils' embarrassing tendency to flare with emotion: She'd call herself a psycho, preempting mockery from others, and she'd make one eye squint a little for effect, and her friends would laugh.

The Rodriguez sisters lived in the projects on the other side of Medford Street, block after block of square brick buildings, with the NO LOITERING POLICE TAKE NOTICE sign stenciled on the cinder blocks right outside the metal door to their apartment. Inside there was a common room, where they cooked and ate and washed and ironed and watched TV and played dominoes and did homework and let the bird, Pito, fly out of his cage. Beyond a beaded curtain were three little bedrooms, one for Jacinta, one for Sefina and Candi, and one for their parents.

The girls had nicknames for the men they were afraid of: Crusty, Booty Guy, Carrot-Head. They talked about running from rapists, about a man everyone *knew* was a rapist who lived on the other side of the housing project, about rumors and disappearances and newspaper stories and cops. They knew the cops by name: There was Desi, and another one named Paul, and when they glided up in their cruisers at two and three and four A.M. on summer nights, the kids still out playing in the heat would come up and say hi and the cops wouldn't even tell them to go home, they'd just say hi back. The girls in this neighborhood wore heavy rings and baggy clothes, and sometimes a knife inside their socks. Nikki and the Rodriguez sisters all used to street-fight before boxing. Not anymore, they'd say. You could lose your license to box. And Raphi had personally forbidden it when she took them on. Although she almost changed her mind a few weeks before I met them all.

It was the night of a big Tito fight. Felix "Tito" Trinidad against Bernard "The Executioner" Hopkins at Madison Square Garden. Raphi had gone over to the Rodriguezes' to watch it on TV. In the weeks before the fight (immediately following September 11, 2001), Hopkins had raised eyebrows even among the boxing community by publicly throwing the Puerto Rican flag to the ground and calling the upcoming match a war. When the time came, he did not fight a clean fight. He kept hitting Tito after the bell, and punching him in the back of the head and in the legs during clinches. Hopkins, who had served five years in a maximum-security prison for aggravated assault, and who had won four national penitentiary boxing championships while there, had been quoted as saying, "Boxing saved my sanity in prison. Boxing was my best therapy."

Midway through the fight, Raphi and the girls' parents heard terrible screaming coming from outside. Maria and Raphi went out on the back steps of the building. About ten girls had surrounded Jacinta, Sefina, and Candi, some showing knives. The whole ugly assemblage turned out to be the progeny of a fight between Maria and another girl's mother. An all-night grudge match passed on to the daughters and their friends. One girl punched Sefina—naturally, Sefina, of all the sisters the one who couldn't hold her tongue or her temper any more than her tears. Jacinta held her younger sister back. Maria screamed at her for not letting Sefina retaliate. It was after midnight, sultry and sooty out in the dark lot between the squat buildings.

When at last all the girls could be persuaded to disperse, Raphi and the Rodriguezes holed up back inside. They were in time to see the knockdown on TV, Hopkins felling the great Tito, who did manage to struggle to his feet by the count of nine. And they were in time to see the utterly surprising thing Felix Trinidad, Sr., father and trainer of Tito, did then. He climbed through the ropes, before a stunned crowd of nearly twenty thousand, and stopped the fight there. Raphi thought of the scene a few minutes earlier—Maria barking at the girls to fight back; Sefina's arms pinned behind her; Jacinta's face looking older than it was; Candi, so little, barefoot, ready to leap into the fray—and wondered what she was doing in these girls' lives. Was it anything good, anything useful to them?

Raphi's own trajectory was unlike that of the girls. She did not grow up in poverty, nor amid notable violence. She was born in 1969 in, of all places, a Red Cross hospital in Finland. Her American father was an AP reporter stationed in Moscow. Her French mother crossed the Baltic alone to spend the last weeks of her pregnancy in Helsinki, since no one knew, during the height of the Cold War, how easy it would be to travel out of the country with a baby born on Soviet soil. Raphi grew up in

Moscow; Paris; Tarrytown, New York; and London, where her parents still live. After high school, she came back to the United States for college, got an MFA in illustration from the Art Institute of Boston, and, before settling into her current position as a graphic designer at Gillette, spent a few years scrabbling to make a living as a freelance illustrator. It was near the end of this particularly rootless, hopeless time that she began to box.

"Why box?" I asked Raphi this question an unreasonable number of times, and she served up a number of different answers, some clearly better rehearsed than others. It had to do with anger. It had to do with size and femininity and power and control and resistance. It had to do with self-esteem and confidence and mastery and self-respect. It had to do with pressures to be pretty, and nice, and little, and sweet. "Yes, but why *box*?" I'd ask. "*Why* box? Do you know? Do you think you understand why?"

Once her old coach, Franky, asked her the same question. They were down by the Charles River, where he'd sometimes take her to run sprints. The sun was going down. The Rollerbladers and dog walkers, the bikers and joggers, the Harvard crews in their shells cutting across the bright water. A public place at rush hour. She answered him at honest length. He was the only person she ever told.

To me, she said simply that she did come to have clarity about her reasons for boxing. She shared pieces of her story, hints at what lay beneath her need. Sometimes she spoke to the issue in a fairly general way. "I needed to know I could hit a man and really hurt him." Sometimes she would offer something more specific but ask me not to repeat it. For a long time I was fixated on one day learning the whole of Raphi's unique story. I thought if I could understand one woman's concrete motivation to box that it would count as a kind of explanation, even a justification, of why women might hunger for this experience more generally.

But the more serious reason I wanted her story was that I imagined it somehow would explain to me why *I* felt the desire to box. Three weeks after my first visit to the gym, I couldn't stand it any longer, and I asked Raphi if I could start training with the girls.

It was late; the girls had left, taking with them all their irreverence and crazy sense of play. I had noticed that they alone among the gym members treated the place like a playground. Oh, they could focus and sweat, all ferocious concentration one moment, but the next they might be break-dancing and throwing wadded-up balls of sports tape at one another. I wondered what the boxing gym meant to the girls. It didn't seem to figure identically in their lives and in the lives of the boys, who never acted out in such ways, who breezed into the gym with a kind of quiet entitlement and just plain worked, just trained.

Raphi came out of the locker room, having changed back into street clothes, nice street clothes: She was going on a date with Candi's godfather, Richardson Cruz. Raphi was the godmother, Candi having been baptized only that fall. Just as September 11 stirred in some people an urgent need to stock up on gas masks and Cipro tablets, Maria had responded in the most practical terms she knew. She didn't want the girls' souls going to purgatory, so she did something she'd been meaning to do for, well, ages: got them baptized. That was how, a few weeks after the towers collapsed, Jacinta, Josefina, and Candida came to find themselves in white dresses, in church, being spoken over in Latin, anointed with holy water and oil. And how Candi—absolutely pleased with herself—managed to secure an eternal holy tie to her boxing coach.

And how Raphi hooked up with Richie. They met that day over the font, as it were, the little gringa and the towering Puerto Rican, with his gleaming shaved pate and his shy, halting English. They'd been dating nearly two months. *Madrina y padrino*. The godmother and the godfather.

Raphi looked so pretty that night, and not a little impatient: her frosty pink lip gloss applied fresh a minute before, with a tiny wand in front of the locker-room mirror. I thought, She's forgotten her promise to show me how to work the speed bag tonight. But she hadn't; she stopped by and brought me over to where the small leather bags hung. The gym was buzzing with men; the after-school crowd had gone home to dinner and been replaced by the after-work crowd. In my mind the gym was always awash in reds and oranges, primary heat and glow, and this night was no different, the room somehow bathed in fire colors, a palette of blunt desire. A speed bag freed up, and I felt embarrassed to be occupying it, but Raphi adjusted the backboard, then dragged over the low wooden platform that would make us more the right height. She was unapologetic about our tying up this station. Behind me, a middle-aged guy had a good rhythm going. *Chuddica, chuddica, chuddica*. His fists on the leather teardrop a smooth blur.

"All my coach really ever told me," said Raphi, "is you let it touch three times before you hit it again." She manipulated the bag with both hands in slow motion, showing me how it should ricochet off the back, front, and back before swinging forward into my fist.

I felt ridiculous. I knew from watching others work the bag that it was harder than it looked. The man behind me shifted his weight from the ball of one foot to the other and switched hands as he did, and he looked languorous, he looked like Gene Kelly, and the bag was going so fast it was like a magic thing with invisible hummingbird wings.

"So, basically, this," said Raphi, and she stepped up and hit the bag, churned it up into a nice rhythm of her own. "You try." She stepped down.

I got on the platform, struck the bag with the side of my fist. It came shooting back at my face, and I leaped out of the way.

"Lighter," said Raphi.

No kidding. I stilled the bag with two hands, tried again. This time it careened wildly on its swivel, going round and round instead of back and forth. I looked to Raphi for a tip, a correction.

She shrugged. "Do it again."

I hit it lightly, and it swung straight this time, three laps, and I hit it again, counted to three, hit it again, counted to three . . . It kept coming back, responding to my touch, and the one-two-three got in my head and I kept making it happen and I wouldn't have stopped for anything.

"Good!" said Raphi.

"Is this it? What I'm doing?" I asked without taking my eyes from the bag.

"That's it." A moment later: "You can try switching hands." Another moment later: "I'm sorry I have to leave early tonight. Next time we should wrap your hands."

I said, "Thanks, Raphi," still not taking my eyes off the bag, and she left, and suddenly I was just in it, inside the rhythm, and all around me were the men and boys and the movement and the equipment and the light and heat and pounding music coming out of the boom box, and nobody was paying much attention to me, and I was concentrating on staying with the rhythm, and every so often I messed up and the bag went spastically every which way, and then I stilled it between my hands and started up again.

"Nah, don't stop it with your hands like that." Vinny Busa, the pebble-eyed guy who sat at the desk, had sidled over and was scowling at me. He reached out a thick fist and batted the leather teardrop a few times, getting it back in line. "Do it with your fist, see if you can catch it." He spun it off course for me. I tried to hit it back on a linear axis. "Get your elbows up." He manipulated my elbow to stick out at ninety degrees, on a line with my shoulder; he observed me another minute, then moved on.

John Curran passed me on his way from the locker room. He was one of the three USA Boxing certified coaches at the gym. Barrel-chested, with a trim, grizzled beard, and astonishingly light on his feet on those rare occasions when he broke into a time step. He cranked my elbows down to forty-five degrees. "You want 'em here," he muttered.

I worked one more round. Naturally, Vinny Busa happened by and paused when he saw what I was doing. "No, no, no." With real irritation. "I showed you. Get 'em up!"

I smothered a smile. Raphi had told me how furious her coaches would get when other trainers tried to offer unsolicited advice. I didn't mind the advice, neither the fact that it was unsolicited nor that it was contradictory. Really, I liked it, for the acceptance it implied. I didn't feel I was seen as a woman at all; it was only my form, only my goddamn elbows that mattered, and it was lovely. I loved their terse orneriness. I felt admitted and I felt free. Was this what the girls got at the gym, was I experiencing what brought them here?

At home that night I noticed sharp, neat purple and blue bruises along the outsides of my little fingers, and when I lay down in bed and closed my eyes, I had the rhythm of the speed bag saved in my body, like the feeling of the ocean after a day spent in the waves.

2

HAND WRAPS

Saturday morning, ten o'clock, at the gym. Raphi, her hands bound already in their layers of protective cloth, laced her fingers around an enormous Dunkin' Donuts take-out cup and sipped. Two newish boys were there; white, solemn, the one soft and unboxerlike, the other with the emergent muscles of preadolescence. They had been coming for a couple of weeks. Nikki was there as well, in a tank top with the word ARMY configured in sequins. She had Rollerbladed two and a half miles from Charlestown, following the Mystic River, past the old Schraft factory, one gray city to another, through the autumn blankness.

"All right, jewelry comes off," said Raphi. Anthony, the more rakish of the two boys, removed a gold chain from his neck. "Did you eat?" she asked them. She wanted to know what. Cereal, they reported. Yes, with milk. She reminded them how to pick out jump ropes the right length: Step on the middle of the rope and the ends should reach a little above the hips. "Two rounds." The time clock blared. Nikki was already jumping, her feet barely leaving the floor, tiny rhythms of heel and toe. The boys stopped and started. The pudgier one, Danny, panted, waited out a stitch in his side, smiling ingratiatingly. Raphi sat on the velvet pew with her coffee. When the clock sounded again, two and a half minutes into the round, Raphi yelled, "Thirty seconds. Pick up the pace!" Nikki showed off some, suddenly jumping high and turning her rope so fast it whistled and passed under her feet twice before each landing. Ten seconds of this. Hotshot. Then the round ended and Raphi had to remind the boys—who were not yet accustomed to the pattern of three minutes of work, one minute of rest—to stop.

The kids were transient, would show up for a few weeks or a few months or, rarely, a few years, and then drop out, vanish, without ceremony, sometimes even without warning. Some of them stayed long enough to spar, and some stayed long enough to get their USA Boxing passbooks and an actual sanctioned bout somewhere, but most of them did not. This was not so much the case with the older boys and men who trained with the other coaches. Some of these, over time, acquired a serious air of promise. For them, it might be a realistic goal to compete in the national Golden Gloves, the Olympics, to turn pro.

But these were not the fighters with whom Raphi was most concerned. She was friends with them, had them work her corner, spar with her, take her out for beers. They went to the same wakes and funerals; she cheered for them in live arenas and at home in front of her TV. But they were not why she was here, in general, or here specifically on a thoroughly gray Saturday morning. She was here for children, for boys and girls but mostly girls, most of them "at risk," in the jargon of her Boston University professors.

All of them at risk, Desi would amend. He and Raphi shared the conviction that people who box hold in common, almost as a kind of prerequisite, some scarring hurt or deprivation. Desi once put it in clear-cut terms: "You don't have two parents at home, food in the fridge, and come in here and make it." Raphi put it more broadly but no less emphatically: "If you're a well-adjusted, basically happy person, you don't box." Then Desi laughed his deep contagious laugh, and Raphi chuckled and shook her head, looking away as she did, because of course they were implicating themselves, too.

Since meeting over the girls the previous spring, they had worked together closely. Raphi asked Desi to go to the Nationals with them, to help her work Nikki and Jacinta's corner, and the best part of that story was Desi's leaving the coach's meeting—the one where all boxers get paired with opponents—in order to throw up, being literally sick with worry over who the girls would end up facing in each of their first-ever bouts. His face was strong and lively when he was relating a story or reacting to one, and the warmth and humor spilling forth with this confession were so evident and layered: Why bring them, then? Why teach them to box and set them up for this, an event so potentially laden with real physical and emotional danger that the prospect made this Charlestown cop vomit? There was a counterweight here, something of such great value that it justified the risk. But only, perhaps—this was what Desi and Raphi were saying—for those who come from a certain kind of damage to begin with.

Nikki Silvano had as much need, as much anger, as anyone Raphi had ever coached. The first time they met, when Jacinta brought her along to practice in Charlestown, Raphi was doubtful about the lanky white girl, so unsmiling and silent, until it was time to hit the mitts. Then she knew Nikki was in exactly the right place. Not that she always made it to practice. Periodically, when she didn't show, it was because her mother wouldn't let her out again—or because her mother didn't give her a message about the time or day of practice being changed. For a while Nikki's mother was calling Raphi almost daily, often threatening to stop Nikki from boxing altogether. The infractions varied. Once it was having left a bowl of Cheerios in her bedroom.

Nikki, for her part, wore her hostility toward her mother openly, almost saucily. "My mother's a very violent person," she would announce, chin high, the color bright all through her neck and cheeks. The proclamation carried the flavor of high drama, and she would flash her beach-glass eyes around as though daring anyone to flout it. Other times she threatened to run away. "My mother was homeless at my age," Nikki would say casually, which chilled Raphi more than the bravado of the first statement. It had the sound of a refrain, or of prophecy.

Raphi didn't know the circumstances of the two new boys here today. She looked at them, duplicated in broken mirrors as they shadowboxed over by the wall. Hard to say whether they would stay. The one had a good punch. But she couldn't feel anything coming off them yet, any particular hunger to be here. If they kept at it, she was sure to learn their circumstances. She was continually amazed by the brevity of the kids' silences; it usually took only a few weeks before they began to bring the raveled pieces of their stories to her.

Now the gym was warming up. Raphi called the boys over, was about to have Nikki demonstrate to them how to pass the medicine ball behind their backs, when the Rodriguezes burst in, merrily late as ever. Maria was first, grinning. "Hey, girl!" Hugs all around, and not trifling ones. Candi rushed at Raphi, who said, "Uh-oh," and just had time to set down her coffee before the kid landed—"Oof"—in her lap. After a minute Candi slid over onto the pew and held out a hand for Raphi to wrap.

The length of time it takes to wrap a hand is part of its ritualistic quality. First the rolled-up ribbon of herringbone-weave cotton must be unwound, all fifteen feet of it. The stitched-in loop slides over the thumb, and then the wrist is bound, around and around, and the cloth brought up diagonally across the palm and around the knuckles, over and over, and then around the thumb, and the hand again, and back to the wrist until the last bit is used up and everything Velcroed firmly in place. Some people wrap between each finger individually, and some secure the whole thing with tape; it depends on how you were taught and whether you're wrapping your hands for sparring or a bout or simply to hit the bags. Boxers generally wrap their own hands unless it's for a fight. That Raphi would do it for Candi, for practice, was rather doting. There was something nurselike about it, not just because the final product resembles a cast, but because it involves tending to someone's well-being in an entirely prescribed manner. The contact is intimate but purposeful and free of inflection. When a trainer wraps a boxer's hands before a bout, it can take on a spiritual solemnity, become devotional as prayer.

Candi got the rich, distant look of a dog being scratched between the ears as Raphi encased her wrist and hand bones in layer upon layer of cloth. She was as close to Raphi as she could be to any adult who was not a blood relation. She liked to enumerate the ways she knew she was special to her coach. A drawing she made had pride of place on Raphi's fridge at home. It was a big red heart sporting pointy horns and a forked tail, inscribed, "I Love You To: Raphiella from: Candi 4 p.m." For Candi's birthday, Raphi had given her a real gym bag. She was always bringing Candi little gifts of chocolate and gum from the cafeteria at work. And once, when Raphi took her out to eat and they both ordered grilled-cheese sandwiches with pickles, Raphi had said, "Great minds think alike," something Candi always liked to remember.

Raphi was equally smitten. This was how she recorded their first meeting, the previous spring, in her journal: "I taught at Charlestown today and it was terrific. I found me a new little fighter named Candi who can kick ass and is totally into it. It makes me feel like all the hard work is worth it when you get a little boxer like her."

Hands done, Candi popped up off the pew, going to get a rope. Along came Ashanti and Ja Rule on the boom box. Jacinta and Nikki glanced meaningfully at each other, and Jacinta cranked the volume. "I'm not always there when you call / But I'm always on time . . ." Jacinta mouthed the silky-voiced lyric, her eyes half closing, her head weaving like a snake's. Her lip-synching matched the recorded voice with spellbinding fidelity. "Wrap your hands!" barked Raphi. "Where's Sefina?"

Maria shrugged. "The car. Her body hurts her." She rolled her eyes, smiled a sideways kind of smirk. Sefina often had a reason not to box. Sometimes she had a hurt ankle, or her period, or the wrong clothes, and she would sit sullen on the pew the whole time. She was growing fast that year, shooting up taller than her big sister, and when she walked down the street, she got whistles and nasty comments. She had just started middle school. Her nickname for herself was Thunder.

At last, as if waiting for someone to notice her absence, she came slinking in, eyes dark and faraway as if she'd just roused from slumber. Still in her jacket, she slouched onto the pew. "Hey!" barked Raphi. Sefina struggled up again, came over, and hugged her trainer. She gave her body over for the moment, letting Raphi say something in her ear, then sat back down.

"All right. Wrap your hands!" Raphi yelled again, mock tough, and feinted a right at Jacinta, who didn't flinch. She smiled her secret tranquil smile and disappeared into the locker room, Nikki bounding along after.

The friendship of Nikki and Jacinta had a kind of gorgeous shimmer, like something you'd encounter in a fairy tale. In fact, in freshman art, they had collaborated on an assignment to create a painting depicting mythical alter egos. Their teacher loved it so much that it now hung in the school library: an eight-foot-long atmospheric tableau on birch plywood, with swirls and eddies of the wood grain showing through and incorporated into the watery scene, which showed a number of dragons (Jacinta) trying to rescue fairies (Nikki) from a cave-dwelling Medusa figure. The picture-story was complicated by the fact that some of the fairies were trying to hold some of the smaller dragons back from the serpent-haired monster; and also by the written statement that during a full moon, the dragons would become indiscriminately violent, a danger to the fairies.

The written statement was not part of the assignment, but the girls insisted on producing it anyway. What their teacher remembered most indelibly about this work—both the painting and the paper that accompanied it—was the paradox that formed the crux of the story. It had to do with the quality of the dragons' rescue efforts. Very specific, these had to be, with enough force to pull the fairies free of the marshy suck around the gorgon's cave, but gentle enough not to hurt their delicate bodies. But strong enough to save them. But gentle enough not to damage. The explanation went on this way, circularly, with pains to be understood, so earnest and crucial that the art teacher could not forget it, discussing it two years later in her office with a furrow between her brows, as if still trying to sort through the message: both the complexity of the mandate, and the girls' urgent need to articulate it.

Jacinta and Nikki shared the unusual distinction of being visual arts majors at Boston Arts Academy, a four-year-old pilot school with four hundred students, situated across the street from Fenway Park. When a Red Sox game was being played, they could catch free glimpses from certain parts of the yellowish-brick building. They liked reporting this, with the delight not of avid baseball fans but of dedicated scammers. They seemed to feel that they'd gotten into BAA on a scam, too—as if good fortune could not come to them otherwise.

Boston has one of those huge school systems where students from all over the city may apply to attend any of about two dozen public high schools. At Edwards Middle School (the antecedent to Charlestown's "Dum-Dum High"), eighth-graders were treated to a day of shopping among the alternatives, with representatives from different schools set up at tables in the cafeteria. Nikki had been leaning toward a military school program when she happened upon the BAA table. BAA really was a kind of haven, one of a handful, within the Boston public high schools. The school's lobby was free of metal detectors. The cop assigned to the building seemed to know most of the students by name. The building lay within walking distance of Boston's major art museums, and the visual arts students traipsed regularly across the Fens to visit and sketch. Nikki and Jacinta's class even had an installation at one of them, the Isabella Stewart Gardner Museum—an ephemeral piece done in grass. It lasted a few weeks and then turned brown.

The girls' special status as artists notwithstanding, they were nevertheless fifteen. They filled their notebooks with ballpoint renderings of cartoon characters and pop stars. Their joint aspirations were to be veterinarians and fashion designers. They had a series of mind-bogglingly choreographed secret handshakes, one for pinky swears, one for big secrets, and so on. They exchanged notes all day long in school, and they saved these notes in shoe boxes to "look back on in ten years." Their claims to practical telekinesis were supported by their ability to conduct entire conversations like this:

JACINTA: Remember that thing? With the...
NIKKI: (*coloring*) Oh my God!
JACINTA: No! Not— The other.
NIKKI: Oh. (*giving A Look*)
JACINTA: What?
NIKKI: (*elaborate sigh*)
JACINTA: Wait, yeah? (*receiving A Look*) Ohhh. That's what I *said!* (*dissolves in fits of laughter, falls on floor, somehow dragging Nikki with her*)

They referred to themselves as *loca* and *blanca*. They had code names—Chicken, Cow, Dog—for the girls they hated. They shared the same lucky number, eight; their unlucky number was twenty-five. They dreamed, with purported frequency, the same dreams.

And they refused to spar with each other.

Once they participated in an exhibition match at the Knights of Columbus Hall in Charlestown, about a week after Nikki first came to the gym. Exhibition matches are what they sound like: for show, and not officially sanctioned; the outcomes are not entered in the boxers' passbooks. Nikki was her unchecked taurine self, but Jacinta refused to raise a glove against her. Desi was the referee and nearly had a heart attack thinking Nikki was going to kill her best friend. The whole experience threw the girls off center, making them temporarily unsure of who they were supposed to be to each other. Ever since they had flatly declined to get in the ring together.

I think of the painting they made in ninth grade, the roles they spelled out for themselves in watered ink. In the story, Jacinta's doppelgänger is strong, both potentially dangerous and potentially a savior. Nikki's is fragile but steadfast and brave. In school, they played nearly opposite roles: Nikki the leader, Jacinta the follower. In the gym, they were both recognized as strong boxers, but Jacinta's power was seen as more controlled, Nikki's as more volatile. The deeper I went into their stories, the more I was reminded that neither girl could be easily categorized: They were each, ultimately, irreducible.

It was nearly eleven A.M. Other people had trickled into the gym—men, a few of their offspring, a young mother in acid-washed jeans, wielding a disposable camera. Now everyone in here was hot, though the back door, propped open, let in a crisp breeze with the smell of wood smoke in it. Raphi had just finished working the mitts with Nikki, who hit so hard it was like a trick of gravity that Raphi didn't get knocked right over backward. They were winded and sweaty at the end of the round, and Raphi was sitting on the ring apron, still catching her breath, when Candi headed toward the heavy bag with a pair of gloves on.

"No," called Raphi. "I don't want you doing that now. Save your energy." Candi showed signs of what looked like disobedience, continuing toward the bag. Raphi belted, "Hey! You have to do what I say," and tilted both her eyebrows and palms upward as if to say, "What's it going to be?" Because that was a gym fact: Nothing, *nothing* could go forward if they didn't mutually acknowledge Raphi's authority as trainer. She sat there, legs in their baby-pink sweats dangling well above the floor, hunching her shoulders a bit as she was wont to do, everything about her frame wiry and delicate-looking except her powerful arms. Her eyes protruded slightly, leveling this silent question at her goddaughter, her student, this little impish girl she loved.

Candi sighed elaborately and weaved off course. The pull to hit the heavy bag at this moment was partly nerves. Raphi was going to have her spar today for the first time ever. Not to say she was nervous. But she had been awaiting this day for months, not sure when it would arrive or who her sparring partner would be when it did, knowing only that these questions would be decided at Raphi's discretion. This day she learned it was going to be Anthony, the more promising of the new boys. At twelve, he was two years her senior and taller by half a head, but he'd been boxing only a few weeks, and he was amiable, with his endearingly raspy voice and eyebrows cocked, full of character.

"Are you ready?" Raphi asked him. He and Candi both came to the ring. The absence of coercion seemed counterintuitive, that both children, still slender-necked and clear-skinned, young enough to be tucked in at night, should come willingly, wantingly, to this meeting. Because it was the first time sparring for both, there was added interest, and the other girls and Maria drifted over to the ring to participate in some way, even if just as spectators. Raphi would usually dole out the responsibility of working as cornermen to the other kids. This could backfire occasionally, as when Candi worked Jacinta's corner and, between rounds, devilishly squirted water into her sister's eye instead of her mouth. But no one was messing around like that today. There was a current of sporting excitement, and under that, faint but unmistakable among Maria and the girls, a palpable feeling of competition, of pride.

"Sefina. You work Anthony's corner with Danny. Show him what to do." Whichever kid was skulking around the margins on any given day, Raphi was most likely to corral into service. Up Sefina got, finally shedding her jacket, and helped Anthony's friend locate a water bottle.

Candi was wearing a yellow tank top with a sunburst on it, black Nike shorts, and sneakers—no boxing shoes yet, although her sister had gotten a pair for Augusta the summer before. Real boxing shoes would be nice, Candi thought, mad cool, the ones that go halfway up the calf. Her ponytail grazed the small of her back. Her face—which seemed to flicker between that of a ten-year-old sprite, ready to break in an instant into her infectious, multi-octave giggle, and that of an undersize but serious pugilist—got circumscribed by the headgear Raphi pushed into place and strapped under her chin. Anthony, in his neutral corner, was similarly fastened into protective gear and gloves and got his mouthguard inserted and clamped down between his teeth. Danny offered him the water bottle prematurely, uncertainly. Anthony waved it away. Sefina, prompted by Raphi, checked that his gloves were on tight. Maria, Jacinta, and Nikki pressed up against the ropes, smiling with frank anticipation, their eagerness notable for its apparent lack of ambivalence.

The bell sounded. The kids touched gloves and boxed. They got busy right away. Anthony, with his longer reach, could have used his jab to hold her off, but Candi was dauntless and kept coming in under it to throw clusters of punches up into his body and face. It was strange to see them react to their first blows to the face. Neither of them did what ought to be instinctive and turned his or her head away, and neither of them looked scared, although they blinked. A certain redness came to the neck and about the eyes, a minor adjustment, a thought or resolve; the mouthguard shifted around and was bitten into place again. Anthony backed Candi into a corner, then she got out and around him and was landing the combinations she'd been practicing for so many months on Raphi and the mitts. Maria and the girls shouted things, mostly Candi's name. Raphi watched with total concentration. She was, in effect, the sole sanctioning body for this event, responsible in the moment for the well-being of these two children she had put in the ring together.

If she had looked over her right shoulder just then, in the direction of the men's locker room, she would have seen the single locker, the narrow gray tower, that had been left to stand outside it, on the edge of what was once an altar and was now where the dumbbells and weight-lifting benches were crammed together. Written small, on a frayed piece of tape, was the name of the last person to use this locker: TOMASELLO.

Bobby Tomasello was the first person Raphi ever saw box up close. A few days before her coach decided it was time to let her spar, he had her watch Bobby and his father, Big Bob, go four rounds. Perhaps it was meant as a test, a cautionary tale, because the two men went hard, and Bobby got the worst of it. After the final bell, the younger man bounded down, his nose bleeding, and cheerfully complained that he must've eaten too much before getting in the ring. Raphi's coach turned to her and asked if she still wanted to try sparring. "I can't wait!" Her eyes were gleaming.

Eventually, she and Bobby were both working the amateur circuit. For her first fight, Bobby lent her his lucky blue trunks. They sparred once; he had difficulty modifying his style for her diminutive size, and he nearly knocked her down with a shot to the liver. By the time she turned to coaching, he had turned pro, but they still saw each other all the time at the gym. He had his nose broken in the ring, and his orbital bone; still, he was bent on becoming a champion. They spent time together at the gym a few nights before his television debut. He promised that after the fight, he'd start helping out with the kids she trained. She took his hand and told him to be careful.

She saw him twice after that. Once was on TV. His big fight, at the Roxy in Boston, was also his longest, ten rounds. Raphi made popcorn and watched it in her bedroom. He started out well, light on his feet, landing combinations, but the opponent was tough, and about the fourth round, Bobby's familiar style morphed into a sick parody. He began dropping his hands, taking a stomach-churning number of blows, and his usual quick footwork looked sluggish, off. The fight went all ten rounds, though, and was declared a draw. At least that won't mar his record, thought Raphi, but she felt ill inside, and after he left the ring, her eyes filled with tears.

The last time she saw him was in an intensive-care unit, his head so bandaged and taped to life-support machines that all she could see of his face was one eye, swollen and encircled with black and blue. In the locker room after the fight, he had complained of a headache, and when his coach went to get the doctor, Bobby fell into a coma. He was twenty-four. He died five days later without waking.

Raphi was not unaware of the ugliness this sport can deliver.

Yet here she was, returning as if thirsty and dipping her head to the only source of drink, and she was not alone but had brought children with her to the watering hole. She leaned lightly on the ropes and watched everything in the ring, absorbed, alert.

Time for the third round. The bell. Candi and Anthony left their neutral corners, advanced on each other, circling, throwing jabs and blocking, coming closer and farther. They were looking more sluggish from fatigue. Good, thought Raphi, with coachly satisfaction: Now they could begin to understand just how long three minutes can be. Who would guess that after a measly nine minutes of activity, with two sixty-second rests built in, a person could be so tired, so out of breath and jelly-legged, that the simple task of keeping one's hands up could feel Sisyphean? This would help them understand the importance of jumping rope for three minutes straight, three rounds in a row; it would help them understand the need to run sprints and the need to run miles outside the gym on days they didn't have practice. The need to practice the speed bag, not just for rhythm but also to learn what it was to keep their hands up for a full round. The need to work the heavy bag in fast bursts, so they could gain the strength to keep throwing punches at all, let alone punches with power behind them.

The bell signaling the last thirty seconds sounded, and both kids registered relief, beginning to drop their hands, back off, glance at the time clock. "Go!" yelled Raphi. "Thirty seconds!" They started circling again, the boxerly shuffle of left foot forward, right foot dragged behind. "Keep going! Fifteen seconds! How many punches can you land?" Candi, hearing her godmother's challenge, surged forward with a combination and popped Anthony hard in the mouth. The bell.

When Candi went to hug Raphi, she practically flew into her arms. The coach scooped her up, and the girl's legs wrapped around her waist. The hug lasted close to a minute. They didn't say anything but seemed to be telling, together, a story they both knew.

Then everyone talked. Candi did this, Candi did that, Anthony has long arms, did you see how she got out of the corner? Jacinta and Nikki, the seasoned ones, with real USA Boxing passbooks and real bouts recorded in official script, hovered around Candi, excited and welcoming. Maria was beaming, her broad face and lively eyes shining on the little one. She replayed some of Candi's moves with her own thicker fists. Everyone knew she'd be tough once she got a chance to spar.

"If you hit like that when you have a fight, you'll definitely win," said Anthony when the girls were done giving their two cents. He was sitting on the ring apron. He nodded at Candi, charming in his good sportsmanship, his authoritative gruffness. Raphi saw him feel around with his tongue, touch his fingertips carefully to his chin.

"Did she hurt you?" asked Raphi sharply, coming up to see how he moved his jaw.

"Naw. I mean, I just . . ." He grinned, nodded. "She hits hard!"

Anthony's simple acknowledgment of Candi's power was sweeter to Raphi than he could ever guess. "You did well," she told him. "You both did. Did you like it?"

"Yeah," said Anthony gamely. "It was good."

"I liked it," said Candi almost shyly. And then her crackly giggle: the absurdity of having stated the obvious.

Raphi was pleased to have found someone at last for Candi to spar with. It was difficult to get sparring for all the girls. Jacinta and Nikki would have been well matched but refused to be paired in that way.

Candi was so small, and Sefina so unruly . . . Sometimes Raphi did put the sisters in together, but this invariably ended with everyone in tears. Raphi herself avoided sparring with the kids. One piece of her wariness was purely practical: They were so young and hungry, and she was getting older and had started smoking again. But more than this was the tricky issue of distance, that distance she felt she needed to maintain in order to warrant their respect as coach. There was an intimacy to sparring that could make it as dangerous emotionally as physically. It was a fine line, Raphi knew, between sparring and fighting. She could not risk hurting them in any way, or having them hurt her.

Fifteen minutes left to practice. Nikki and Jacinta got on a mat and did leg throws. Anthony and Danny were instructed to follow suit. Maria picked up a hand weight and worked her biceps. Candi, still basking, sat on the ring apron and watched a couple of grown men shadowbox. The platform creaked under their moving weight like a boat. Naturally, now that practice was nearly over, Sefina felt the urge to work out. She roamed over to a speed bag and began, essentially, to kickbox it.

"Sefina!" her mother snapped. "Cut it!"

Her final spinning kick, defiant and very Charlie's Angels–esque, missed the speed bag by a lot—good thing, since the bladders were old and had been patched and repatched. She could have split it for good. The long, long leg, clad in distressed denim, came back down with a clunk. She got on the scale, slid the weights around, stepped off. She shoved open the back door. Cold air and sunlight came surging into the gym. "Sefina! Shut it!" Damn. She always had to get blamed for everything.

This was how Raphi ended practice that day: with a game of musical chairs. Special rule: After each round, a chair was removed, but every player had to stay in the game, finding a seat on another's lap, until by the end, six kids were piled on top of one another for as many seconds as their giggles would allow. "Go home!" she barked. Then she broke out a box of granola bars and some clementines, a whole bright glistening crate of them, and the kids descended.

"Can I take five?" asked Candi, right away.

"As many as you want."

Sefina started juggling with them. Maria, sorting through the girls' necklaces, which they had left in a tangled pile near the boom box, told her to stop.

Jacinta, all dimpled and quiet, took two. And a granola bar.

The boys had to be encouraged to help themselves.

Nikki pocketed a couple of the shiny globes. "Thanks," she said, with a certain embarrassed flatness. Then she smiled a secret smile and grabbed one more.

"Can they really have this many?" Maria asked. The crate was just about empty. The kids were acting all happy, snatching up and tossing around these tokens of their coach's abundant care.

Raphi shrugged. "That's what I brought them for." She was winding up hand wraps, a monotonous task. How many hundreds of times she had done this. A hundred and twenty inches of cotton. Twenty-seven bones in a human hand and wrist. As if remembering something, she whipped around and adopted her fiercest voice to address the kids: "And I don't want to find any peels on the floor!"

Boxing has long been a shady business, operating way out on the margins of society. Even though it has been entrenched in our country as a sport and big business for nearly a century, its existence continues to come under attack from the American Medical Association on one hand and from state legislatures on the other. While detractors and proponents debate the physical dangers of boxing relative to those of other sports (race-car driving, horse racing, skydiving, hockey, and even football may have higher rates of serious head injury and even death), virtually everyone now acknowledges the existence of dementia pugilistica, a chronic encephalopathy caused by the cumulative effects of multiple subconcussive blows to the head. Also called punch-drunkenness, its symptoms can include slurred speech, foot dragging, tremors, and memory, hearing, and vision impairment. No one can deny that boxing is the only one of these sports in which blows are not incidental but the very means to winning.

Disturbingly valid comparisons have been drawn between boxing and cockfighting, or dogfighting, or gladiatorial combat among Roman slaves—all forms of exploitation in which a powerless object is forced to bleed, and draw blood, for the pleasure of powerful subjects. Failure to recognize the aptness of this analogy and that the vast majority of boxers come from backgrounds with compromised access to money, education, jobs, or high social status—that they "come from want"—constitutes a kind of injustice. But a too-neat acceptance of this analogy constitutes another injustice. By neglecting to wonder what else boxing *means,* and *does,* and *is* from the perspective of those who practice it, we commit an act of blindness and condescension.

Yes, there was the terrible hollow monument of Bobby Tomasello's locker on the former altar. Yes, there were the framed portraits of the Quiet Man up in the office, shimmering cruelly in the kids' eyes, perhaps, like mirage pots of gold. Yes, there were the dues no one could pay, and the ex-cons who worked the desk and worked the bags and worked the kids' corners at fights. Yes, there were the old-timers who came in slurring and smelling of alcohol, and the boxers who sneaked out for a cigarette or a joint; there was the sweet curly-haired young heavyweight who wore a bracelet on his ankle as part of his probation for a drug bust, and the handsome white-haired gentleman who was a prominent figure in the Charlestown Mob.

Yes, it was a place of brokenness, of "little wanderers," as Raphi called them sometimes, called herself, too. It was a place around which milled some danger, some ugliness. But why, then, did it also feel like a hearth, a place to come and be fed? What was this mixture of safety and freedom—and danger—that seemed possible here as nowhere else?

Several years ago, shortly after she'd won the Golden Gloves, Raphi was invited to appear on the local public-television program *Greater Boston.* The topic was women's boxing, and the other panelists were politely but clearly opposed to it. Raphi looked tiny on-screen. She was sitting in a huge chair, her feet barely reaching the ground, and her hair was pulled back so tightly that she appeared as a pale oval face with huge eyes.

Bill Littlefield, the host of National Public Radio's weekly sports program, *Only a Game,* was also on the show. He said that the only convincing argument he'd ever heard for boxing came from a state police officer who maintained that the confidence he'd found since taking up the sport had made him less likely to draw his gun. "If all policemen would feel that way," said Littlefield, "I think it would be better."

"What about all *people?*" interjected Raphi. But the camera cut to her too late; three voices overlapped in confusion, and her query was lost.

The assertion that boxing is cathartic and therefore makes people less likely to engage in physical aggression is debatable, to say the least, and faces opponents in the physical and social sciences who assert just the opposite: that boxing normalizes the use of physical aggression, thus making people *more* likely to engage in it. Although many studies have been conducted, no definitive proof exists for either position. From here it would be easy enough, and logical, to make reference to such studies, and to all manner of data and statistics supporting one view or the other—precisely what most of the experts I interviewed for this book did. Which often proved absorbing, helpful, provocative, or orienting, but failed to take into account the specific existence of individuals and their unique relationships to and experiences of boxing. The experts—largely physicians and public-health advocates concerned with the problem of violence and cultural factors that may contribute to its prevalence—tended to ask and answer questions about boxing in a policy-driven way that dealt in generalities and made little allowance for paradox.

These were intelligent, sensitive, sincere people, but they had *decided*. They, like the others on the television program, were as certain of their views, I reminded myself, as I had been before stumbling upon the boxing club. Before I'd encountered the troubling person of Raphaëlla Johnson. Everything about what Raphi-the-boxer represented was difficult, counterintuitive. Not so awful to think of cops boxing, but this slight woman, pale-faced and bird-boned, huge-eyed and earnest—she seemed aberrant. She looked the classic victim. How monstrous of her to insist otherwise.

In the *Greater Boston* segment on boxing, the moderator wrapped up by questioning whether breaking into the sport of boxing really constituted a victory for women. The guests, except for Raphi, opined that it did not. Littlefield, in a final indictment of the whole sport, declared, "To endure pain for money and the entertainment of strangers sounds suspiciously like prostitution to me."

My problem, both while watching the segment and while interviewing experts, was that the people opposed to boxing made a great deal of sense. They spoke to the subject in what I would have called, for most of my life, the only sensible way. My own voice and views, once firmly and serenely held, would have supported the arguments I now found myself scrambling to refute.

The one thing that is truly monstrous is the idea of another person being unreachable. I think this is what lies behind our fear of people we imagine to be evil: the belief that they are wholly beyond our reach, beyond our appeal and our compassion, because they have alienated themselves completely from the rest of humanity and thereby rendered themselves inhuman. My childhood impression of boxers, and of the crowd that hungered for the spectacle of boxing, was exactly that: These were people who had at least temporarily emptied themselves of those human qualities I could recognize, converse with, touch.

But there is mutuality involved. For us to accept another person's alienation is simultaneously to alienate ourselves from him—to become complicit. When we decide to accept that another person is unreachable, we may cut him off, send him away, but we have set ourselves adrift as well. I wonder what was more frightening about my childhood glimpses of boxers: the idea that these men had put themselves beyond my reach and I could never evoke their recognition, gentleness, humanity—or was it the idea that these men *were* human, like me, and that I might therefore have the capacity to go where they had gone, to experience appetite for force, desire for the aggressive use of my body? Perhaps what I shied away from was not the fear that they would prove immune to my imagined appeal, but the fear that I might prove susceptible to theirs.

That I found the world of boxing disturbing didn't make me want to walk away from it. To the contrary, I was repulsed and entranced. Earlier in my life I would have honored only the repulsion. But it had come to seem possible—*necessary*—to open up a space in which the innate will and power to do violence could be considered. Not as a foreign entity but as a part of us: of humanity in general, of women in particular, and of myself in the most specific instance. Each of these three seemed exponentially scarier and more troubling. Yet each also seemed crucial to consider.

In the gym that afternoon, the kids stripped clementines of their bright rinds, and the gym air got stippled with sweet mist. They were laughing, Anthony putting slices gingerly into his mouth since he was beginning to get a fat lip, Candi not gloating but holding it in, wearing her new pride like a nimbus. I was drawn here as nowhere else. The experts all assured me that whatever benefits the kids reaped at the gym, they could get just as well on the soccer field and without the ugliness. But these kids had not chosen to be on the soccer field. Anyway, I was beginning to think the experts were wrong.

3

TIME CLOCK

My brother was a star wrestler in high school. I never played anything, had no use for sports. Once, as an adult, I got referred to a psychiatrist because I weighed so little. After we talked for a while about eating habits, he said, "Oh, so food is your sport," and I thought he might be an idiot, or else I might be. "Does everybody have a sport?" I half whispered, growing warm. In sports there is a goal you are meant to achieve with your body, and this was something I had long refused.

My brother had a beautiful body, the proportion of muscle to skin to bone in exquisite balance, and he was very kind and funny, and although he was this incredible athlete and well liked by teachers and peers and everybody, it had not always been this way. He'd spent the first four years of his life in foster care and in an orphanage, and after he became a member of our family, it took him twice that time to win some measure of peace within himself. Whatever equilibrium he had now, he'd struggled long and hard for, and I could not think of him without some residual ache that was an awareness of his old terrifying vulnerability. Anyway, he was this wrestling star, and I never went to see him at any of his matches. My parents almost always went ("Kick some ass for Mother," our mom used to tell him, dryly, just before he wrestled), and my sister was the team scorekeeper, so she was always in attendance. But I was— I don't know—busy. I can't have always had other plans during his meets, but it seemed to work out that way.

Just once he had a home meet in our high school gym, and I was wandering around the building at the same time—waiting for play rehearsal to begin, probably—and I ran into my mother in the hall. She said, "Come in, Andy's just about to wrestle." I followed her through the door. The building was a little old-fashioned, so the gym had a balcony, and that was where we stood, high above the mat. He was down there, barely recognizable in his blue singlet and headgear. He is thirteen months younger than I am. He wore his hair shaved close to the skull back then, and I was looking down on the top of his dark round head. The wrestling match began. Within seconds he and another boy were down upon the mat, entangled, struggling against each other with all their might. I was racked with sobs. Somehow I came to be standing out in the hallway, alone, convulsed. My mother found me a few minutes later. She sounded compassionate and amused. "Lele, he *won*," she reassured me. As if that were why I'd been crying.

The only thing I ever liked to do with my body was dance. I was, vain but true, a very good dancer. When I was little, I did quite a bit of folk dancing, and this is how good I like to believe I was: When I danced, I was an alchemist. I could change my arms into wings and my feet into air. I was so light and could travel so seamlessly inside the rhythm that it was nearly flying. I hated to dance with anyone touching me, the weight and sweat of another person's hands, arms, shoulders. If my partner was another little girl who was a very good dancer, that was all right. But best was alone, outside, on a warm night. The gypsyish strains of Floricica Olteneasca coming out of a couple of loudspeakers set up on a folding table on the grass, my bare feet landing on the earth only to push off again higher into the dark air. When I danced, I could get a trapdoor to open in the prison that was my body. I had access to enormous power. Speed and flight. I could use my body to be free of my flesh. Always, that beacon, that hope: to be free.

And later, that other avenue toward lightness and flight, keeping the flesh negligible. A different way of using the body, or abusing the body, to be free, to simulate freedom, from flesh. I didn't think it through. I was in my fourth decade before I understood that I wasn't just genetically on the thin side. But I don't think food was ever my sport; there was nothing sporting about my thinness. If anything, it was closer to religion, offering the illusion of transcendence.

When a woman's body, a girl's body, is construed as unpowerful at best, a liability at worst, then the idea of shedding that body, escaping it somehow, holds beautiful, seductive promise. To become flight, to become air, what a dance!

I trained. My night on the speed bag left me sore and happy. After Raphi's exit that night, Vinny Busa took it upon himself not only to adjust my elbow height but to guide me through part of a workout, with weights and lots of leg throws, and the next day my muscles sang with their private, aching secret. I was alert to a new possibility. I had worked out on occasion before but felt silly, a pretender, playacting at something I was not, at something I would not risk letting myself want. In the grittiness of the boxing gym, in the unprettiness of it, in the peculiar, revolting honesty of the sport—and in the person of Raphaëlla, who could have been my carnival-mirror image, limning an alternate route to agency than any I had envisioned for myself—I found myself able to relax my prohibition against inhabiting my body. To train as if I cared.

At the next practice I jumped rope. I had jumped a little with Candi before, where we faced each other and jumped with a single rope; she liked to do this, and it made me laugh. But I had never jumped a whole round, and even with lots of starts and stops (I kept hitting myself in the back of the head with the rope), I was ready to collapse after three minutes. Still, I was wildly happy. I found Raphi's water bottle and drank from it; we all drank from her bottle.

It was a Tuesday night, the first week of December. Jacinta had shown up with a swollen right hand. She had punched a wall at school earlier in the day, when a teacher made her angry. After practice, her mother would take her to the emergency room to make sure it wasn't broken. She wanted to work out; promised not to hit with her right; then wrapped both hands anyway. *Loca.* At least this night she wrapped them—half the time she'd work the bags bare-fisted and scrape up her knuckles.

Raphi showed me the four basic punches in front of the mirror, then left me to shadowbox. Torture: the reflection of my pale face, my ludicrously slight build (somehow more ludicrous in me than in Raphi, who was scrappier, less elongated). I was aware of my arms, so unlike Jacinta's, which felt like telephone poles when you hugged her. I was aware of my brow line, so unlike Nikki's, whose seemed sculpted in iron. In the ring behind me, the girls ran sideways, stopped, threw combinations at thin air, reversed direction. Except for Candi, who was mad at Sefina and sulked against the ropes, sticking out a foot to trip Sefina every time she passed.

The men were all around that night, young and old, training for the Golden Gloves. You had to be sixteen to compete. Raphi hoped to bring her girls instead to the Silver Mittens in the spring, a kind of junior Gloves event for the eight-to-fifteen-year-old set. The men were also around because John Ruiz was in town, getting ready for his fight with Evander Holyfield in ten days at Foxwoods Casino. Ruiz would be sparring at the gym in preparation. No one was exactly sure when, but members of his entourage were filling up the little office, warning people they'd be towed if they parked out back, going about in their TEAM RUIZ jackets and talking grimly into their cell phones.

Raphi called me over to hit the mitts. I was surprised. This was only my second time working out. She put gloves on me, warm and damp inside from the last person: a flicker of revulsion, quickly dismissed. I shoved my hand in deep, and she fastened the Velcro around my wrist. She told me one was my jab, two was my right, three was a left hook, four was an uppercut. She yelled, "One!," and I threw a jab at her left mitt, and she brought it a little forward at the same moment, and it connected. I mean it *connected*. All I wanted in the world at that moment was to repeat the action. The sound it made was pure, visceral pleasure. "One!" she yelled. "Two!" And then, "Put your body into it, your hip." She showed me. "Two! Beautiful. Again. One! Two! Turn your hip! One, two! One, two! One, one, two!" I was backing her up. "Faster!" She pivoted out of the corner. "Now try a hook." I tried a hook. "Keep it tighter, close to your body. Good. Again. Keep your hands up! One! One, two! One, two, three! Hands up!" Three rounds were over so soon. Not a moment *too* soon, because my muscles had turned to water and my punches were barely carrying though the air, but still, disappointingly soon.

"You're strong," Raphi told me later in the locker room. "And you have the anger. Where did *that* come from?"

"I do? Really?"

"You remind me of Nikki. She looks so willowy, but then you get in the ring with her, and there's this fire."

"Really? I mean, I do?"

"You should buy your own hand wraps."

The seven nicest words I ever heard.

I am ten or eleven, at a baseball game, bored. Underneath the boredom I am bothered. The players are people I love and admire, my camp counselors and the counselors-in-training, but they are acting unlike themselves, invested in winning, in beating. The camp is called Kinderland. We kids like to say it's a communist camp, but this is because we like getting a rise out of people. It's really more socialist. All the bunks are named after heroes of the oppressed.

The custom at Kinderland is for any athletic competition to end in an official tie. But today is different, today people are keeping score, and it has made them look different and sound different to me. These are the people I hope to be when I grow up—smart and brave and funny, with orange sneakers and guitars. They stay up late talking on picnic tables under the millions of stars. They know the words to all the songs; they drink coffee and patrol with flashlights while we sleep. But today they have disappeared inside their bodies. Beneath the game lurks something that is not a game. Low chatter on the field, a jagged-toothed tension. Bluster and clapping. A scowl; spitting; taunts.

I want to remind them they don't really care. That this game is a game. They must stay vigilant, these older ones whose responsibility it is to take care of us, they must not slip away into other selves. I must have heard about this somewhere: the thing of dusting off home plate. I find a leafy branch on the ground. Between batters now, I dart out and sweep the dry yellow dirt off the base. I know it's a silly thing to do, but in a way, that's the point. The obvious absurdity of my twig broom might break the spell this sport has woven over them.

As I spent more time at the gym, I got to know some of the boys who regularly worked out alongside us. Moses was from Uganda. He worked two jobs: in a lab during the week at MIT and at a nursing home on the weekends. And he was taking a computer-programming course. "In case the boxing thing doesn't work out," he told me, and I laughed before realizing he wasn't kidding. Whenever he sparred near the end of the week, he made an effort to throw more body shots than blows to the face, so that his opponent wouldn't have to go on a date with a black eye.

James was from Bermuda. He worked out but didn't spar; he wore a prosthesis, having lost a leg to childhood cancer. He had a small son, and dreadlocks, and was a reggae musician.

Tonio was from El Salvador. A sophomore at Somerville High School, he wore a red bandanna around his head and had the silkiest, sparsest black facial hair. He jumped rope with incredible, effortless grace, as if his blood type were helium. His trainers called him a natural. He was the rare kid they allowed to switch up, to box south paw and righty within a single round.

Pierre was Haitian, Tonio's friend from school. He came less regularly, and the coaches got on him for slouching. His father had been shot dead when Pierre was a toddler, drug related.

Cal was a super-heavyweight. He was on probation for taking part in a drug deal. He had curly black hair and an affable, ready smile, full of humility. His role model was his younger sister, a gymnast.

Ngozi had strict parents, his mother from Kentucky and his minister father from Nigeria. He'd lost his first three fights—one by decision; the other two were stopped by the referee because Ngozi was losing too badly. His parents were considering making him quit.

The boys were uniformly friendly and respectful toward the girls, although the groups kept separate. These young men, every one, possessed a surprising gentleness—within the gym, at least. They comported themselves with something like quiet nobility, which their coaches said was what came of boxing: the outward measure of the confidence and self-control they earned from the sport.

I was talking about this one day with their coach, Gene McCarthy. We were standing near the fire door, Gene with his arms folded over his broad chest, appraising Tonio on the double-end bag, while he carried on this conversation with me, this genial, proud monologue rife with words I was beginning to anticipate: broken homes, poverty, discipline, self-esteem—the same story I had already heard and would hear many more times over the coming year—when the sound of crashing metal rang out from the girls' locker room behind us. This was becoming a familiar sound, too, and I didn't need to look in order to picture what was going on in there.

Sure enough, a moment later, Jacinta came flying out with a shriek, dimples flashing. Sefina tore after her in a fury and kicked her in the leg. Maria aimed the back of her hand at Sefina's cheek but missed, since now the sisters had dropped to the floor and were wrestling on the mat, right in the middle of everything. Mild glances from the men, who did not stop their workouts. Raphi yelled at them to get up, prodding Jacinta with her foot. "You can't do that out here!" she admonished. Half laughing, half furious, they chased each other back inside the locker room, where the crash of bodies against lockers briefly resumed. A lewd rap was playing on the boom box, and Candi hopped up off the pew to dance to it, mostly with her butt. Nikki did a chin-up, not on the chinning bar but by grabbing onto one of the wall-mounted speed-bag boards, and narrowly missed kicking in the wall at the precise place where the girls had managed to put a hole in the plaster the previous week, "while running sprints." Maria and Raphi rolled their eyes at each other. So much for quiet nobility.

Gene was not wild about girls in the gym, nor about women boxing in general. Almost none of the male coaches were. Oh, they *supported* it, they'd tell me affably. Then they'd lean in: But they didn't *like* it. They were disarmingly, endearingly frank about their distaste. The number one reason they gave was that women were too pretty; why should they want to mess up their faces? Real concern and bewilderment over this, you could see it in their eyes as they shook their heads: How could a woman risk destroying her best currency, her looks? I was also told that women didn't have as much anger as men to discharge, nor as much reason to be angry. I was told that it was inherently revolting to want to watch a woman being beaten. And by another *woman* . . . Here, inevitably, the complaints petered out, words giving way to nonwords, to a discomfort so deep it apparently could not be pursued, and so the list would end with its final image: woman, in all her yielding softness, turning the tables and making her body an instrument of power and mastery and violence. With the list's end came, I thought, the truest objection, whose roots lay in fear.

Girls tend to seek power through obedience. In her book *The Secret*

Lives of Girls, Sharon Lamb points out that this is less true for girls living in certain underserved communities: the poor, and those from black and Latino families, where a measure of resistance may be prized. But in a society that usually tries to squash or deny female aggression, it's a struggle for all girls to understand and value themselves as potentially aggressive beings. And, she says, "This realization is crucial to growing up whole."

If what boxing offers girls is qualitatively different than what it offers boys, it is no less valuable. It might well be more valuable, if only for being more rare. Anyway, I told myself, as the sounds of the Rodriguezes' locker-room wrestlemania reverberated behind me, self-control might not be uppermost among their needs.

In response to a query of mine, Raphi e-mailed: "I was wondering when the sparring bug would bite you. I didn't want to mention it first because I didn't want to rush you. Before you spar I'd like to do some defense drills with you, because sparring is really scary if you can't defend yourself." She briefly outlined a training plan to get me ready for sparring. "I am not worried about your offense although you need some more work," she said. "I see fire in you." What surprised me most about the note, when I came across it later, was the date, December 10. Less than two weeks after I first hit the speed bag.

In my memory, I had been slow to broach the question of sparring. I would have thought I'd trained for months before raising the possibility. In reality, it took me thirteen days. She said *she'd been waiting for me.* And spoke of fire in a way that made me rise from my chair and stand before the mirror. How can a person be so blind as not to recognize herself? How can a fire be so well hidden as to conceal its heat?

Female aggression carries all the burden of the unacceptable. In *Real Knockouts: The Physical Feminism of Women's Self-Defense,* the sociologist Martha McCaughey writes that our very construction of femininity hinges on the taboo of aggression. "Cultural ideals of manhood and womanhood include a cultural, political, aesthetic, and legal acceptance of men's aggression and a deep skepticism, fear, and prohibition of women's." We begin the twenty-first century with this taboo largely intact.

But before considering the issue of female aggression, it helps to have an idea of how our culture understands human aggression. The argument over whether human beings are inherently aggressive and must learn to be peaceful, or inherently peaceful and must learn to be aggressive, extends back centuries, at least. Thomas Hobbes said man's only drive is for self-preservation and power, and civilization alone saves him from his destructive impulses. Jean-Jacques Rousseau said man is at heart peaceful, and civilization corrupts him. The debate has carried straight through to the twentieth century, with scientists and scholars disagreeing over whether aggression is a drive or an instinct; whether it is ever present and requires continuous reining in or is summoned only by an inciting event; whether it discharges hostility or reinforces it, and on and on, without ever reaching consensus. In fact, the leading theorists of the twentieth century sound remarkably like Hobbes and Rousseau in their utter discord, so that we have Robert Ardrey telling us, "Man is a predator whose natural instinct is to kill," and Ashley Montagu saying, "No human being has ever been born with aggressive or hostile impulses, and no one becomes aggressive or hostile without learning to do so." The heatedness with which the experts duke it out on paper is itself eyebrow-raising: Certainly the question has puzzled and plagued us for ages, and the answer *matters* to us. It is not an academic question but an elemental one that goes to the heart of who we are and what we are doing on this planet.

Once, in tenth grade, one of my teachers scribbled on the blackboard: HUMAN NATURE IS BASICALLY GOOD / HUMAN NATURE IS BASICALLY EVIL. Then he went around the room, making us cast our votes out loud one by one, while he kept a chalk-scrape tally. When he got to me, I said, "I don't believe in human nature." I didn't know whether I believed in human nature or not, but it seemed important to smash his neat dichotomy and the way we were falling like pins in the face of it. He was physically the largest teacher in the school, had a propensity for wearing lab coats even though he taught English, and was mildly famous for having once purportedly slapped a student and called her a bitch. When, hearing my response, he growled, "Oh, don't give me that," I caved immediately. "Basically good, then," I squeaked.

There was no doubt in my mind that the right answer, as far as he was concerned—the answer revealing a more sophisticated intellect and greater emotional maturity—was "basically evil." I felt obliged to vote the other way. Whether this was because I needed to make a feeble, last-ditch effort at defiance, or because my vote would somehow contribute to the possibility of good in the world—and I felt, as a girl, under duress to answer this call—I cannot say. The moment was strangely fraught—for him, it seemed, as well as for me. And although it passed without any further notice, it left a kind of residue. It seemed to me a queer battle, misfought, and I felt ashamed for having put up so little resistance.

Why, I wonder now, does that moment have such lasting power, enough to disturb me two decades later? Probably because it evokes a thousand like it: all the tiny moments of acquiescence and shameful surrender that mark a girlhood. In hewing to his either/or model, I not only relinquished my own view; by choosing the option I felt I had no choice but to choose, I narrowed the scope of what was possible for me to embody. It cannot be incidental that most of the girls in our class voted as I did, and most of the boys the opposite.

Of course, the issue here is aggression, and aggression is hardly synonymous with violence, let alone with evil. But how often it is mistaken for those two! Or at least presumed to be evil's antechamber. The literature on aggression is rife with short leaps from the one to the other, and the energy invested in explaining, rationalizing, contextualizing, prescribing, and distancing ourselves from any such primal impulse belies a serious discomfort—one that makes it difficult to speak of aggression as something valuable to us. The word is so diffusely applied, it is really, as Anthony Storr says in *Human Aggression,* a portmanteau term encompassing the forms of aggression we deplore as well as the forms we need for survival. Although the pendulum of public opinion swings wide, deplorable aggression tends more often, predictably, to obscure the other, more constructive form. And so at the beginning of the current millennium, it is fashionable to regard aggression as a public-health dilemma; a learned behavior (learned largely from television); and something that should and can be greatly reduced, if not avoided, in part through ameliorating poverty and other social stressors.

I have no quarrel with these ideas. But to regard aggression exclusively in this light is a mistake. And no one group suffers the cost more than girls.

When we think of aggression, we most commonly think of anger, and this is one aspect of aggression that many girls must work to reclaim. The expression of anger, says Lyn Mikel Brown in *Raising Their Voices: The Politics of Girls' Anger,* is "intimately tied to self-respect, to the capacity to realize and author one's life fully." But other researchers speak of aggression quite apart from any anger or hostility. They refer to it as linked to agency, curiosity, power, and creativity. Dana Crowley Jack, in her book *Behind the Mask: Destruction and Creativity in Women's Aggression,* identifies aggression as essential to human development and well-being. "If conflict is necessary for growth, if one needs not only empathy and attunement but the ability to oppose others and express one's will, then healthy aggression is mandatory to the development of self and to positive connection."

The renowned British child psychiatrist D. W. Winnicott spoke of the infant's primitive experience of its own aggressiveness—or, in his term, "ruthlessness"—which he described as the baby biting and scratching and kicking. He said that when the mother survives the baby's aggression, "the baby will find a new meaning to the word love." Winnicott called this experience—of being at liberty to exercise one's own aggression in the fullest, and seeing that the world survives it—the basis for healthy human development.

Yet by the time they are one or two, girls are receiving the opposite message: that the world will not withstand their attacks. Sharon Lamb again: "Girls and women fear that their anger could destroy others . . . that to express anger threatens annihilation." Dana Crowley Jack: "The fear of women's destructive potential is learned early." Study after study shows that parents and teachers, wittingly or not, stifle aggression in girls and encourage it in boys. And so, in a phrase coined by Lyn Mikel Brown and Carol Gilligan, girls grow up under the "tyranny of the nice and kind." Colette Dowling, in *The Frailty Myth: Women Approaching Physical Equality,* speaks of "girls' overwhelming need to be small," and of the "flight from self" that many of them undertake during their pre-adolescence and adolescence.

In other words, although the rebuke to girls' aggression originates in the voices of others, it soon takes up residence within girls themselves.

Very early, girls become complicit in their own diminution. If the process of internalizing the rebuke is really successful, girls not only comply with it but believe in it, and the cultural myth is insidiously realized. One tiny measure of aggression is allowed for women defending their children; other than that, women are "by nature" nonaggressive.

In her book *Woman: An Intimate Geography,* the Pulitzer Prize–winning *New York Times* science writer Natalie Angier dismisses this notion. "Of course they're aggressive. They're alive, aren't they? They're primates." But, she says, scientists and society alike ignore this fact, ritualistically and reflexively. "The problem of ignoring female aggression is that we who are aggressive, we girls and women and obligate primates, feel confused, as though something is missing in the equation."

The confusion she names would be tricky enough to negotiate when it *is* felt, something acknowledged and nettlesome aboveground. How much more poisonous might it be when the faulty equation is not recognized as such, when the missing thing has been stuffed so deep, for so long, as to have been stricken from consciousness?

One result of aggression driven underground is what academics call indirect aggression and relational aggression, the now famous tactics of mean girls or, should I say, of girls, since we have recently been enlightened that girls are by definition mean. I refer to the recent spate of books (Rachel Simmon's *Odd Girl Out,* Rosalind Wiseman's *Queen Bees & Wannabes,* Emily White's *Fast Girls,* Phyllis Chesler's *Woman's Inhumanity to Woman,* Leora Tanenbaum's *Slut!* and *Catfight*), as well as cover articles in both *The New York Times Magazine* and *Newsweek,* identifying the problem of meanness in girls and the proliferating school-based interventions aimed at rectifying the crisis. What has failed to find similar prominence in the media are various studies showing that although these kinds of aggression (gossiping, excluding, withdrawing, etc.) are more common among girls than boys, they occur with *equal frequency* among adult women and men. According to Sarah Forrest, for example, in a 2002 study presented at the British Psychological Society conference, "We found no differences in the sexes at all. Men were just as bitchy as women." Never mind. The whole notion of mean girls, the very phrase *mean girls,* is so sexy, so media-ready.

Less so are the other ways of redirecting or sublimating female aggression, which researchers say include anorexia, self-injuring, and depression. This last, studies show, becomes more than twice as likely to afflict girls than boys from puberty on. As Jessica Benjamin tells us in *The Bonds of Love: Psychoanalysis, Feminism, and the Problem of Domination,* "Obedience, of course, does not exorcise aggression; it merely directs it against the self." But this is a story we are less willing to read, in part because keeping blind to such repercussions dovetails so beautifully with what we want and need to believe about women. In *Civilization and Its Discontents,* Sigmund Freud puts the paradigm neatly, stating that aggressiveness at once forms the basis of every human relationship and constitutes the greatest hindrance to civilization. But rest assured, civilization will not crumble, because we have women. And women, he says (specifically mothers in relation to their children), represent the "single exception" to this rule of aggression, and are therefore a kind of fire wall, the one thing standing between civilization and its destruction.

With stakes that high, no wonder we're willing to look the other way when a girl won't eat, when a woman privately cuts or burns herself, or when she simply—and far more commonly—commits the nonviolent violence to herself of disengaging, disappearing, going softly, unobtrusively, half dead. In all but the most severe cases, looking the other way isn't even terribly hard. For if these are the symptoms of aggression disavowed, tamped down beneath both individual and collective consciousness, they are also, as a rule, easy to hide. If female aggression is all but unacceptable, the symptoms of its suppression are nearly invisible. Or so commonplace as to pass for normal.

Imagine for a moment that we all had what Winnicott calls "good-enough" mothers. Imagine our mothers survived our infant aggression. Sometimes we scratched and kicked, and they were not destroyed; they did not withdraw; they remained intact, and we received the message that the world would bear us in all our fiery spirit and vigor. Imagine, then, that as we grew, the girls among us had this message rescinded; at the eleventh hour the promise was betrayed. And then—the story's ugliest twist—we became collaborators and began to betray ourselves.

Defense turned out to be hard. It was the first time I felt really cloddish at the gym. Raphi and I were in the ring; hip-hop was filling the church to the rafters, men were beginning to trickle in as late afternoon turned to evening. The girls were doing heaven knows what behind us; we didn't want to know. (They'd managed to put another hole in the wall the week before; soon somebody was going to notice that the posters kept getting moved around.)

"You're going to block a jab like this," said Raphi, and showed me. The move consisted of turning her right glove out.

I was kind of thinking, That's it?

"Throw a jab," she said.

"Just—at you?" I'd never thrown a punch at her when she wasn't wearing the training mitts, and I was not quite sure how you did this. Did I aim for her glove itself? Or for her face, trusting that she would block me before I connected? I compromised, aiming a lackluster jab somewhere in between, and she rotated her wrist, bringing it forward just a little, and knocked my glove away.

"Again."

I threw a few more jabs, little elfin blows, and got the idea.

"You try blocking."

She threw jabs at me, light and easy, and I rotated my glove to catch them. I felt silly. I was able to block her punches because I knew they were coming, and I knew they were coming because, well, it was a drill, and she was throwing them slowly, in a rhythm, but I didn't see how I could apply that in a real situation. "How does this work if you're really sparring?"

"Same." A shrug.

"But I mean, how do you know, like right now I know to expect a jab, but how do you—"

"Practice!"

"Oh." Jab, block, jab, block. "Am I holding my hand right, is it supposed to be more of an angle?"

Later she would tell me that I would have driven her coach mad with all my questions. I knew, I could feel it myself, the ridiculousness of asking them. I'd seen the other boxers, seen how they just listened and did. But I wasn't liking being in my body then; I wanted to climb out of it. For the first time, I was feeling self-conscious in the ring. My mind was wanting to scramble up to the rafters. With my questions I was affecting a kind of dopiness, a guise. I knew this guise, I had worn it often, more as if by instinct than by intention.

When I practiced defense, there was no denying I was in the ring with another. When I hit the mitts, it was almost possible to think of it as a solitary activity: my power alone, directed outward, unchecked, toward those grandly impersonal targets. But suddenly it was impossible to ignore the fact that we were *two* in the ring. I had no alternative but to regard, receive, and respond to this other's intention toward me.

Raphi showed me another defensive move: how to slip a punch by dodging sideways from the waist. I was really bad at it. I'd learned everything pretty quickly until this point, but my body was stiff and clumsy, and it was hard not to laugh because a dozen times Raphi would have clocked me if she'd been throwing with any force at all. This was all pretend! My old confusion around sports came flooding in. If I tried to defend myself, that would be as good as admitting the game was real, and then it *would* be real. These moves ran counter to what I already knew to be the best, the only, defense: vacating my body. Staying outside the game.

I got to the gym one afternoon shortly after New Year's, and Raphi was in the ring, sparring with the same tattooed man I saw my first night. It was her first time sparring in eight months, and her first full week without a cigarette in that same length of time. She had started smoking in Catholic school at age eleven, then quit at twenty-four when she arrived at the Somerville Boxing Club. It was Franky, her old coach, who laid it on the line before he agreed to take her on, even as he held one of his own long brown cigarettes between stained fingers. No smoking, no drinking, no drugging; eat right; get to bed early; and start running. By her own account, Raphi was at that time depressed, skinny, lost, angry, and jobless. There were Franky and Ralphy both, the pair of them like grizzled old bulldogs, taking no guff. I could imagine how ready she was to put her trust in a regimen, put her body in the hands of these two old men who would train her to fight.

I felt shy to have walked in on her fighting. The tattooed man was Jerry Lee Johnson, a good friend, her earliest sparring partner. She had done his portrait in gouache; it hung, along with his old fight posters, behind his cluttered desk at work, in his furniture-repair shop in Everett, in the same "rat-hole" neighborhood where he grew up. During his brief professional career, he had earned the moniker Jerry "The Crowd Pleaser" Johnson, but she referred to him as Jerry Lee.

I sat on the pew, started wrapping my hands, looking up from time to time. I was curious to see them spar. Jerry had told me his story. His father was stabbed to death in a Reno, Nevada, alley before Jerry was born. He grew up abused, left home at fourteen, spent a few years in foster homes and lockups run by the Department of Youth Services. He shoplifted, robbed houses, stole cars, had a daughter at age seventeen, used and dealt drugs, and slept on people's front porches and in their cellars and hallways, in a crackshack for a while, and then in a wooded area called the backfields. Eventually he did prison time for beating a man who owed him money. Released from jail a month before his twenty-first birthday, he had his first amateur fight a year later and turned pro at age twenty-four. At twenty-nine, having received a total of 160 stitches in his face, he retired. He was a little worried about brain damage. Now he had three kids, a wife, the furniture-repair shop. His oldest daughter was expecting: He was due to become a grandfather at the age of thirty-five. He credited boxing with having saved him.

Raphi was terribly fond of Jerry. Whenever she got hit in sparring, she would get angry and use this anger as her fuel. She had to have a sparring partner she trusted enough to let herself unleash some of that anger. Jerry pulled his punches, of course, with Raphi, but he made himself a formidable sparring partner, acutely attuned to provoking her, igniting her fuel. He aimed to get her "worn, torn, tired, pushed around," and for his part, he got to work on defense, his footwork and feinting. For Raphi, what was the draw? Working on skills, of course, but also this: She was free, free to rail, to attack, to be as large as she wanted.

Now my hands were wrapped, but the girls hadn't arrived, and there was nothing to do but give the ring my full attention, to watch her *want* unapologetically. I couldn't see their faces for the headgear; only their bodies, the one a good sixty pounds heavier than the other, their strange dance, intimate and impersonal. Jerry blipped her—that's what he called it, *blip blip blip,* in her face and gut—and she unleashed herself at him. She'd given him a few black eyes in her time, but not today. Today he'd forgotten, perhaps, how much bigger he was, or that she hadn't sparred in so long. Perhaps she'd forgotten what three rounds with a strong boxer felt like, or that she had stopped smoking only ten days earlier. In any case, he landed one too hard, and she took herself out of the action, went to her neutral corner and hung on the ropes, breathing with her head down, very pink, waiting for the stars to clear.

From the pew, with an ache and fear, I knew this: I wanted to spar.

.   .   .

A new girl was using the gym. White, slight, with a shaved head except for a handful of skinny braids that dangled across her brow. She came to the gym in the baggiest pants I had ever seen. Sometimes Candi would snicker when the new girl crossed to the locker room to change, always in a beeline, head down, furiously making no eye contact with anyone or anything. She didn't train with us, but with Vinny Busa from the front desk, and I found it odd that she would gravitate toward him, with his alcohol haze and pebble eyes. He was still young, mid-thirties, but his fighting career was long over. His nickname in the ring used to be Boom-Boom, as in Vinny "Boom-Boom" Busa, a detail that served to embarrass him now.

The girl's name, it took me some weeks to learn, was Trini Molloy, and she lived out in Milford, an hour away. Her mother brought her to the gym three times a week, six hours of driving. She was fourteen years old. So well did her clothes, hair, and attitude camouflage her that it was several more weeks before I registered, with surprise, that her face had an almost fairy-tale lyricism, a simple and searing loveliness.

Her work in the gym was serious: no antics, no horseplay, no *warmth*, or apparent appetite for warmth, of the sort that I had grown used to witnessing among the boxers and trainers. The word that came to mind was *enlisted*. She was like a baby soldier, with her peach-fuzz scalp and bone-deep sobriety and way of being perpetually at attention before the sergeant, Vinny Busa. Later I learned the reason she didn't want to train with the girls: She didn't want anything like connection at the gym, only hard work. In Trini I saw a third reason for being here—not to cultivate a noble discipline and holding frame for aggression, nor to encounter the freedom and license to explore it, but to test oneself, with a kind of ruthlessness, in order to prove something about an ability to survive. I saw in Trini a quality that I associated with my image of young Raphi, arriving for the first time at the gym, dripping wet, bicycle seat in hand, a tough look in her eye. And I saw in Trini—was it true?—something of myself.

It would be months before Trini told me her story. It would be nearly that long before she'd say hello to me. But in those first few weeks I became friendly with her mother, Linda, who sat in the office on the beige leather sofa with a schoolbook in her lap; she was studying for her bachelor's degree in psychology. She wore jeans and sneakers, her wavy brown hair fell below her shoulders, and her smile was at once open and grounded.

I was on my way out of the gym one day, still sweaty and loose, and I paused in the office to say hi to Linda. I'd just passed Trini and Vinny Busa in the gym, working on her hook in front of the mirrors. They were equally unsmiling, that pair, and deeply engaged, as if what Vinny had to teach her was the single most important lesson in Trini's life. I said something sympathetic to Linda about how much Trini's boxing had become a part of *her* life. I was thinking about the thrice-weekly commute, driving back and forth through the snow, and all those hours she now had to spend doing her studying at a boxing club instead of in a library or a quiet room at home.

"It's worth it," said Linda. "The way it's helping her deal with anger."

"Has that been hard for her?" I asked.

Linda smiled gently. "She was in anger-management classes this fall. But they didn't really . . ." She shrugged. "The truth is, I don't even care about the anger. It would be worth twice the commute. She was really bad. Suicidal. Before this. Since the boxing, she says she hasn't had any suicidal thoughts."

I felt the strangest sensation up the back of my legs, as if they were vanishing. I thought I might need to sit down. I had a vivid memory of a moment in late summer, perhaps six weeks before I first entered the boxing gym.

I'd been standing in the kitchen of my apartment, alone. I'd lived there only a few months and had failed to notice a seemingly unimportant detail, which was that both doorways leading out of the kitchen could be sealed. Such a simple observation. I hadn't noticed it before because one of the doors to the kitchen swung both ways, and it had been propped open out of sight, against the wall of the next room, so I'd thought of this as an open archway instead of a door that could be closed. But in that hot, still, engraved moment, I apprehended two things: that the kitchen, a little room, could be completely sealed off, and that the stove was gas. The terrible significance of these paired facts made me strangely calm and grateful for their promise.

The time clock in the next room blared, and I was back in my body in the homely gym office, the dark space of fake-wood paneling and discarded sofas, the desk cluttered with racing sheets and fight magazines and the phone that hadn't worked properly ever since Vinny Busa accidentally dropped it in the sink, and my heart was racing, there was a prickling all over my scalp, and I thought: Since I started boxing, I haven't had any suicidal thoughts, either.

It was like a child riding in a car at night and looking out the window and seeing the moon and saying, "The moon is following us." This was how I felt about my body, an epiphany, leaving the gym, pushing open the heavy door and walking out into the frozen sunshine, the dingy parking lot. I thought I'd effectively shed my body, left it behind long ago, and here it was, it had been following me all this time. Constant in spite of me.

PART 2

4

BLOWS

Nikki knocked Raphi out. She didn't mean to. They weren't even sparring. It was just a Saturday morning at the gym, and Nikki was in the ring hitting the mitts. The rest of us were waiting our turns, working on the speed bag or the heavy bag, lifting weights, shadowboxing, whatever. We were scattered in the gym's pretty midmorning light. People were always telling me this was the nicest space the Somerville Boxing Club had ever occupied. I never saw its earlier incarnations, but as I visited other gyms, I began to get the idea: cement floors, no windows, low ceilings, exposed ducts, a sheen of dubious moisture coating every surface.

Who knows why Nikki's glove missed its mark that day, why it skirted the mitt and connected instead with Raphi's face. There had been a sudden, dramatic midwinter thaw. All the snow had melted and the mud had dried. So Raphi had sent the kids running that morning when they first arrived, downhill to Davis Square and back again in the bright, thin sun. A little over a mile, round trip. Maybe it was a premature burst of spring fever that made Nikki swing a little wild.

Or maybe it was the knowledge that at last, six months after Augusta, another fight was coming up: the Silver Mittens. When they had returned from the Women's Nationals the summer before, Raphi's plan was to get the girls as many fights as she could before this late-winter event. But they hadn't had a single one. It was so hard to find opponents.

So hard to find fights, period. Promoters called Raphi from time to time, asking whether she had any girls of a particular age and weight, but nothing ever quite materialized, and now the Silver Mittens were almost upon them and Jacinta and Nikki's USA Boxing passbooks were exactly as inked in as they had been in August, which is to say hardly at all: two bouts for Jacinta, a win and a loss, and Nikki's single entry: a loss.

Yesterday at school, during an assembly on drugs, Jacinta had passed along the news of the upcoming bouts. Raphi had called Maria the night before with the date of the Silver Mittens, four weeks hence. The girls had been sardined in with a couple hundred other students on stackable chairs at one end of the cafeteria. The speaker was a probation officer, regaling them with true stories of kids their age doing time. Jacinta and Nikki were dead bored. The *loca* reached over and touched the *blanca*'s sleeve. "The fight's going to be on your birthday," she whispered.

Nikki made her eyes huge while the rest of her body froze. The clown. With theatrical care, she swallowed. "The twenty-fifth?" she whispered back.

Jacinta nodded. Great solemnity. They were big on portents, these two, or on acting as though they were big on portents. The grandeur of life at fifteen.

"I better win, then," Nikki whispered: a statement of fact.

So maybe the accidental blow that knocked Raphi out was a result of the knowledge of the upcoming bout, an outcome of the nerves and adrenaline rush, even though it was still a month off. But no one who knew Nikki could entirely discount the other possible factor, a simpler and perhaps more obvious one: anger. Unconscious, unbidden, and misdirected, but present and desperate for outlet. Nikki had told me more than once that when she first started boxing, she was "really angry, I don't know why," but now she was not. Her anger was gone; she had none anymore. She told me this with her beach-glass eyes at once clear and flat, her mouth set, her chin lifted. So be it: Somehow Nikki Silvano, devoid of anger, on a mock-spring morning while training for a fight, knocked her coach out cold.

Trainers do not as a rule wear headgear or mouthguards or any protective devices when they hold the mitts. The question of protection does not arise, it's that rare for a punch accidentally to strike the trainer full on. So it was an almost surreal surprise when Nikki's left hook missed the mitt, not even grazing it, to connect full force with the right side of Raphi's jaw.

The coach dropped to her knees, and all of us who had been dabbling at our workouts around the periphery of the ring stopped what we were doing, although no one had made a sound. Maybe it was just that that had alerted us: the sudden absence of sound and motion in the ring. We drifted over, unsure of what had happened and whether anything was required of us. Raphi stayed down for what began to feel like a long time, her forehead on the mitts, not responding to Nikki's suddenly childlike, sweet-and-scared queries as to whether she was all right. Finally Raphi waved Nikki off and rose, and then it was to retreat to her neutral corner, finding her way there by blind instinct, her head still down. She knelt again, face shielded against her mitts, incommunicado.

My single conscious thought, absurdly, was that Raphi should get up. I was frustrated with her for not being quicker about it, and somewhat anxious on Nikki's behalf. Get up, Raph, I thought, tell her you're okay. Nikki seemed jilted, stranded in the middle of the ring, her long, powerful white arms dangling awkwardly at her sides, ending in their somehow clownish red gloves.

A story about Nikki. When she was small, she had a problem with falling out of bed, and this was coupled with a horror of strange creatures crawling across the floor. Sometimes she actually saw them, these creatures, which were malevolent; she was convinced they were the ones that kept knocking or dragging her out of bed in the first place. So her mother, Maureen, devised with Nikki a game of securing the girl in her bed by tucking the covers tightly all around the perimeter of her body. They called this ritual the mermaid.

Alone in her bed, mermaided, Nikki would stare straight ahead, at the dark depth of the ceiling, as long as she could to avoid sighting the bestial intruders she knew to roam her bedroom floor. Inevitably, the temptation to look, to check, would make her sit up, and the mermaid would come undone. This was a grave wrongdoing. Messing up the mermaid, within the night logic of her scary bedroom, was a terrible act; loosening the sheets that held her body still meant she was a bad person. Nikki would cry herself to sleep for having done it.

The poignancy of that tale—the recurring tableau of safe boundaries and dislodged boundaries, the maternal protection that hinged on not

seeing, not moving, the guilt coupled with fear—which Nikki had managed to tell me not with her mouth but with a ballpoint pen and a spiral
notebook handed over to me unexpectedly one day at practice, was
evoked in that moment by the childlike quality of Nikki's expression in
the ring, and by the childlike quality of her voice as she repeated, at long
intervals, "Sorry . . . Are you okay? . . . I'm sorry."

At the back of my mind hovered some ready concern for Raphi, but
the idea of her being really hurt was so unlikely, unthinkable, that I
brushed it aside. Why was it unthinkable? As a measure of our necessary
faith in Raphaëlla-the-coach's absolute impregnability. To follow her
where we followed her, to unleash our bodies the way we did, with her
knowing blessing, we needed her to be immune to us. For if we could be
too much . . . the whole thing would collapse. We would have to moni-
tor our strength, fall back into roles of nipping and tucking at our own
power. It would render this experience either too dangerous to be borne,
or else a sham, and both possibilities felt calamitous.

As we waited, a tense question mark ballooning over the scene, I remembered Raphi's words about why she was reluctant to spar with the
girls: "I can't risk hurting them in any way, or having them hurt me." A
worry did occur to me, though still, absurdly, not a worry about Raphi. It
was of a much more selfish nature: whether this would upset the intimate balance and trust we all needed, coach and boxers, to do the work
we came here to do. The threat of loss hovered, shadowing these moments as we gathered ringside, shooting one another glances, waiting for
Raphi to give a sign.

Nikki went to the neutral corner and bent down and gave Raphi a
hug, an awkward thing made more awkward by the rare and bashful ten-
derness in it, as she leaned her head briefly against the top of her
coach's. The embrace went unreciprocated. Nikki straightened, backed
up a step. We were all close to the corner now, waiting. The round,
which had ceased to exist except in the abstract, ended; we learned this
from the time clock, which blasted its indifferent tone, at once harsh
and reassuring.

For those of us charged with being good, with being ever-constant in
our ministrations to a world in pain, how sweet was the sound of the
clock. Here was the real balance for which we were all striving within
those walls: We wanted our strength to affect, but we needed it not to
ruin. We needed to smash, and we needed the world to survive our

smashing. It was as unfair and dangerous a proposition to make Raphi the bastion of resilience as it was to make women the bastion of gentleness. But if it couldn't be the trainer, still we required something to assume that mantle. And we had something. The time clock reminded us of it. We had the sport itself, with its rules and conventions, its physical and temporal bounds.

In another moment Raphi got to her feet. The one-minute rest between rounds ended with a triple trill from the clock. She put the mitts up to work another round with Nikki, who came in tentatively at first, until Raphi barked, "Hit hard!" a couple of times, sort of goading the girl back into her strength—"One, two . . . one, two, three . . . one, one, uppercut, uppercut, hook"—working so hard that Nikki had to pause: She couldn't breathe. She couldn't get air in. She rested her gloves on her thighs, very red in the cheeks. No air.

Asthma was a condition Nikki and Raphi shared. In fact, ever since Nikki threw out her inhaler at the Nationals the previous summer, fed up with how the medicine was making her heart race, they had shared not only the same condition but the same inhaler. From time to time, during practice, Nikki had to take a hit off Raphi's. The inhaler was not on hand at the moment, though; it was in the locker room. Nikki, bent at the waist, openmouthed, concentrated. Everything now was the oxygen's path to her lungs.

"Breathe," said Raphi.

"Lift your arms up," advised Jacinta, peering up through the ropes, brown eyes liquid and fixed on her best friend. Her T-shirt advised the world at large: SIX MINUTES TILL MY NEXT MOOD SWING.

"No!" yelled Raphi. Then, less sharply, "The blood has to run to her hands." A cardinal rule in boxing: Between rounds you keep your arms down. But there was something off about Raphi's tone, and the logic seemed off as well, the issue being asthma at that moment, not Nikki's preparedness for a hypothetical next round.

It wasn't a bad attack. Nikki's airways expanded. Raphi touched her shoulder, spoke to her; Nikki nodded, nodded again. Mitts came off, and gloves, and boxer and trainer both bowed low to pass back through the ropes together. That was it for the day. No more practice.

I would wonder at this forever: what had just happened, the role reversal, and the double reversal. The one incapacitated and then the other. As though the figure of the strong one, the caregiver, needed to restore itself to the person of the trainer before they could leave the ring. I would think of Nikki-the-child, mermaided shut by her mother's hands; and the inevitable breaking loose, sheets stirred up; and her shame and fear: the horror of her own ability to disrupt what her mother had wrought. I would think of Nikki-the-adolescent, bristling with a strength surpassing that which is commonly held to be useful for a girl, and with a burgeoning beauty she must either disbelieve or yank into submission: the wish to dull her eye color, the hair raked into slick partitions on her scalp or hidden under a hooded sweatshirt. And I would think of the gym, its constancy, its grim routine and rough regimen, and Raphi, the stalwart, the steward of it all.

Some of the explanation for what had happened also must lie with Raphi, who must have let her attention waver for a second. A trainer's first responsibility, while holding the mitts, is to protect herself. But the fact is that a few weeks later, while working the mitts with Richie, Nikki would miss again and land a blow so hard to his stomach that Richie would throw down the mitts and walk out, half crouched, to spend the rest of practice sitting in Raphi's car. And Desi, the trainer who was a cop, would act out for me, bubbling with his gorgeous sense of humanity and humor, a similar experience he had with Nikki that left him comically preoccupied with trying to make light of the devastating effects of her punch. If none of this was proof enough that Nikki, on some level, chose to let herself lose control in the ring, the timing of her asthma attack seemed another kind of evidence.

I don't mean I believe Nikki faked distress or willed it. But she didn't get asthma attacks often—in my three months of observing practice, this was the first time I had even heard she had asthma. That she had an attack on that day, within minutes of having knocked out her coach, seemed, if not an outright manifestation of anxiety, then at least strikingly synchronous. It was as though something unspoken had to be put to right.

That night Raphi revealed over the phone that she had no memory of working a second round with Nikki, or of talking Nikki through her asthma attack, or even of driving herself home after practice. "Autopilot, I guess," she said when I asked her how she managed any of it. "You see fighters do it in the ring sometimes, when they're knocked out on their feet but keep fighting. That's what's so dangerous." Then she confided that she had temporarily lost any sense of how the gym was laid out, to the extent that she couldn't locate the locker room at the end of practice. When she said this, I recalled an image of her meandering out to the office after having climbed down from the ring; I remembered thinking it odd at the time. Was she making a phone call? But the cordless had been in here with us, on a pew, where we'd hear it if it rang. Now I understood: Not wanting to alarm anyone, she had wandered around looking for the locker room instead of asking. Later that afternoon she'd stopped by the hospital, where she'd been diagnosed with a concussion, kept for a few hours of observation, and then discharged with instructions not to be alone for twenty-four hours.

"Will you tell the girls?" I asked.

"I don't know. I think they kind of know already, because I spoke with Maria, but I might kind of downplay it."

A few days later, her head feeling better, Raphi mulled over the episode some more. If she had any anger toward Nikki for knocking her out, it didn't show. I heard only forgiveness and a heightened sense of her own responsibility. "The thought of that entire day still scares me," she said. "I always have guilt, but now it's worse, about exposing the girls to this danger. Even though this won't likely ever happen to them, because their heads will always be protected."

She was talking about the headgear all boxers are required to wear for amateur fights—padded leather contraptions that covered the boxer's forehead and ears, fastened with Velcro straps under the chin. Protective gear, shorter rounds, fewer rounds—these factors were always cited as evidence of a great divide between amateur and professional boxing. Also, the fact that scoring in amateur boxing derived exclusively from the number of legal blows landed; in theory, how hard a boxer hits had nothing to do with it. In reality, of course, the strength of one's blows had a direct effect on the opponent receiving them. Still, the emphasis in amateur boxing was supposed to be more on technique and sport than on damage wrought. The divide was real; these differences did add up. In professional boxing, where the fighters might go twelve or fifteen rounds with no headgear, the potential to inflict serious damage was far greater. But it wasn't an accurate corollary to say that amateur boxing was therefore safe.

"What's the worst one of your boxers has ever been hurt?" I asked.

"Oh, none of them have ever gotten hurt," said Raphi quickly. "Well, I mean, you know, of course bloody noses, black eyes, bruises . . ."

She trailed off, looked over quickly at me. We laughed then, a small laugh, very tinged, that ended with our eyes, full of knowing and puzzlement.

A few weeks later, on a Saturday morning when the gym was empty except for Raphi's crew, Nikki's grandmother dropped her off at practice and stayed to watch. Raphi exchanged some pleasantries with her. They sat on the pew and spoke of Nikki, who stood nearby, pleased and shy, taking it in.

"I know she's strong," said Mrs. Silvano with quiet affection.

"Yeah," agreed Raphi. "We're all scared of her!"

It was meant as a compliment, in jest, but the way it came out, it missed its mark, and Nikki, hearing it, blushed and swiftly dropped her head, and what was going on behind her eyes was anyone's guess.

Raphi put me in the ring with Sefina. Of all people, Sefina, the loose cannon, the middle child, the stormy, sulky one. Thunder, indeed. And twelve! I was nearly three times her age, though lighter by some fifteen pounds, and less experienced. Of all the girls, she was the one I knew least. One week she'd come decked out in diamond studs, lipstick, and her big sister's low-cut wraparound sweater, her hair covered by a do-rag printed with the Puerto Rican flag. The next week she'd be all child: messy ponytail, floppy T-shirt saying EFFORT IS THE KEY TO SUCCESS— ANTHONY EDWARDS MIDDLE SCHOOL, and jeans she was outgrowing fast, an inch of white-socked ankle showing beneath the cuff. Her attitude toward boxing seemed to change from week to week as well. One week she'd fairly shove her way into the gym, declaring, "I'm first on the mitts today!" The next Raphi could hardly persuade her to wrap her hands or haul her body off the pew.

I had seen Sefina spar, and she looked a dizzying mix of fury and fear. She'd close her eyes and turn her upper body away from blows, which was kind of disastrous to her, but she'd flail, too, in anger or panic, punching any which way, landing blows on the back of her opponent's head, legs, wherever, which could be harmful to the other party. I felt warily tender toward this girl but was hardly champing at the bit to get

in the ring with her. Yet in a way I was. The mounting urge to test myself, to test this *thing,* had begun to inflict an almost physical ache, so
that I felt slightly reckless about whom I'd get in the ring with, just to
have a chance to see how I would be.

I had by now read enough accounts, and been told enough stories, of
people's first sparring experiences to know that involuntary tears were
not an uncommon reaction to being hit in the face for the first time; this
was the possibility—and, I feared, the likelihood—that disturbed me
most. Also to be overcome was the natural enough instinct to turn away,
an instinct to which I had seen Sefina succumb. And would I remember
to keep my hands up? Another pitfall for the novice. My feet: Would I
be able to move around the ring and keep them always shoulder-width
apart, remembering never to cross them, which would put me off balance? Who would start? How would I know when to throw a punch, and
would I be able to see her punches coming early enough for my brain to
tell my body to block or slip them the way I'd been taught? It was one
thing to block and slip punches when Raphi and I were drilling and I
knew exactly what was coming and when; it was quite another in the
ring, unscripted. And what kind of mood was Sefina in today? I checked
her out: inscrutable. She was either shyly pleased or shyly reluctant; I
could not tell, only that her smile looked charged with ambivalence, and
that she was struggling to smother it.

"Do you have a mouthguard?" asked Raphi.

I shook my head.

"I think I have one in my locker you can use."

Sometimes Jacinta and Nikki would wear mouthguards when hitting
the heavy bags, just to get used to exerting themselves and breathing
with it in there. I could understand why you'd need to acclimate yourself: The thing was awful, a thick plastic crescent, and I had to concentrate on not gagging when I put it in my mouth. It was an almost panicky
feeling. One of the things I always hated about sports was the equipment, the paraphernalia you had to strap on, commit your body to—
from the most innocuous pinny to the terrible encumbrances of skis
locked to your feet (I tried this exactly once) or snorkel and goggles and
flippers (also once). Running alone appealed, although even that, when
I imagined it in its ideal form, would occur not on a track but over field,
barefoot, thistles be damned.

"Ah wong shay ih," I said, and spit the mouthguard into my gloved hands. "It won't stay in, Raphi."

"Bite down on it. Breathe through your nose."

I didn't want to; it was worse this way. It made my heart jittery to hold it wedged in so tightly.

"You ready?" Raphi asked Sefina, who nodded. Her mouthguard had already been properly fitted at home, which is to say, tossed in a pot of boiling water for a few minutes until soft, then molded to the shape of her own teeth. Hers was the color of a marigold. She grinned at me, this absurd slice of orange flashing, and hit her gloves together a few times, as if belligerent. I laughed and promptly lost my mouthguard. Raphi picked it up off the floor for me, since I was disabled by my gloves, and rinsed it with a squirt from the water bottle. "Bite down on it," she reminded me. "You ready?" I nodded.

This was a far step from real sparring. We weren't even wearing headgear; Raphi didn't want us to go that hard. It was what some call controlled sparring, and some call moving around, or working, as in "You're just gonna work." Raphi had told us to limit ourselves to the jab, that was all, jabbing and blocking, getting a feel. We were going to move around the ring a little, she said, just jab and block, jab and block. She told us this about five times. "Remember, you have more experience than her," she told Sefina, who nodded gravely, then shot me a glance that looked young, filled with uncertainty. "Also you weigh more," Raphi reminded her, which made me cringe for Sefina, since Maria had started making jokes about her middle daughter getting fat—which she was by no measure—but Sefina simply nodded again and eyed me soberly, and I realized Raphi was smart to charge her with all this specific responsibility. It might help her focus, which she often had a hard time doing.

We got in the ring, waited for the bell, touched gloves, and smiled like a couple of fools. We moved around, threw feathery jabs that managed to disturb a few air molecules, moved around some more. I was offended. Sefina wasn't even trying to hit me! More than that, I was appalled by my own lameness. Why had none of my blows connected? They all seemed to stop about two inches short of her face. I tried again: the same. It was like that old practical joke with a dollar bill on the sidewalk—each time the innocent pedestrian bends to retrieve it, an unseen thread jerks it an inch out of reach. I tried again. It wasn't that Sefina was slipping my punches; the target remained constant. We were at least a minute into the round before I comprehended that I was positioning myself two inches too far for my reach to extend to her face. Even as we moved around, I maintained this distance: a little bit too far for contact. I told myself to move in, and I did, backing her up by moving in more aggressively with my feet, but I still couldn't override a stubborn switch in my brain that wouldn't let me hit her face. A few body shots grazed her, and under my glove, her side felt soft and small. She flinched. I worried that she didn't want to be there. Her eyes looked so dark and wary, she was so young, and I was an adult, a woman, a mother. It was wrong.

I dropped my hands. She should have hit me then. I was completely open, but she dropped her hands, too, smiling uncomfortably and worse: looking away, over at Raphi, an appeal. "Don't look at me!" yelled Raphi. "Look at her! Keep your hands up. Come on! You have forty seconds! Box!"

The round was nearly up. I was exasperated, a little bit with Sefina, because I thought she had decided I wasn't worth trying to hit, but mostly with myself, for being in the ring and failing to break free from my own constraints. The thirty-second warning bell came, and I jabbed, with full extension this time, and hit her lightly in the mouth. She flinched again and looked as surprised as I felt, for a split second only. I had knocked her mouthguard off center. She readjusted it. I mumbled, "Sorry"—bad form, but I couldn't help it—and then she came back and hit me, not flailing, not retaliatory; she hadn't gone stormy and teary, this wasn't wronged Sefina windmilling at one of her sisters, but controlled Sefina, a little pissed off maybe, but pretty controlled, and at last deciding to employ her skills.

Her punch landed on the side of my face. It didn't hurt at all. A momentary sting. I had remembered to keep my chin tucked, so my neck didn't snap back, and more than anything I felt solid. The discovery that I was not afraid, that I didn't mind it, that I could take a punch, was exhilarating. Oh, *fun!* The switch had been flicked. And now I was thinking: Look, we are smiling at each other with our eyes! How perverse and also not perverse—and this was when we began to trust each other, to circle each other more purposefully, to concentrate on timing and anticipating the next jab. But of course, the bell, damn. The round was over. I was breathless. How could that be? After only three minutes.

Raphi gave us water and asked us how it felt. She told me not to block with both hands, only one. She told Sefina to keep her attention on me, not look away. "You want to go another round?" she asked. We looked at each other, shrugged, smiled. "Okay," we said. I was dying to. "Still just the jab," she told us. She gave us more water. We slipped our mouth-guards back in.

In this round we were better. We threw more punches and landed more, too—this due in no small part to the fact that neither of us managed to employ a whole lot of defense. I'm sure my footwork was pitiful, but I didn't really care, because I'd gotten past the first essential mystery of training, which was *How will it feel to hit and be hit?* The answer: winged. Truly, winged: a new dimension in which to move. A couple of Sefina's punches in this round did snap my head back—"Leah, tuck your chin!" shouted Maria, altruistically, from the other side of the ropes—and it didn't hurt; I only felt embarrassed to have left myself that vulnerable. But mostly I took the punches and felt strong, stronger for having taken them, and completely focused on looking for my next opening to get a shot at her. None of my punches landed hard—maybe one, right at the end, that brought brief rosiness to her nose, the slight-est moisture to her eyes. But you couldn't help that when you were hit right on the nose; Raphi had told me so, and now I had experienced it for myself.

When we finished this round, we were done for the day. We hugged, lightly and in gratitude, the way boxers do. I had until now found the boxerly hug perplexing, in its own way more unsettling than the violence that has preceded it, *because* of the violence that has preceded it, and because of the apparently instantaneous shift from the impersonal to the personal. The only way my mind could make sense of it was to as-sume that the hug, too, was impersonal, coerced by ritual, full of hypocrisy, the final and most revolting gesture of the fight. But when Se-fina and I met for our small embrace, it was natural and heartfelt. Her soft gray T-shirt wrinkled for a moment under my arm. I was sincerely grateful to her for getting in the ring with me. The thing I was testing had nothing to do with her, yet I could not have done it without her.

When I was a kid, I went with my family to see the gospel musical *Your Arms Too Short to Box with God.* I was pretty young; the only memory I have of the show is this scene right after Judas has betrayed Jesus to the chief priests. They've paid him the thirty pieces of silver and left, and he is alone on the stage. In a wild frenzy of self-loathing, he dances. I remember the actor, his muscles, his bare upper body, the caged fury with which he danced, as though he wanted to destroy his body, tear himself to pieces, escape himself. And the terrible, devastating absence of anyone to fight.

One of the dominant figures in the local boxing scene, a gym owner who was also a USA Boxing official, asked me to be sure not to refer, in writing, to amateur boxing matches as fights, or to the athletes as fighters. It was important, he said, to call them bouts and boxers, in order to distinguish the real sport of amateur boxing from the corrupt business of professional boxing. I respected his wish to improve the image of amateur boxing, but I knew even in the moment that I would not honor his request. For one thing, just about everybody I'd met in the boxing world used the terms *fight* and *fighter* freely; changing the jargon would be misrepresentative. But even if that were not the case, I would have hesitated to do as he asked. The more I saw people spar, fight, even simply shadowbox before their reflections in the long, dirty gym mirrors or before the figments of their imagination up against the sweaty walls, the more certain I was that this was *fighting*, that these were *fighters*.

It wasn't the opponents in the ring they were fighting. The opponents were rather like the gift, the happy eventuality that permitted them to take their own measure. Now, when I saw boxers embrace at the end of a bout, I felt it as real and was moved by the thought of what they each had been willing to provide the other. Of course, our arms were too short to reach our deepest hurts, our fears and regrets. But we could enlist surrogates, and with their aid might dance and smash around some of what we burned to know and do.

I sat in the tiny girls' locker room after that first taste of sparring, unwinding my wraps from my hands, then winding them slowly back up on themselves in tight, dampish rolls, surveying again as I did so the pictures taped and tacked to the plywood walls, the newspaper clippings of female boxers, the notice in ballpoint on a scrap of legal pad: NOTHING WILL WORK UNLESS YOU DO. On Raphi's locker was a piece of white sports tape on which she had written her name. Beneath it another hand had possessively scrawled, GODMOTHER OF CANDI. Also taped to her locker was a piece of loose-leaf on which we each recorded our weight every day we came into practice. On the opposite wall hung the mirror, whose silver backing was starting to go, rendering all visages reflected in it slightly mottled with black. Being alone, I indulged myself in a quick scan for any signs of redness or swelling.

Nothing hurt, not my cheekbone, where I had received a couple of solid strikes, not even the inside of my lip, where I thought the edge of the mouthguard had dug in under the force of Sefina's glove. I began to doubt myself, to wonder, Did we really work in there, or did we take it too easy, was it all too safe? I was uncomfortable with my own disappointment at not finding a bruise, and unsure about my relationship with Sefina. Yes, we had hugged at the end. But I wasn't certain I wanted to get in the ring with her again. I couldn't really tell if she had liked it, nor was I sure I could tolerate my mixture of elation and guilt over hitting her. I had little doubt she could kick my ass in a street fight, but within the constraints of the gym and our relationship, I didn't know whether she felt particularly free to hit me. What unsettled me most was the realization that our blows had connected cautiously: We both had continued to be cautious with each other.

Later Raphi would tell me she thought we both did well, exactly as we should have for this first not-quite-sparring session. But I was dissatisfied. Even before my heart rate had entirely slowed to its regular rhythm, I was hungry to step it up.

I stole a glance at my arms in the mirror. They weren't as whispery thin as I was accustomed to seeing them. The record of my weight on Raphi's locker door showed that I had gained a few pounds since starting training, about three, to be exact, which I privately realized was momentous. My gaze lit on a pull quote from one of the old press clips tacked to the wall: THIS SPORT IS AT TIMES AN ADDICTION.—RAPHAËLLA JOHNSON, BOXER. What I really, really wanted was to get in the ring again, soon, with someone other than Sefina, someone older and more confident, with whom there would be no unspoken obligation—for either of us—to hold back.

I started going to the Golden Gloves. They began in January, in Lowell, a frozen old mill town north of Boston. Lowell Memorial Auditorium looked huge and Grecian, whitely lit against the purple-black sky. The sidewalk was treacherous with black ice. The boxers' entrance was unmarked, around the back, and then around the back some more and down a short flight of stairs, and you would knock on this featureless black metal door. It would swing partway open, and a big guy would look you over. The first night I explained that I'd called ahead and gotten permission; he shrugged, said, "Okay," and let me in.

This was where Raphi had made her bit of history, and where, six years later, I could easily imagine how shocking her presence must have been, because even now the basement of Lowell Memorial Auditorium on a fight night was overwhelmingly male. The hopefuls were mostly young, mostly tattooed, and in varying states of undress as they waited in the hallway outside the makeshift doctors' examining room. Across from them was the glove table, where pairs of red and blue ten-ounce Tuf-Wear boxing gloves were laid out at the ready, along with terry-cloth sweatbands to cover the laces (in order to reduce the risk of cuts) and a bottle of Fantastik for wiping clean the leather between fights. Down the hall were the locker rooms, where fighters and trainers stashed their gym bags. Farther down the hall, a large storage room served as the officials' headquarters, where boxers in their underwear stepped on the scales and got matched up with opponents—or not. Lots of kids would get sent home without a bout, told to reappear the following week.

The Golden Gloves is the famous annual amateur boxing competition started by the New York *Daily News* in 1927, joined a year later by the *Chicago Tribune*. The phrase "Golden Gloves" refers not to a single event but to a series of events that take place in multiple locations across the country, progressing toward eighteen regional competitions (including four within the armed forces) and culminating in a national competition some months later. The Lowell Golden Gloves, sponsored by the *Lowell Sun Times,* occur weekly at first, then semi-weekly, over the course of about six weeks every winter, beginning with the novice division and moving on to open-class and then regional finals. Boxers from Maine, New Hampshire, Vermont, Massachusetts, Connecticut, and Rhode Island travel here to compete.

The locker rooms were buzzing. The light, steady *whup-whup* of jump ropes, the short, sharp exhalations of shadowboxers, and the cracking report of gloves on mitts reverberated off the metal lockers and cinder-block walls. Already, the fighters who had been slotted into the early bouts were getting their hands wrapped by their trainers; they straddled chairs backward, in utter silence, while the lengths of gauze got wrapped and wound and layered in the intricate pattern particular to each trainer. Corner buckets sat at the ready, stocked with towels, gauze pads, cotton swabs, tape, ice. A metal device for swelling reduction was allowed, but ammonia, smelling salts, and coagulants were all prohibited at amateur matches. Some boxers disappeared into the bathrooms to change into their protective cups and satin shorts. Some laced up flashy boxing shoes in crayon-box colors, rising to midcalf and dangling tassels. Some would box in flat-soled sneakers. One kid crouched in a corner, monkish in his black hoodie, apparently praying. One literally bounced on his toes around the room until his coach said, "Save it, Eddie. Don't blow yer wad."

Out in the hallway, in line for the doctor, a white man in a black knit hat was eating some florid concoction from a two-quart plastic tub. In front of him stood a tall, doe-eyed Dominican kid with eyebrows sculpted into an almost feminine arch, a style prevalent among many of the Latino fighters. The red-faced kid before him looked nervous and surprisingly plump. The next guy up was a towering beauty, black and built, with a high-wattage, impressively easygoing smile. They all clutched their USA Boxing passbooks. You were supposed to be a citizen to get one, but Massachusetts was infamous for its slovenly accountability; while in most states you'd have to produce a birth certificate, many kids here got by with lying. The inside joke was that Moses from Uganda had been passing as Puerto Rican.

Upstairs the auditorium was filling in. From the ornate ceiling, chandeliered and medallioned, painted pink and cream, hung an American flag and a pair of banners: the New England Golden Gloves and *Lowell Sun* Charities. In this same space Shakespeare was performed, but tonight the stage, flanked by pieces of pipe organ twelve feet high, was filled with spectators' folding chairs, with the boxing ring erected where the orchestra would normally be. The Lowell police, wearing uniforms distinguished by a large badge on the left shoulder that read, incredibly, ART IS THE HANDMAID OF HUMAN GOOD, patrolled the area in a leisurely way. A fat, mustached coach came through the door that said BOXERS ONLY and patted the cop's beer belly. "What's up, Coco?" greeted the cop. Ringside, imposing, the judges took their seats.

The judging of amateur boxing—all the governance around amateur boxing—is carried out according to the highly intricate, not to say Byzantine, rules and regulations put forth in the USA Boxing handbook. This is issued annually, and it's important to stay updated, since the rules and regulations (lest they become too comprehensible, one supposes) are constantly being altered and tweaked. Some sample copy from the 2002 edition:

Concerning the awarding of points.

1) End of each round. Twenty points shall be awarded for each round. No fraction of points may be given. At the end of each round, the better (more skillful) boxer shall receive 20 points and the opponent proportionately less. When boxers are equal in merit, each shall receive 20 points.

2) Points determination. The awarding of points shall follow these principles: one point for three correct hits; one point for a warning by the referee or judge; if the number of hits differs from three, six, nine, 12, etc., the table shown in figure 43.1 is to be used.

(Further illustrating the near-incomprehensibility that is apparently the commission's goal, points are actually awarded by *subtracting* them from the opponent's score.)

Back downstairs, the remaining officials buzzed back and forth, ferrying messages, lining up the order of the evening's bouts, making sure everyone was weighed in, had seen the doctor, turned in a passbook, come with a certified trainer. One young hopeful was somehow without, and he went around the locker rooms asking if anyone certified would agree to work his corner so he could fight. In the nick of time he got an affirmative and dashed, panting, out to the glove table to inform the officials. "Hey, Billy, what color is that, silver or white?" an official asked another kid, referring to the trim on a boxer's satin shorts; the announcer upstairs would need it for the introduction. A moment later: "Ramirez to the glove table! Anybody know who the hell Ramirez is? Tell him he's up!" An official in latex gloves whisked down the hallway. "Who doesn't have his passbook? You need to leave it with doctors. Hey, Mikey, good luck tonight. I can say that now, the ref's gone up."

Everybody fighting on this night, the second of the competition, was considered a novice, with ten bouts or fewer. Even so, many wore the look of the old guard. Some were slouchy and slit-eyed, from boredom or fear or habitual masks of toughness. Some were upright, affable, clasping hands with old acquaintances. But there was very little talk. In the claustrophobic makeshift examining room, the two docs greeted the last few boxers with recognition. "Back again this year? You know the routine. Take off your shirt. Is that a new tattoo?"

At the front of the line, the white guy in the black knit hat spooned the last bit of the reddish-purple paste into his mouth. It was hard to guess his age: His face looked at once youthful but battered.

"What was that?" I couldn't help asking.

He smiled shyly. "Oatmeal and raspberries."

Oatmeal and raspberries! Nursery food.

"Next," said the sentry at the docs' door, and sticking his head into the examining closet, "This is the last." The oatmeal-and-raspberry kid went in, already tugging off his shirt. His muscles told of a boy driven to spend hours in a boxing gym; there was a hard story here, I guessed, beneath the beauty of his sculpted strength. Or not. Was it possible he'd been swept up in a fantasy of the noble warrior, full of the adolescent male will to pump iron and boast a six-pack, to draw his bit of blood if he was lucky, to strut and crow about it? The basement halls felt too gray for that, too tense with fear and need—and gentleness! The surprisingly gentlemanly manner of the men and boys.

Not that there weren't eruptions. When there was a dispute at weigh-in over a kid who was supposedly disqualified the previous week, his trainer started cursing out the official. One man, after losing his bout this night, would ram his fist through the wall inside the stairwell outside the auditorium, leaving a nice big hole in the plaster and causing a Lowell cop to haul him and his coach down into a basement hallway, where they could figure out who was going to pay for the damage. In the back locker room, a young man getting ready for his fight was nearly hopping out of his skin with tension. He had his gloves on already and punched the cinder-block wall a few times, then slammed his fists against his own headgear. He blew his nose into the garbage can with a vigorous snort, paced, pounded the sides of his head again. "This is gonna be a war," he promised under his breath. "Relax, Joey," said his trainer. "Just stay nice and warm."

But given boxing's public persona, I was surprised by the quiet goodwill and respect exhibited by most of the people back here—boxers, trainers, officials, everybody. More than anything, there was a sense of all being on the same side, or perhaps more accurately, and more meaningfully, of having come from the same place. I tried to picture Jacinta and Nikki here—they would be old enough the following year. I tried to picture Raphi here. There were still so few women. The previous week, the first week of the Gloves, one woman had shown up amid the nearly forty male boxers, but she hadn't gotten a match. This night, out of seventeen bouts on the roster, one would be between females. I slipped upstairs in plenty of time to see it.

The auditorium looked well packed to me, although one of the cops told me it was nothing like it used to be five, ten years ago. The caliber of the boxers, too, had gone down, he said. The economy had been too good, that was his explanation: Hardship bred the best boxers. One of the fifty-fifty raffle girls came by, in her *Lowell Sun* Charities T-shirt, with her apron full of raffle tickets and cash. "Fifty-fifty!" she called. She wore blue eye shadow and a high ponytail. She looked like a high school sophomore. "Hi, Uncle Joe," she greeted one of the men standing near me by the door. Uncle Joe and the cop traded comments on the refs. "The one in that last bout was hanging so far back, he shoulda just gone out for a beer."

The bout before the women's ended in a technical knockout. I'd never witnessed anything like it. It was an uppercut that actually lifted the boxer off his feet and landed him flat on his back. It was like something on Saturday-morning cartoons. And then he didn't get up. By now I'd seen guys get standing eight-counts, and I'd seen guys get knocked down and then get up on one knee and rise again, and I'd seen guys dazed and stumbling, but I had never seen anyone not get up. Maybe fifteen seconds went by. The ref was kneeling over the kid. I was thinking about the ambulance parked out front during all boxing matches. Then the kid did get up, and the crowd cheered for him, the same crowd that had cheered, shrill with excitement, when he went down. Below the ring, he got stopped by the doctors—all the fighters had to pause here postbout and submit to a penlight shined in their eyes. Apparently the kid's pupils contracted satisfactorily. He was waved on, unshepherded.

The crowd was over it before the kid even reached the stairs. They were ready for the next fight. The spectators craned around and leaned forward to check out the women, coming now through the boxers' entrance with their entourages, one at a time. They reached the ring, stepped through the ropes. A trainer pushed a lock of hair more securely under a boxer's headgear, and the heckling started.

"Make 'em leave their hair down and wear heels!"

"They can't even pull hair with gloves on!"

"Shave the bastards!"

"I'm for that."

"I'll help!"

"Woo-ooo! I'm the barber!"

The ref had them touch gloves. The bell rang, and they started.

"See that ass moving? Two shots in the head'll slow that down."

Laughter.

"Jesus Christ!"

Laughter. Whistles. Catcalls.

Then: "Oh! Oh!"

"Did you see that?"

"Holy fuck!"

What was happening was that the women were boxing well, which is to say keeping busy (the crowd hated it when the boxers spent more time sizing each other up than throwing punches). They were landing hard punches, and neither boxer retreated or even tucked into a well-guarded position in order to wait out her opponent's flurries, but instead moved in to unleash a little counterpunching heat of her own. In other words, both fighters demonstrated skill as well as heart, and by the first bell they had won over the crowd, even the most virulent of the hecklers, who rose to their feet for a standing ovation. ("This oughta be a training manual." "Jesus, fuck. You see all the head shots at the end of the round?" "They oughta bring back the guys from the last fight and make 'em watch.")

Later, in the locker rooms, I happened upon the kid who had gotten knocked out. About seven fights had gone by since his bout. He was alone, hand wraps still on, straddling a chair and squinting as if in disbelief. He stopped me and asked if I had seen his fight. He asked whether it looked like he was winning before he got knocked out. There wasn't a bruise on him, but his eyes were dark and hollow-looking. He had his name tattooed on his forearm, and a couple of hands pressed in prayer tattooed on his bicep. He said he had no family or friends there for him. "I was doing good, though, wasn't I? I'm so mad. I don't even remember it. Was I fighting good? I looked strong, right? Was it in the third round? Didn't it look like I was winning up till then?"

"Yeah," I told him. "You looked really strong."

In the next locker room I found the smaller of the two female boxers, blond, from New Hampshire. She had won by decision. Now she was icing her many cuts and bruises, glowing with delight and more or less wordless with disbelief. Her boyfriend, who worked her corner, was very tall and boyish, brush-cut, and tending her like she'd just given birth. Her uncle, who trained her, was beside himself with pride. He insisted, gravely, on giving me one of their yogurt-peanut energy bars.

"Did it bother you, what the crowd was yelling?" I asked the boxer. She was eighteen. She looked up at me from under the ice pack. Her face was kind of a mess, and I was rattled to find myself jealous of what she'd done, of what she'd been through. It seemed important to know what that would feel like. I was afraid I might need to know it for myself.

"What were they yelling?"

"You know, the obscenities, just sexist stuff."

She shrugged, shook her head. "Oh. I didn't hear it."

"That's good."

This was it for her, she said. Probably. She just wanted to see if she could do it. She was planning on going to community college in the fall. She might want to model, too. She had a sizable egg, already purpling, on her left eye, a cut on her lip, and some nasty bruising on her shoulder. She kept exchanging amazed glances with her boyfriend. Her uncle couldn't resist repositioning the ice pack on her brow. The happiness was coming off all three of them like sparks, and I excused myself from their intimacy.

When I left, the night was all black and so cold each breath entered my nose like shards of ice. Behind me, in the auditorium, the crowds were still rasping out encouragement and derision in their flat, sprawling New England accents. I shuddered; there was relief in leaving, but wistfulness, too, and I knew I'd be back the following week. But more than wanting to return to Gloves, I was hungry to get back to the gym. Even as my feet echoed over the ice and away from the ivory hulk of the auditorium, I itched to get in the ring again myself, and to go harder this time.

5

FEINTS

Raphi and Richie, windshield wipers going, crept through the open iron gates of Mount Auburn Cemetery the first Sunday in March. They had been a couple ever since the party held a few weeks after Candi's baptism in September. Since then, Richie, who had moved here from Puerto Rico six years ago, and who worked as a cook in a Boston University cafeteria, had moved out of the Rodgriguezes' apartment, where he'd been stretching his long frame out partway on their sofa each night, and into his own room in another apartment. He had applied for and received his provisional USA Boxing coach's certification so that he could work the corner with Raphi at the girls' matches. Two weeks ago, he had presented Raphi with a preengagement ring made out of paper, with their initials, *R* and *R*, inscribed back-to-back: their trademark, Raphi explained to me.

So now they were linked by a dream of a shared future, or a provisional shared future, contingent on a real proposal, contingent on a thousand things, really. Raphi was in love, but she was cautious, too. She had not prepared her parents, across the ocean, for the prospect of Richie as a son-in-law. And Richie, tall, quiet, the second youngest of sixteen siblings, critically impoverished in his own expectations of himself, had *little wanderer* written in Day-Glo all over his kind, lost soul. Raphi was no fool. She knew little wanderers were her weakness; in a way, her compunction to heal was her principal characteristic, but whether in so doing she brought herself healing was less certain.

Richie—on documents Richardson Cruz, to his family Ñoin (for reasons apparently inarticulable)—liked the idea of their getting married in the ring. Raphi thought this might occasion a heart attack in her mother. Maybe the ceremony in a chapel, then pictures afterward at the gym. They were talking about waiting a year and not moving in together until then. Although early autumn seemed attractive. Or late summer.

The white sedan wound slowly along the snaked cemetery roads, along which snowdrops and crocuses had begun to nose through the earth. The day was warm and impressively gray. Mount Auburn Cemetery, situated right off a busy street in Cambridge, was hushed, and Richie and Raphi were hushed as well, passing the footpaths charmingly named, according to the curlicue lettering on the signposts, BUTTERNUT and FUCHSIA, SORREL and ORANGE, COWSLIP and EGLANTINE. The car threaded among hills and dales toward the flat far corner of the modern part of the cemetery, where the graves had been decorated with the occasional Mylar balloon, in defiance of the signs declaring that only natural arrangements were allowed. This was where Frank Murphy, Raphi's old coach, had been buried one year earlier. She had been coming almost weekly ever since.

Near the back gate of the graveyard, they pulled over, and on foot found the modest horizontal slab that Franky shared in death with his favorite aunt. Raphi held two long-stemmed roses, yellow with orange frilled edges. Richie, who had learned the routine, reached down and took the metal canister from a hole in the ground before the grave, and brought it over to one of the slender spigots that dotted the property. He turned the knob. "No *agua.*"

"That's okay," said Raphi. "She gave us those things." She: the woman in Store 24. Those things: plastic tips on the ends of the stems, keeping the blooms in about a half ounce of water. Raphi and Richie each placed a rose in the dry canister. He came around behind her and curved one arm across her midsection. He was more than a head taller, and he kept his scalp shaved bald. A wire-thin beard traced his jawline. He was soft-spoken, with a slight sibilance in his speech, and his two front teeth overlapped slightly and beguilingly. Now he lowered his face and kissed the top of Raphi's head.

They had just come from Lawrence Memorial Hospital, in Medford, where Raphi's other former coach, Ralph Palmacci, Sr., was on life-support machines following a heart attack following an angioplasty. He had looked terrible; Raphi was almost sorry she'd seen him like that. Two years ago he'd had reconstructive surgery on his knee, and when he was wheeled out of the operating room, still under the anesthetic, the nurses reported that he'd been throwing punches in the air. But there was no brain activity now; the family was on the verge of giving consent to disconnect the machines. So there would be another funeral soon. First Franky and now Ralphy, her surrogate fathers. It was sad to think that Franky never got to meet Richie. Raphi thought her old coach would have liked him. Actually, she thought her old coach was *like* him, in a way that was hard to describe. More than once she'd had the fleeting fantasy that Franky and Richie shared souls, that Franky had somehow passed his soul into Richie and sent him to her six months after his death. She wished she could ask him for his blessing.

Ralphy at least got to meet Richie. It had been classic—even in her sadness, the memory made her smile. The soft-spoken twenty-nine-year-old with his heavily accented English, and the hard-of-hearing eighty-four-year-old, bent over his cane, tilting an ear. "Where are you from?" Ralphy had asked.

"Puerto Rico."

"Ah, Billerica!"—a town north of Boston—"I know it well!"

She had shared a secret self with Franky and Ralphy, unlikely confessors, the pair of them. It must have occurred as a function of their ability to receive her secrets as much of her willingness to reveal them. One secret: After sparring, she often cried, not from being physically hurt but as part of the release. Franky and Ralphy were the only two she ever let see. Not that they understood. The thought of their puzzlement still amused her: the grizzled ex-pugilists laboring desperately to understand women. They'd been better at it than they knew.

Oh, they'd been her champions! Franky with his Frankisms: "You can't eat an elephant whole, doll. You have to eat it in sandwiches." (Which meant: Take it easy, one step at a time.) Or: "Why do you think, when you pick up a pencil, the eraser's been worn out?" (Everyone makes mistakes.) Ralphy wordlessly preparing to wrap her hands before a fight, setting up the two chairs, white towel draped over the back of one. Franky's ludicrous insistence, after she finally lost at the Nationals, that Raphi's nose was not broken: "For Christ's sake, it's not broken! Look at her *sister's* nose!" (Raphi's sister, naturally, had been a little put out by that remark.) Franky helping her visualize sunsets before a bout, and refusing to let her give up when once, in tears after losing a bout, she'd vowed to. ("Honey," he'd told her kindly, "you're not fucking quitting.") They hadn't been perfect, those two, but between them they'd offered something she could trust. They had taken her seriously, seen her for a fighter; perhaps it was this she was most grateful for.

Richie had both arms around her now, encircling her waist. An ambulance went by, interrupting the cloistered hush of this garden of thought and memory, linking it to what it was, after all, linked to: real life and pain. Raphi blinked at the grave. Her turtleneck was white and ribbed and emphasized her slenderness. Her top fighting weight was 119. Now she hovered somewhere around 105.

"Okay," said Raphi at last.

With no more speech than that, they got back in the car. They were on their way to buy a spit bucket, towels, and tape.

Two of the girls finally had fights coming up.

It had been a grim winter. Two more losses at the boxing club, not deaths this time but disappearances no less haunting. Mick Murray, a stalwart at the gym, a trim man, polite, of few words, unshowily handsome in middle age, had vanished. He used to come several days a week, to work out alone or to train his seventeen-year-old twins, and he was someone Raphi thought of as a friend. He'd worked her corner at fights, had even taken her out for a beer once, to cheer her up, when it was her birthday and Bobby Tomasello had just died and they were losing the gym and everything was so sad. She'd heard something or other of his shady past, knew he was an ex-con. Once, when one of the Somerville fighters had a bout in New York, a bunch of them from the gym all drove down in the same car, and every time they passed a bank, the driver would slow and ask Micky if he ought to pull over. From this joke, Raphi gathered that he'd been some kind of bank robber. But she'd thought it was in his past. She liked Micky. A lot.

Then the story broke that he was under federal indictment. The papers were calling him a Charlestown gangster with links to organized crime in Montreal and the Irish Republican Army. The papers had him stealing from UPS trucks; involved in a scheme to collect thousands in unearned health care from the Teamsters; shaking down a bookie. It made Raphi feel queasy, dizzy; she didn't want to think about it.

But it was hard to ignore what seemed like an unnaturally close relationship between the criminal-justice system and the Somerville Boxing Club—a relationship that sat uncomfortably with the picture of the gym as a wholesome environment for the kids who sought it out. So many of the gym's members had had brushes with the law, or close friends or relatives who'd had brushes with the law. And it wasn't just the fighters in off the street; it was the people who made up the base of the club, its founders and funders. One of the board members, an attorney, was regularly referred to in the papers as a prominent Mafia lawyer. The fact that boxing traditionally drew people from the most disenfranchised strata of society—immigrants, the impoverished, the underserved— lined up neatly with the fact that these groups disproportionately populated the correctional institutions. But whether this relationship was causal in any way was harder to say.

Did the ritualized brutality of the sport foster a kind of lawlessness? Or was it a curiously apt remedy—almost homeopathic—that, at least much of the time, saved people from criminal temptations? No one I met in the boxing world espoused the former view. Almost everyone, from the old-timers to the current crop of kids, had offered up some version of the latter: "Boxing saved me—continues to save me—from the road I've seen my friends take."

Boxing hadn't saved Vinny Busa. His was the second disappearance from the gym, or imminent disappearance; he was bound for the same general destination as Micky—prison—though in Vinny's case the departure was less shocking. It seemed everyone had known for some time that Vinny would be going away, soon, for a while. No one batted an eye, as though this was something that happened with Vinny from time to time. In the weeks before he started serving his sentence, Ann Cooper, the gym's talcum-scented, crinkle-eyed den mother, bought him a sweater, "From the club, to kind of tell him thank you, because he does so much for us." It was true: Without Vinny, who would be here to open the gym each afternoon?

Vinny had started boxing twenty-two years earlier, at age fourteen. By his account, he'd work out for a few months, then get himself "in trouble" and disappear into the labyrinths of the Department of Youth Services, only to resurface and drift back to the boxing gym for another respite from the street. Even after giving up his own boxing, he'd maintained a connection with the gym. "Every minute you're here," he pointed out, "you're not on the street." Now, with Franky dead and Ralphy out of the picture, Vinny had become the guy who was here six days a week, the guy who answered the phone (sometimes, anyway), the guy who opened each afternoon and closed each night. "I'm the only nitwit with nothing else to do" was how he put it, rolling his toothpick to the other side of his mouth. He'd train new kids who came in, the ones who hadn't made it onto the "team" of boys licensed for competition. At least he'd train them if he felt like it. Some days he wasn't in the mood to hold the mitts; then he'd tell the kids to jump rope or hit the bags. Or better yet, go running.

That had all changed, kind of, two months earlier, when Trini Molloy came to the gym. Not that Vinny supported girls' boxing. And he didn't think females should spar. But Trini had a kind of determination he'd never had. It was funny how that kid took a liking to him. With her shaved head and baggy pants and all. To Vinny's mind, she respected him because he was tough, because he'd yell at her, swear at her. Well, maybe that wasn't exactly why. But he treated her seriously, and she treated him seriously, and they had worked something out, the two of them. It was like he was a real trainer when he was with her. She came from a long way, he knew, to train here in Somerville. He knew, too, that she might not want to keep coming when he wasn't here anymore; it was funny to admit it, since he wasn't used to forging real attachments with any of the kids who came in, but he felt like he was letting her down.

He'd told her about it last week. "They're taking me away," he'd said, and he knew she knew what that meant. It had been easy to tell she was mad. She hadn't said anything, but she'd hit the mitts hard that day. She about killed the speed bag. Actually, she'd had her best day at the gym ever.

Now they were saying the gym might close. First of all, basically nobody paid dues. Vinny had made a big sign to hang next to the sign-in sheet by the door in the office: DUES IS DUE NOW! It was pointless, of course: The sign had been roundly ignored. Pretty much everyone ignored the sign-in sheet, for that matter. On top of that, the longtime crew of people running the club had been vastly depleted. Some had died, some had retired, some had relocated to Las Vegas. Without Vinny

Busa to provide a more or less regular presence, it was unclear whether anyone would be around to unlock and staff the place during posted gym hours.

In the end, the trainers cobbled together a haphazard schedule, on a week-by-week basis, according to who could come on which afternoons to open the place up. Most days it still managed to open. Some days boxers came, kicked up the gravel, hunch-shouldered, in the chilly parking lot for a while, then gave up and went for a run or a drink. They tried not to take seriously the prospect of the gym closing, of it one day not being there. The threat of the gym closing wasn't novel; every couple of years that tired old rumor got dusted off and trotted around, and every time the club managed to resurrect itself with an infusion of new blood, or new cash, or a move to new digs. But this time it was hard not to wonder whether a certain critical mass had shifted.

Vinny Busa's last days on the outside passed like any others, a little work on the mitts with Trini, taking out the garbage, reading the racing sheet at the desk, flipping through an old issue of *Ring* magazine, drinking a Diet Coke with his elbows on the ring apron, looking up through the ropes to watch the boys spar. Then one day one of the guys from the gym dropped him off, for a while, and he had gone away. The seedy little fake-wood-paneled office was exactly like it was before, and the desk with the sort-of-broken clock and the duct-taped phone was exactly like it was before, and the gym itself was exactly like it was before, except he wasn't in it.

At last: fights. Sefina's and Candi's passbooks had come in three weeks ago, and Raphi had brought them to the gym, where they'd been examined with intense absorption: the pebbly white covers all shiny and stiff; the passport-size photographs staring back, almost as if foreign, scrutinized for traces of the familiar; the pages and pages of space in which to record an entry for each bout pristine. Jacinta and Nikki had looked over their books, too, only slightly broken in, with their new validation stickers affixed. Everybody had signed their books, checking off the box that promised they'd never competed professionally, and returned them to Raphi for safekeeping. She'd given them strong embraces, commemorating the moment, an exciting if uncertain one. Because there had been so many half-promises of upcoming bouts, none of which had transpired, it was hard to gauge how much significance the moment merited.

The difficulty girl boxers had in getting ring experience was significant almost everywhere in the United States. Massachusetts was no exception. The boys from the gym had boxed, collectively, some seventy bouts since the fall, according to their trainers, Gene McCarthy and John Curran. Raphi's girls, by contrast, hadn't even wound up competing at the Silver Mittens, the event she had assumed was a sure thing, for lack of opponents.

When at last a promoter from the South Shore, Mike Cappiello, called Raphi and offered her a fight at the Roseland Ballroom in Taunton for a 106-pounder in March, she accepted immediately for Nikki, and when he called back a few days later to offer her a 102-pounder, she said yes for Sefina—in spite of her doubts: Sefina was the least ready. Never mind that the weights were a little off—both Somerville girls had about ten pounds on their opponents, but as Raphi said, who even knew if the gym scale was accurate? A more serious obstacle ought to have been the age difference. Sefina's opponent was fourteen, and Sefina was only twelve. This matchup was technically not allowed, but the promoter said the other girl had just turned fourteen, and Sefina would turn thirteen in July, and after all, this was Massachusetts, not exactly orthodox about the rules.

In the end, the most serious problem looked to be the girls' own behavior. This, from an e-mail Raphi sent me, filled me in on a day I had missed, when Raphi's old sparring partner Jerry had agreed to stick around to help the girls in the ring:

> Yesterday's practice was a disgrace. Jerry was mad when Nikki and Jacinta were late. And during sparring they both quit before 2 rounds were up. Jerry is a stickler about doing three full rounds. So he yelled at Nikki, said he was ashamed of both of them. He said she was better at boxing the very first time she sparred. Then he left without saying goodbye to anyone. I don't think Nikki felt too bad. She bounced right back. Then Candi and Nikki sparred, but Candi first was laughing and then acted like a baby when she got tapped in the stomach so SHE quit. So then I threw Sefina in with Nikki. Talk about girl fight.

She was just flailing her arms with her eyes closed, no form or skill whatsoever, punching Nikki repeatedly in the back of the head. When it was all over I wanted to shoot myself. THREE WEEKS, we have!

And the next week:

The French girl, Sylvie, who has been training with John Curran, agreed to spar Nikki and Jacinta, one round each. Nikki went first and of course almost knocked Sylvie out right away, and was just beating her with some of the hardest blows I've ever seen. I felt bad for Sylvie and kept telling Nikki to cool it but she wouldn't. She was like a mad-woman. Then Jacinta went in with Sylvie and it was pretty normal until Nikki started shouting out names of girls that Jacinta hates. So Jacinta got wild and tried to kill Sylvie. She got her in the corner and they were half fighting/half wrestling and Sylvie was so scared she got Jacinta in a headlock and tightened it and wouldn't let go and literally almost strangled Jacinta to death. Jacinta passed out for a moment on her feet and there were about fifty people watching and four people in each corner, and no one stopped it. Everyone was just stunned. Nikki was screaming at ringside to Sylvie in her high-pitched screaming voice "YOU FUCKING BITCH!!" Finally Nikki ran in and almost killed Sylvie and then EVERYONE jumped in and Jacinta was crying and legless and her neck was all bruised. And you should've seen Sylvie's face, COVERED in bruises and scrapes.
    Of course I am insanely bothered by the fact that Nikki stopped it and not me and I don't know why I didn't. It happened so fast and yet it was slow motion.

Two weeks later Ralphy died. It wasn't a shock—the only surprise was how long his body had continued to function after being taken off life support. Still, the finality of it hit Raphi hard. On the Monday afternoon of his death, five days before Nikki and Sefina were scheduled to fight at the Roseland, the awareness of his absence reverberated among the older boxers and trainers at the gym like a sorrowful chord, sweetened only by the understanding that it was shared. Ralph Palmacci, Sr., was the first trainer many of them had worked with.
    In spite, or maybe because, of the pall of mourning, the gym felt al-most cozy, packed with the usual suspects, the air ripe with sweat and

teeming with the pounding rhythms of fists and hip-hop and the homely familiarity of everything. Raphi and Candi huddled close on the pew beneath the altar, bent over a slim paperback Raphi had brought, *The Tao of Sports*. Maria had mentioned Candi's trouble with reading in school, so Raphi tried to practice with her now and then. " 'Mystery,' " read Candi, her raspy voice concentrated and low. She read slowly. " 'The Game is bigger than any game. The Game is beyond the scope of all games.' " She shot Raphi a sidelong glance. "I want to hit the mitts."

"I just don't feel like it today," said Raphi. She did look rather drawn.

"I want to," Candi persisted.

"Give me a break."

"I always give you a break."

"Yeah, right." Raphi rubbed her knuckles against the girl's head.

Candi was saved from being simply pretty by her eyebrows, which were black and thick and widely arched. She deployed them to great effect, and she bared her beaverish white teeth now, too, for good measure.

Raphi rolled her eyes.

Candi, who was sporting four candy necklaces, pulled one forth and bit at it as though it were corn on the cob.

Sefina emerged from the locker room wearing a tank top and boxing shoes purloined from Raphi's locker, satin boxing shorts purloined from Jacinta's.

"Nice outfit," commented Raphi.

Sefina grinned and checked herself out in one of the wall mirrors, which was glazed with dried saliva.

"That's disgusting," observed Candi mildly. "Why don't people use the spit buckets."

"Don't ask me," said Raphi. "Warm up. Come on! Get up!"

Candi finished nibbling the necklace, removed the other three, and slipped them into the pocket of her mother's jacket, beside her on the pew. Little sticky dots of color ringed her neck. Maria was doing biceps curls with a ten-pound hand weight.

Jacinta and Nikki streamed in, having taken the train and then the bus from school. A new thing with them: They didn't want to get picked up anymore. Jacinta had blown her hair out straight and glamorous today, but it was Nikki whose appearance was the more striking for its divergence from her usual dress, which ordinarily included one of her brother's loose shirts, a pair of sweatpants, and sneakers. She was wearing stretch jeans with a flare at the ankle, and a skinny stretch T-shirt in shades of cantaloupe and saffron, fading to pale peach over her breasts.

Maria did a wolf whistle, and Nikki shimmied her shoulders a little, blushing at the same time.

"Hootchie mama!" hailed Candi loudly. Then Sefina took it up; together they chanted, "Hootchie! Hootchie!" until Nikki started to get a vacant look in her eyes and Maria hissed, "Shut up!" to her daughters.

The male boxers had paid this scene little mind, immersed in their private worlds of shadowboxing, pounding bags, and skipping rope, churning up the rising steambathy atmosphere, which would grow increasingly moist and pungent as the evening brought more men into the gym. These girls and their antics stood for the most part outside the gaze of the men, which could be attributed to two things: the consuming involvement of the men with their workouts, and the age of the girls and the fact that they were chaperoned not only by their female coach but also by the brash, steely guardianship of Maria. The tenuous nature of this exempt status was never forgotten, however; certainly not by Raphi and Maria, whose collective empirical knowledge of men was not reassuring. In spite of the Ralphys and Frankys and Desis they'd known, they seemed to regard such men as anomalies. One reason so few women had followed Raphi down the path she bushwhacked into the gym six years earlier was surely the difficulty of finding a trainer willing to focus on working with them and not on having sex with them. Franky had once told Raphi about walking into the club office in the middle of the day and finding a young female boxer, barely out of adolescence, on her knees, bent over the trouserless lap of the decades-older married man who was supposed to be her trainer.

Without commenting on the consensuality of the sexual acts, or expressing shock that such acts occur, it is worth observing that lacing on the gloves doesn't automatically confer on women a sexual bye. For all that the ring itself is roped off, scoured and purified of sexual intent; for all that the surrounding square footage of the gym functions primarily as a workplace dedicated to the single purpose of practicing this most demanding of sports; for all that the male boxers tend to come across as good guys and noble warriors—nevertheless, boxing remains overwhelmingly a male environment, informed by a particular strain of masculine culture, one of the ramifications of which is that female boxers are constantly reminded (by the round-card girls in bikinis and stilettos, by the lyrics that blast from virtually all gym boom boxes, by the heckling taunts of spectators at matches, and by the inevitable advances from male trainers and boxers) that they are more easily regarded as sex objects than as athletes.

An irony of this is that among the many established benefits of Title IX (the part of the Education Amendments of 1972 that prohibits federally funded programs from excluding or discriminating on the basis of sex), and of girls' athletic programs in general—benefits that include higher grades in school and lower rates of school dropout, cigarette and marijuana use, and depression—one of the most touted is the lowered rates of engaging in sexual activity and of teen pregnancy. Several studies have found that participation in sports gives girls an avenue to power, respect, and confidence that they might otherwise seek through sex. The idea that a girl might come to the boxing gym out of a need to feel power, and once there find herself subjected to the same sort of duplicitous messages about the relationship between her power and her sexuality that she encountered outside the gym, is heartbreaking.

If Candi, Sefina, Jacinta, and Nikki were as yet relatively innocent of such hassles, Raphi and Maria were not. Their low opinion of males was one part of the reason they both felt so good about the girls' learning to box. Raphi regarded her positive relationships with a handful of men as exceptions that proved the rule, and she was not without wariness regarding even those, as though she half expected them to change without warning. She traced her decision to box directly to negative experiences with men in her childhood and adolescence. "It was important for me to know I could hurt a man," she had told me early on, and although she never elaborated much on the details of those experiences, their impact remained a motivation for everything she did at the gym, both her own workouts and what she imparted to the girls. Raphi's message was punctuated by Maria, who, on a daily basis, was saucily and colorfully forthright about her disparaging views on the opposite sex. Such views seemed only reinforced by her husband, Hector, who readily agreed that the need to deal with men was one of the most compelling reasons to teach girls to box. "I feel good about them boxing," he said of his daughters, "so they can be strong, protect themselves. If any of them's going to wind up with a guy who likes to hit"—fatalistic shrug and grin here— "then it's good, you know? So she can hit him back."

Hector came into the gym on occasion. He used to drive a truck for Sweetheart, the company that makes paper cups, but he'd injured his back on the job a few years before and now was home on disability. He was always ready with the same greeting for me—"Hey, baby! How you doing?"—accompanied by a hug and a broad grin with a streak of Lothario in it. But this would be generally followed by a wince, and he'd been limping more lately as his back caused him increasing pain. Sometimes Jacinta would give him a massage, which alleviated his suffering temporarily. As did pain medication. And how did it make him feel to watch his daughter get hit in the face when she was boxing? "Good, good." With the Hector grin, feline and spreading. "It makes me feel good. She can take it. I don't have to worry about her."

Not that boxing ought to be confused with self-defense. The most skilled and powerful 110-pound female boxer is still, in a dark alley against an attacker, 110 pounds. Being fleet of foot would serve her better in such a situation than her best blows or her most leonine heart. But the confidence, rooted in physical self-knowledge, that a person can get from sports can function as a deterrent to attacks and abuse. Girls are not only more likely than boys to be the targets of attacks and abuse (83 percent of girls in public schools experience harassment, according to the American Association of University Women's 2001 study "Hostile Hallways"), they are also less likely to use their own aggression as a defense against such encounters. The same study found that girls are far more likely than boys to report feeling less confident because of an incident of harassment, and to change their behavior as a result (by not talking as much in class and by avoiding their harassers). By as early as fourth grade, writes Colette Dowling in *The Frailty Myth,* boys associate aggressive acts with self-esteem, while girls associate aggressive acts with guilt.

The more time I spent with these girls in and out of the gym, the more I was aware, as I never had been during my own adolescence, of what a treacherously muddled passage this could be, from girlhood into womanhood. I thought of the way Candi, age ten, during warm-ups in the ring, liked to convulse everyone by doing imitations of sexual writhing so note-perfect as to shock. But later she would tell me—with what aim did she impress this upon me; what question was she hoping to settle for herself?—that at heart she was a small kid. "Everyone tells me I have the brain of a forty-year-old, the face of a thirty-year-old." She rattled this off as though it were a perfectly standard observation, and fiddled some with the lollipop stick in her mouth before confiding, with a trademark Candi chortle, low to high in two notes, "But I feel like I'm five."

I thought of Sefina, age twelve, who was adding inches and pounds so rapidly this year that to witness her was practically like watching time-lapse photography. The other day she had lost herself beautifully inside the ring, alone, spinning, arms out, red-gloved fists going round and round, a centrifugal dream of dizziness, and I had thought, The *baby!* and been pleased she still had the freedom and innocence to do that, be the center of her own world. I thought of her walking in her own neighborhood, where by her own account, she was the object of more and more wolf whistles and stares, which she neither suffered nor enjoyed quietly, but which incited her to confrontation: "Why you did that? What, you got a eye problem or something?" she'd demand, right up in the guy's face. I felt almost joyous when I heard this about her, but was brought up short by the others' sobriety. Even Candi told me she worried for Sefina's safety, felt the need to protect her.

Most of all, I thought of the big two, Jacinta and Nikki, themselves beginning to articulate the complexities of giving up childhood for womanhood. Jacinta had done a report earlier that year on the Middle Passage. Describing it one day in the gym, she had mentioned the fact that some Africans helped furnish the Europeans with their human cargo. Her mother had piped up and corrected her, explaining that the Africans were the enslaved, the whites the enslavers. Jacinta explained what she had been taught, quietly and with deference, but Maria insisted her daughter had the facts wrong. Jacinta had accepted this. There was something sad and familiar in the way Jacinta relinquished her own truth in order to keep intact the peace with her mother, and her mother's superior authority.

Nikki and Jacinta brought me one day to the place in Charlestown they called "The Spot," partway between their respective homes. They had been excited to show me this place, which had, I gathered, some kind of mystical properties for them; they looked upon it as their secret hideout. They had met here and told each other their dreams here and burst into tears here, and when they brought me to it, I was a little surprised by how unremarkable, and not even really hidden away, it was. The Spot was a cement structure, like a scorekeeper's or announcer's perch, overlooking the athletic field of Dum-Dum High. It was hardly private; if the Rodriguezes lived just one building over from where they resided in the housing projects across the street, they would theoretically be able to keep an eye on the girls from their windows.

But its charms were undimmed for Nikki and Jacinta. "If we climbed up on top," they told me, splicing the sentence several times between them, "you'd be able to see everything—the whole field, down to the houses where Nikki lives, by the bridge, the water, the sky, everything." It was a cold, sunny day, however, so we huddled on the cement bleachers below the Spot, out of the wind. The romance of this place might have been lost on me, but clearly not on Sefina and Candi, who, hotly aware of being left out, scampered across the street. One of the big two kept rising to shoo them away, in increasingly threatening tones.

With the three of us alone, they filled me in on details of their joint history. They parsed for me, in painstaking slow motion, their secret handshakes. They wrote out for me a glossary of the teenage slang they shared. *On dogs*—no lie; *mad wug*—really cool; *be oust*—leave. They seemed shyly ravenous to talk with me here. As they sat facing me on the cold bleachers, I understood slowly that I was here to witness their prize creation, which was their friendship.

When I asked them about boxing, their answers circled back to their friendship, as though the appetite for and benefits of each were one and the same. The picture they presented of their friendship was of a safe haven, a semi-magical resource that could be leveraged against tangible pressures to do drugs, to have sex, to change. They spoke of the girls in the neighborhood, "with all their cell phones and girliness," as embodiments of the threats to their most cherished selves. They told me they had a fear of becoming more feminine.

"We have weird guys who follow us home," said Jacinta. She was wearing one of her killer T-shirts, this one stating: GOOD GIRLS ARE BAD GIRLS THAT NEVER GOT TAUGHT. Her strong brown arms circled her knees.

"We get cars beeping at us."

"Boys saying stuff."

"It's like, I want to show my prettiness," Nikki confessed warily, "but then the assholes come out."

Her mother had gotten her a makeup kit this past Christmas, and told me she'd offered Nikki careful instructions on applying it "without coming out too slutty." Now, said her mother, "She's in the mirror all the time, doing her face, making muscles." I could picture it so well: the girl—almost transfixed by the glass—caught between searching the image of her own face, which she was learning to alter with powders and creams, and flexing her biceps, calculating the worth of the part of her that was real and the part she had invented. The looming, insistent question: Was it either-or? Or could it be both?

Their refuge was their refrain: "We're really immature." They insisted upon this, sitting across from me on the cold cement, Nikki's nostrils flaring, Jacinta's dimples deepening, and this statement, which they had avowed more than once, seemed to carry greater depths of meaning than the face value each word might betray.

"We're afraid of changing," Jacinta explained, startlingly direct. "We don't want to lose our tomboyness."

"Yeah!" said Nikki, rounding her eyes, leaning forward. "I don't want to lose the things I used to love. Like"—she cast about—"like sports. And baggy clothes! The things that made me happy. Like I'm not ready to really say goodbye."

The love between them was multifaceted and dazzling. It comprised the intimate and the chivalric. At school, whenever they had to part company (as after lunch, when their schedules diverged for a period), Jacinta would walk Nikki to her classroom, where Nikki would deposit her books, and then Nikki would walk Jacinta to *her* classroom, up a flight, and there drop her off before returning downstairs. By the time the next bell rang, Jacinta (so smooth at stealing out of class a minute early) would already be loitering in the hall outside Nikki's class, out of sight of the teacher, whispering, "Yo, *blanca!*"

Since the previous June, when they'd caught the notice of the entire school at field day, where they had reveled publicly in the mock-boxing activity (wearing the harmless giant boxing gloves the school had rented for the occasion), they had relished being branded the girl fighters, jointly recognized for their participation in this unlikeliest of sports. That label had followed them ever since, casting its rarified light, and it was surely this light as much as their fighting skills that afforded them a kind of barrier against intrusion.

That day at the Spot, they spoke so candidly and shiningly of what they had in each other, in their relationship as boxers and as best friends. Their willingness to name it a precious object made it seem all at once vulnerable, too good to be true. It was like that moment in a fairy tale when the heroine takes her one good treasure and sets off with it into the woods. These girls were already surrounded by woods: by a neighborhood crumbling in places; by a housing project that the federal Department of Housing and Urban Development had called among the nation's most distressed; by the street-corner addicts and dealers they passed on a daily basis; and by deadeningly frequent reports of neighborhood rapes, beatings, and assaults. One day on the way home from school, the girls had watched a man jump to his death from the top of a building. When I asked whether they had talked about what they'd seen and what they'd felt with any adult, they shrugged and shook their heads in a way that made clear the thought hadn't even crossed their minds. But all that was drab and dangerous around them might have served to make them cherish and guard more vigilantly what they had. The real threat to their friendship came from a less obvious source, from the quarters meant to be most nurturing. Their parents had begun to make noises about the girls being too close.

ROSELAND WEIGH-IN: 4:30

Fighter	Coach
mouthpiece	amateur books
sports bra	coaching license
tank top	2 buckets
trunks	vaseline
chest protector	2 white towels
socks	scissors
boxing shoes	headgear
rubber bands/scrunchies	training tape
clean clothes	ice bag—first aid
	Q-tips
	jumprope
	gloves
	mitts
	Gatorade
	power bars
	water bottles
	gauze

Raphi had handed out these lists a few days before Saturday's fight. Nikki, duly equipped, was the first to arrive at the gym, at three-fifteen, a half hour earlier than Raphi had specified. Her father, Enzo, who lived in East Boston, had brought her and waited with her outside the locked building. He was affable, wiry, smoking a cigarette. Nikki had gone to bed at seven the night before, then woken up that morning at five. She couldn't stand still. "I've got my dot," she told me, promptly upon my arrival.

"Your dot?"

"I've got cramps." Matter-of-factly. Then, "You're going bald," she told her father.

"Don't say that!" Enzo, a kitchen worker at Tufts, looked embarrassed.

"It's all shiny."

"It's from wearing a hat."

Raphi and Richie arrived, and Nikki, full of adrenaline and morbid wit, had to run out and pretend to get hit by their car.

Enzo headed off to work, kissing his daughter first.

"Dad, don't kiss me in public," she said, looking pleased. She had brought a watermelon-flavored Baby Bottle Pop and two peanut-butter sandwiches on white bread. Plus her homework, in case she had time.

Inside the gym, Nikki gathered her things from her locker and weighed in: 118 with her clothes on. Oops. It was a little high. Raphi told her not to eat her sandwiches until after the weigh-in at Taunton. We waited in the office. At three-forty-five Raphi called the Rodriguezes at home, twice.

"It's not like they're ever late," said Richie dryly.

"I told them three o'clock," muttered Raphi.

They pulled into the parking lot, all calm, a little past four.

We sped the whole way to Taunton, about an hour south of Somerville, and arrived at the Roseland Ballroom at five-ten to learn that no other fighters had even shown up yet. The place reeked of cigarettes. A couple of guys working with the promoter were sitting at the bar and told us we could go into the main ballroom, where the fights would be. The girls instantly rushed for the pool tables behind the ring. "Ooh, this is nice!" There were about seven tables covered in pumpkin-pie-colored felt. The kids grabbed cues. Nikki and Jacinta racked up. Sefina sulked. "They won't let me play!" She slammed down a cue. "Josefina!" snapped her mother. "Pick it up!" Candi carried in one of the trainer's buckets, looking official. Hector went off in search of an outlet so he could charge the battery for his video camera. Sefina sat on a bar stool. She had eaten a pear and a piece of cheesecake that day. Trying to keep her weight down. Her hair was in cornrows, done by her mother that afternoon.

Other young fighters began to drift into the room, and Maria puffed out her chest a little, engaged in a few staring contests with other mothers. Then she brainstormed with Nikki and Sefina about what she could yell from ringside during their fights to make them mad. "You're fighting like a girl," she tried for Nikki.

"Dyke!" added Jacinta.

Candi started reeling off the names of girls Nikki hated.

For Sefina: "Those are chest protectors, they're not real," taunted Maria. Apprehending the glower on her middle daughter's face, she chuckled. "Okay, that does it for you."

At five-thirty, all the fighters and their entourages were banished from the main ballroom and gathered in the smaller one, where weigh-ins would take place. A disco ball hung from the ceiling. It was cold in there; people hunched in their windbreakers and down jackets. Workers crossed the room with cases of Budweiser on their shoulders. Raphi went to the bar to get her ice bucket filled.

A guy came around with an ink pad and stamp. All boxers and coaches got their hands stamped for free; everybody else was supposed to pay ten bucks admission. Among our crew this led to much surreptitious wetting of stamps and pressing backs of hands together. Jacinta and Nikki sat off to the side singing softly, in imitation R&B lilts, a song they'd made up together: "Should I smile because we're friends / Or should I cry because that's all we will ever be?" The lyrics to all the songs they'd made up could be taken as ambiguously suggestive, and whether they were singing to an imaginary figure or to each other was a question of some concern to the grown-ups in their lives.

Candi and Sefina hung out at a banquette. "Bartender!" cried Sefina in her idea of a derelict's rasping voice. "Bartender, give me some whiskey!"

Candi pretended to mix a drink. She shook it vigorously, then mimed throwing it in Sefina's face. "You're drunk!"

At six-ten the girls were called to weigh in. The officials had set themselves up on the low platform where a live band might have gone. Sefina climbed onto the flat bathroom scale. "No way. No way." The speaker was a blond woman in a red-and-black jacket, scowling down at the numbers on the scale: 120. Her voice was belligerent. She was the mother of Sefina's opponent and had been bragging loudly for the past hour about her own recent bout at the Roxy, in Boston. "Mine is one-oh-two. No way. No way. For her first amateur fight? I was told one-ten."

Maria had been involved in a staring match with this woman earlier, in the big ballroom. "She's not one-twenty," Maria told her now.

"The scale lies, then."

The women grilled each other with their eyes.

The official commented on the obvious: "If the scale is off for one person, it's off for everybody."

"At home she was one-ten," Maria promised Raphi.

"Go take off some of your clothes," Raphi said.

Sefina, completely abashed, slinked off to the bathroom.

"She never weighs one-twenty," Raphi told the official.

Meanwhile, Nikki weighed in quietly: 115.

Sefina returned in her blue satin tank, trunks, and socks and stepped back on the scale: 115.

At a club show, the weight-discrepancy issue was up to the coaches; this would never fly at the Golden Gloves. The other mother made a disgusted sound with her tongue but agreed to the match.

The girls all had to pee: back to the bathroom, where they took turns shadowboxing in front of the wall mirror and reading aloud the writing on the Scent-O-Matic: PERFUME FOR YOUR EVERY MOOD. SELECT YOUR FAVORITE SPRAY. 25 CENTS. But no one had a quarter.

At seven the boxers and coaches were allowed upstairs while families and friends got relegated to the main ballroom. Jacinta and I managed to sneak up with Richie, Raphi, Nikki, and Sefina. Upstairs was a freezing cold, slope-ceilinged storage room where the boxers clumped with their coaches amid old, listing couches, fake Christmas trees, a toilet seat, some rolled-up carpet, crates of empties, and a clear plastic bag filled with multicolored inflated balloons. Down at one end of the room, boys chinned themselves on an exposed duct. "We have to stay here the whole time?" asked Nikki. "I don't want to stay here for two hours."

"It's more like one," Raphi told her, and Nikki's eyes widened sharply. "Who wants to get wrapped first?"

Sefina straddled a chair. Raphi laid a towel over the back. Sefina put her hand out. "You didn't bring the blue wraps?"

"You have to get gauze first," Raphi reminded her, and proceeded to wrap ten feet of gauze around Sefina's hand. Sefina's leg was jiggling, her head turning back and forth, her mouth producing a steady stream of goofy chatter. "Got a little extra energy there?" asked Raphi. She began to deliver a low, steadying talk. "You touch gloves when the ref brings you out and explains the rules. When the bell rings, you don't touch gloves, just fight. In fact, what you should do is come out and throw your right at her nose. If she hits you first, don't worry about it. Just keep your hands up, concentrate, and throw your combinations."

Nikki took the chair. Since coming upstairs, she seemed to have traveled far away inside herself. Raphi began to wrap her hands, breaking away a few times to tell Sefina to calm down and save her energy. The girl could not hold still: She was tapping out rhythms on her thighs, wiggling her ankles, giggling.

"How come you don't fight anymore?" asked Nikki abruptly, quietly.

They both watched her hand, which Raphi wrapped as she spoke, slowly and carefully. " 'Cause I had a full-time job. And I wanted to coach. And they never had an opponent for me. And I fought in the Golden Gloves and the Nationals, and that's what I wanted to achieve."

"Did you win your first fight?"

"I won my first, lost my second, won my third, and lost my fourth and fifth."

"I had one fight and I lost," said Nikki. Just contemplative. Perhaps she was remembering that fight, at the Nationals the previous summer, when her legs had wobbled and the referee stopped the bout.

If Nikki's prefight nerves were making her somber, Sefina's were having the opposite effect. She was going nuts, panting, pinching Jacinta's leg.

Raphi glared. "Sefina, sit down and shut up."

"It calms me!" she protested, parodying what a grown-up might say. But she did sit, heavily, only to work on her burping. She zipped her fleece up over her neck and chin, like a turtle. "Help! I'm stuck in a hole! I can't get out!"

Raphi, her hands jammed under her armpits for warmth, laughed in spite of herself.

Nikki and Jacinta were beeping at each other. *"Beep." "Beep."* They pinched each other's cheeks. "We're immature," said Nikki. "Raphaëlla, what's wrong?"

"She looks nervous," observed Jacinta.

"Are you nervous?"

Raphi shook her head. "I'm *cold*." She was wearing Franky's old corner jacket, light blue with navy lapels and SOMERVILLE BOXING CLUB across the back. She'd found it when she cleaned out his locker after he died.

At eight-ten an official came in and called the boxers in the first three bouts downstairs to get gloved up. Sefina and Nikki were bouts five and six.

"Let me tape your shirts on. Stand," commanded Raphi. She taped the straps of their tank tops to the straps of their chest protectors. She worked the mitts some with Sefina. "Easy. Just break a sweat." She called on Richie to work the mitts with Nikki, and he emerged from where he had been biding his time in the shadows of the eaves. He and Nikki went into the hall, and soon the sound of blows rang out, but only for a minute. "Just a little," called Raphi, stopping them. "Save the rest."

When at last we headed down, Maureen, Nikki's mother, was standing by the door to the main ballroom in a denim jacket with Elvis embroidered across the back. It had a momentous feeling, her being there after so many disputes, all the times she'd threatened to take boxing away from Nikki as punishment for some infraction. Nikki went to her and they hugged, and Maureen, in her raspy voice, told her who else was there: her boyfriend, Nikki's grandmother, Nikki's brother . . . They looked through the door together, scanning the crowd. Maureen draped an arm across her daughter's back, and Nikki let her. "I want to fight!" she said softly, pink-cheeked, turning to Raphi.

We watched the first bouts from the doorway, then edged into the main ballroom, where we stood at the back. Nikki's eyes were on her mother, seated far across the ring. "My mom's all yelling!" she reported to Raphi. "And it's not even me! She's all, 'Go, you fucker!'" The color was high in Nikki's cheeks, and she was giddy around the edges, a laugh shaking from her throat.

Bout number three: Sefina suddenly wailed, "I have to pee!"

Raphi sighed. "Take off your gloves. Jacinta, take her to the bathroom. *Fast.*"

A minute later, Nikki: "Where's Jacinta?"

"She had to take Sefina to the bathroom. Because Sefina had to drink a gallon of Gatorade before fighting."

The third bout ended after two rounds, when the red corner retired. Raphi pulled Sefina into the hall, had her hit the mitts with a few combinations. The fourth bout ended after one round, when the referee stopped the competition. Sefina was up. They made their way to the blue corner. Jacinta massaged her sister's shoulders. Sefina stepped into the ring, dancing foot to foot. Her opponent arrived. The announcer declared a bout of three one-minute rounds, in the 110-pound weight class (the length of the rounds commensurate with their youth and inexperience). The bell. It was over, really, right away. They traded a few blows, and then it was all Sefina. The other girl was backing up, blocking, crouching; the ref stopped it even as the girl turned full away from the fight and retreated to her neutral corner midround. Earlier, her mother had told her, "I don't care if you're dying. I want to see those hands flying. Go the three rounds." I wondered how her mother would receive her now.

But the elation over in the blue corner, among the Somerville crowd! Jacinta was wild with laughter; Candi came running down from her seat, with Maria, and Maureen, and Nikki's little brother, Enzo, Jr. Sefina! Who would've expected it? As if winning conferred on her a sudden responsibility to be suave, Sefina stepped rather solemnly into the middle of the ring when she was announced the official winner and had her arm raised up by the referee, breaking into a smile only when she dipped her head to accommodate the medal being hung around her neck. Upon her return to the corner, the kid got a long hug from Raphi, and now her smile glowed. She descended from the ring and into embraces, back slaps, congratulations.

Nikki was up next. Basking in the pride over Sefina's somewhat surprising triumph, the Somerville crew settled in with knowing anticipation: Nikki was such a powerhouse. Jacinta retreated into the audience to watch her friend's fight from beside her father's video camera. Maureen remained ringside, crossing her arms, smiling faintly, light glinting off her thick eyeglasses, which had been repaired with masking tape at the left temple.

The announcer: "This bout will be three two-minute rounds in the hundred-and-six-pound weight class." The ref brought both girls to the center of the ring and spoke; they touched gloves and returned to their corners. The bell. Nikki came on strong, and so did the other girl. Nikki caught her with a combination but didn't follow up. Something was off. "Box, Nikki, box!" screamed Jacinta from the darkness of her seat. Everyone was yelling, on both sides, except the trainers: People working the corner weren't allowed to coach during the fight, only the audience. "Brenda, rip her head off!" The other girl stepped forward, fired off some jabs and right crosses; Nikki didn't counter. Her head snapped back. The ref stepped in, gave her a standing eight. She looked down and saw her mother at the ring apron. Something collapsed inside her. She shuttered up the way she could, retreated a million miles behind the smooth green surface of her eyes. The ref said: "Box."

Nikki put up her hands, but there was no fight in her at all. "Kick her ass!" yelled Maureen. The other girl moved in, a flurry of punches; Nikki was bent and protecting her face with her gloves. She wasn't fighting. She wasn't throwing anything. It was hard to believe she was scared or outboxed. The other girl was okay; she'd obviously put in her hours at the gym, but so had Nikki. In the darkness behind me, piercing through all the other shouts, Jacinta wailed on a rising note: "Nik-keeeeee!"

The ref stepped in, and the fight was over after one minute and forty-four seconds. I still didn't understand what had happened. Then I heard Jacinta's voice again, plaintive and wondering and carrying somehow high above the din, spelling it out: "She just gave up." Nikki got herself outside the building so fast it was as if she'd flown. She remained hidden for a while, around the corner of the building with Jacinta and Candi and Sefina in the brittle air. Her mother ventured out, then after only a short time hustled back inside the ballroom, rebuffed, shaking her head and scowling. Raphi, Richie, Maria, and Hector all stood around the Roseland's main entrance, smoking.

Sefina came by to report that Nikki wanted to sleep over at the Rodriguezes' that night. "What about her mother?" asked Maria. Sefina shrugged. "I would never leave one of you," said Maria rather grandly, jerking her head toward the door where Maureen had retreated back inside. "It was her mother," they all agreed softly, hunching their shoulders against the wind. "She looked down and saw her mother and gave up."

Weeks later, when Nikki and I would talk about it, she would say the same thing. The idea that her mother had cared enough to come to the fight had pleased Nikki at first. But their relationship was so troubled that the sight of her mother in that instant triggered feelings of failure and worthlessness. At times Nikki would refer to her mother as an inspiration, someone who had always supported her drawing, for example. The way her mother had let her turn the narrow vestibule outside their bedrooms into an art gallery certainly seemed an act of love. But more often when she spoke of her mother, she seemed tensely coiled, full of anger and pain over all the times she'd felt torn down verbally and humiliated by her mother and her mother's boyfriend. Perhaps Nikki had lost the fight as an act of defiance, to punish her mother for excoriating her, to prove her right in her hurtful predictions about her daughter's worthlessness. Or perhaps it had been a subconscious, involuntary act of allegiance with this woman whose own life was circumscribed by poverty, illness, and depression. Nikki could not say. Only that she saw her mother and quit.

When Maureen came outside again, looking wrecked, cigarette in hand, her defenses were up. Nikki wanted to sleep over at the Rodriguezes', she was told. Maureen met this blow with bitterness but no fight, giving up in the early rounds as surely as her daughter. "Fine. I'm her mother. She doesn't want me? She wants to blame me? Fine. I'm outta here." And she was, like an echo of loss.

6

REACH

During my pregnancies, and only then, I grew to meet and surpass the weight the medical charts say is healthy for my height. With such a specific purpose, I found cause to fully inhabit my body. I reached my fighting weight.

When I was pregnant, I wanted steak. So dark and flavorful, this salty bloody craving. Iron for the baby, a medical person would say. Steak is iron rich, as are dark leafy greens. The Rapunzel in the witch's garden would have been iron rich. Broad leafed, I imagine it, the leaves glossy, nearly black, and thickly veined. Iron for the baby sounds rather sweet, but we all know where Rapunzel's mother's craving led: to a desire so overwhelming that she made her husband steal and gave up the baby she was nourishing. A desire so chaotically transforming that it rendered the good mother a kind of witch, and left the witch herself to assume the maternal mantle.

Other than during pregnancy, I never liked meat much. True, I never liked *food* much, but meat held special difficulties. I found it suggestive of my own body. I couldn't help but see similarities between chicken skin and human skin, between cow flesh and human flesh, between pig gristle and the things that slid and resisted within my own body. The similarities insinuated themselves before my mind's eye and in my throat. Only now do I see that my aversion to meat was not unlike my uneasiness with desire, with carnality.

Carnal is a funny word. The mind leaps to sex. Modern standard definitions start with sex and might include something about earthliness, something about the body. My pet dictionary—a 1931 *New Peerless Webster's*, its pages liver-spotted and its binding gone to tissue and strings—puts a finer point on it. Its entry for *carnal:* "pertaining to the body, its passions and appetites; animal; fleshly; sensual; impure; not spiritual but essentially human; secular." A startling lot of linkages put forth in a short space. But how dead-on they feel. The pairing of appetite with impurity. The severing of the spiritual from the human. How immediately recognizable and bitterly accurate they seem.

And of course in the Latin, *carne* is meat.

By mid-March, I had a little more sparring experience under my belt. Raphi had put me in the ring a few more times with Sefina, and with Monique, a friend of Nikki and Jacinta's who came sporadically over the course of the winter. Monique was solidly built, a good bit heavier than the other girls, and there was a narrowness about her eyes that made me think she would prove formidable. But when we got in the ring to work, there was nothing there: She was barely willing to hold her hands up, barely willing to tap me, and as a result I was unable to throw more than the gentlest jabs, and even those I wound up keeping on a leash. They stopped just short of her face, barely grazed her middle.

The effect of all this halfhearted ring work was to sharpen my appetite for real sparring. If before I had been curious but wary, the wariness had come loose and shredded under the steady friction of my curiosity. I knew so little but was acquainted with at least the feel of the canvas beneath my feet, the parameters of the ring, the amount of wind necessary to carry me through a round of constant movement. I was beginning to get a feel for my own reach, for the look of a glove rushing my face, for the look in my sparring partner's eyes—a feel for what it was like to look into the eyes of someone I was trying to hit, someone who was trying to hit me, without anger, without guilt, without *emotion*.

Sometimes there would be a flicker of fun telegraphed back and forth between us, an acknowledgment of someone having gotten in a good shot or having ducked a good shot, a second of recognition when we became two people who knew each other, who were, in gym parlance, teammates and comrades. But these seconds, unwelcome, counted only as lost time. They interrupted the work, and to my surprise I found that I didn't need—didn't want—the reassurance of those flicker-smiles. Anyway, they were not reassuring. In those moments when, say, Sefina and I caught each other's eye, dropped our hands a little, seemed to acknowledge the absurdity of what we were doing, the work was undermined, made crass; doubts were cast. Intolerable ambiguity edged in.

At last Raphi herself offered to spar with me. The first time we did it, she put on my headgear for me, fastened the strap under my chin like a nursemaid securing a bonnet. The girls were all late that day; we were the only ones there, along with some men down on the gym floor, working the bags and weights, peripheral. We put in our mouthguards, slid our hands into sparring gloves, Velcroed them shut, waited for the bell. We touched gloves. "Light," said Raphi, the word contorted by her mouthguard, and whether she said it to remind me or reassure me I did not know.

I had the feeling of absolute safety. I'm not talking about physical safety. In fact, I was acutely aware that this was a Golden Gloves champion opposite me; that part of what fueled her in the ring was anger; that when she got hit, she had a hard time keeping her anger in check. And that "We'll just go light" were famous last words—anyone in a boxing gym could testify to that.

The safety had to do with purity of intent. The moment we began to spar, I saw from Raphi's eyes how straightforward this would be, and I moved into this as from a cave into a clearing. She was not angry, not out to hurt me, but neither was she playing; there was nothing playful in her gaze. And though she was my friend outside of the ring, she was not here as my friend. I was grateful for this absence of complicating affection. This was work, clear and hard, free of pretense, and what a relief. Passions we may have had, but they were not for each other, so there would be no confusion.

How wildly the confusion leaked in with the girls! The last time Sefina got in the ring with Nikki, the fissures had opened up again, evidenced not by contorted smiles and dropped gloves, as when she and I sparred, but by something rawer. I supposed Nikki had gone too hard for Sefina, who'd resorted to her old, unboxerly impulse: turning away, backing up, screwing shut her eyes. Raphi had yelled into the ring for

Nikki to go easy, but to no avail. Sefina had begun to cry in her gravelly, furious way, through her mouthguard. Raphi rolled her eyes, shouted, "Stop!" and went into the ring. She'd brought Sefina into her neutral corner. "Did you get hurt?"

"No."

"Are you out of breath?"

"No."

"Are you angry?"

"No."

"Did you get scared?"

"No."

"Then what's wrong?"

"I don't know!" Raging sobs. Everybody had pressed in, hands reached out to pat her. She'd taken a wild swing at Nikki, who danced out of reach, and the whole time Candi had been clamoring, "I wanna box! Can I box? Me next, Raph! Put me in next!"

All of it had been equally comprehensible: the tears, the unnamable fury, the laughter and gaiety and sympathy and jealousy.

All of these things seemed ever present, teeming just below the surface; part of the edginess of the boxing gym came from never knowing when a leak might occur and what form that leakage might take. Just as Sefina might one day break up a sparring match with giggles and the next with sobs, the older boxers had their eruptions, too, though these tended to occur outside the ring. I thought of Raphi's modest confession that she used to cry in the locker room after sparring. I thought of the disproportionate number of club members who were or had been in trouble with the law. I thought of the club members who told me bluntly they wouldn't want their sisters dating a boxer: Boxers hit.

I thought of Sylvie Forte, the French woman in her late twenties who had sparred so disastrously with Jacinta a few weeks earlier—the session that had ended with Jacinta in a choke hold and Nikki storming the ring screaming, "Bitch!" Later, Sylvie told me about a kind of bottomless, angry energy within her that could never be spent, no matter what sport she tried—until she found boxing. Her French-accented words ricocheted fast and bright around the locker room. "People say, 'You got a pretty face. You want to break it?' They look at my outside. But my inside is in the ring. I love it. Nobody see my inside." When Sylvie described the first time she boxed, she spoke wonderingly of how it *made her tired,* finally, in a way that nothing else had ever managed to do, and her relief in that was palpable.

I thought of Trini Molloy, the girl with the shaved head who had trained with Vinny Busa. She kept in her closet, in a secret drawer, the Eminem calendar she'd requested for Christmas. On it she recorded all her important boxing dates: the day she started at the gym, the first time she sparred, the day Vinny went to jail. I thought of her just a few weeks before she started, wanting so badly not to kill herself that she'd come out of her bedroom and told her mother she needed help. Several months after we met, she told me about the inciting incident, the December night with all the drunk boys—her sister's friends—in her room, and their voices speaking words she would not repeat, and their hands touching her so that she could barely eat afterward, and had lost seventeen pounds by the time she made it to the Somerville Boxing Club.

No one, *no one,* came here just to box. No one even pretended to. What happened in the gym, in the ring, was tightly and plainly bound to griefs unhealed, riddles unsolved, hurts inflicted beyond those walls. I'm thinking not only of the stories that play broadly, the histories rife with abuse, addiction, poverty. For who among us can be called undamaged? It's just that in the gym, the connection between each boxer and his damage was concrete. It was the thing behind what he was doing there. It was potentially the best tool fighters had in the ring, and it was potentially their undoing.

As I got closer to my own desire to box, what remained a mystery was whether, through boxing, the damage could be transcended, or whether it was simply reenacted over and over in the sanctuary of a specific arena. Or worse: whether, through boxing, the damage might actually be aggravated, corkscrewed deeper and blunter into the self's pliant core.

We sparred. I led with a jab, and Raphi blocked it and countered. She blocked and slipped punches so fast; I couldn't imagine ever being that quick. By the time I saw a punch coming, it was too late for my brain to send my body a message about how to avoid it. Essentially I had no defense. So my ring strategy—not that I viewed it in those terms, but my de facto strategy—was not to care. It went something like this: I don't mind getting hit; I'm not afraid; and look! I can even move forward, even back you up a little, even occasionally land a punch! I was so exhilarated by my lack of fear, so proud, even, of my fearlessness, that it didn't occur to me until the next day, when I was feeling the knotty bruises on the side of my head and the stiffness in my neck, that as strategies go, this one was really lame.

But in the moment, on the canvas, it was fun—fun with a narrowed eye and an edge, with rasping lungs and a slamming heart and legs now tiring, going rubbery—but fun like I was unaccustomed to: fun incarnate. Everything, even colors, seemed more vibrant. We were in sepia-gold light; Raphi's face was pink, and her ordinarily pale brown hair, poking out from under the headgear in back, flashed darts of bronze. The whole ring was ensconced in orange. Even the time clock had a color, the blast of the bell shot candy-apple red through my sternum. During the break Richie materialized, low-key, graceful, to squirt water into our hot little mouths. Raphi panted, "Do one more?" and I nodded, got the mouthpiece back in, waited for the bell.

In the second round I dared to be more aggressive. Most of the time, my jab glanced off Raphi's headgear or missed completely, but a few jabs landed with a kind of satisfaction that traveled right up my arm and into my trunk. I got some right crosses in, and those felt even better. I had no sense of hurting her. She never backed off or retreated, not with her feet and not with her eyes. She ratcheted up her own aggression to match mine, landing combinations, which did not rattle me, and a body shot, which did. I had this unbidden flash of the four humors: What were they? Blood, phlegm, black bile, and something. I had dropped my hands. I was demoralized in my gut. "Are you all right?" Raphi asked, the words garbled by the plastic.

I loathed the idea of speech in the ring. Speech was too human, too full of personhood, and therefore a muddying intrusion. This couldn't be muddied. I nodded impatiently, almost as if to shake off her words, and put up my hands, and she put hers back up, and I moved forward and jabbed, and missed, and jabbed again. She wove and came back to land a jab and another, immediately, and I threw a hard right to the jaw. She straightened her headgear, danced away deftly. We were both winded, and we circled, taking those seconds to rest. I heard both of us breathing. We watched each other; we were pure concentration, and breath, and the blood was up, the bell hadn't rung, and I came forward and jabbed again.

.   .   .

The poet Mary Oliver has written an essay called "Sister Turtle" in which she describes finding a pheasant in a field, "its breast already opened, only a little of the red, felt-like meat stripped away." She has startled off the killer, a red-tailed hawk, which had been feasting on its prey seconds before. In the instant, the poet reacts to her find as meat. She imagines with pleasure the pheasant becoming *her* dinner; then she collects herself, eyes the waiting hawk, and continues on her way. "But I know how sparkling was the push of my own appetite. I am no fool, no sentimentalist. I know that appetite is one of the gods, with a rough and savage face, but a god all the same."

She refers to the scientist and theologian Pierre Teilhard de Chardin, who "says somewhere that man's most agonizing spiritual dilemma is his necessity for food, with its unavoidable attachments to suffering."

When I came across this line a few years ago, I thought that she was speaking—and that he was speaking—of the suffering that our hunger causes in *others*; of the fact that our drive to appease our hunger inevitably wreaks havoc, chaos, destruction. I was thinking of the suffering of the killed pheasant. When I read this, I was imagining hunger as an ugly, vicious agent, a force to which we are shackled so long as we insist on existing, but also one which can be, and ought to be, controlled. It never occurred to me that Oliver or Teilhard de Chardin might have meant the suffering of the hungry, the suffering of the red-tailed hawk, the suffering that hunger, unsated, causes in *us*. This was around the time that I weighed the least in my adult life, during the year or two before I began to box. I was walking a line between thin and dangerously thin, the gauzy veils of undernourishment keeping the world at bay. I had no sense of feeling hungry, of suffering. I had an almost literal sense of hovering, slightly, outside of my body. This was good. Sometimes I felt effervescent, as though Pop Rocks had been dissolved in my bloodstream. If I was a little bit afraid, I would not have admitted it.

"By the way," Raphi told me in an e-mail, "it's time to start weighing in more regularly and write it on my locker door. But please don't become obsessed with your weight. It's just so that I can easily match you up with someone for sparring, and also in case there are any drastic changes I want to know."

There were no drastic changes. Boxing functioned for me like a pregnancy: It provided a purpose, an absolute necessity to eat. I'd be damned if I let myself slip, let myself get too thin to maintain the muscle and endurance I was building. I had to maintain enough mass to be strong in the ring. The food, the pounds, were the means to an end I had grown stubborn about. What started as jealous curiosity had settled into steely conviction: that I take this thing to whatever its limits turned out to be.

"Also, to avoid injury and chronic fatigue," Raphi went on, "it's very important that you eat well. As soon as you can after practice you should put something in your stomach. I suspect you are like me and couldn't care less about eating, so I find a shake with yogurt, milk, or ice cream (calcium) and a banana (potassium) is easier to digest. If you want to take it one step further, you could use Met-RX, found at CVS, which is a dietary supplement for athletes. Totally legal!"

Raphi and I had acknowledged that we shared some of the same difficulties around self-nourishment, and it helped me to hear her advice. I tried to follow through on eating the food she recommended, but the special supplement seemed too extreme. When I began training, I'd anticipated, based on what I knew of Raphi's experience, that a transformation might take place in my body, a core strengthening that would announce itself in my very stature. Whether this would be cause for celebration or alarm, I wasn't sure. My fears must have overshadowed my hopes, though, because neither my weight nor my appetite for food increased.

We continued sparring, Raphi and I, and I loved it but was left wondering why I didn't feel more satisfied. I was always a little sore the next day; I could calculate where her best shots had landed by where I felt stiff. Raphi, too, reported aches as a result of our sparring, although I suspected her of just being nice. Once she told me I had a "crashing right," and that she had "the bruises to prove it." I didn't wholly believe her. There was a disconnect between what she reported experiencing and my own experience of what went on in the ring. My punches felt like toy punches; the padded leather encasing our hands and framing our faces was somehow overly protective. When I was hitting the mitts,

I knew, I felt, how hard I could hit. When I was working the heavy bag, sometimes I would hit so hard the force traveled all the way up my arm and jarred my head, causing a dull ache there. When I was holding the heavy bag for Nikki or Jacinta, I'd have to brace myself against it as hard as I could, and still their blows managed to knock the bag loose from my grasp. So even though I had progressed from uncomfortably moving around the ring with Sefina and Monique, to sparring, albeit light sparring, with a grown woman, I was haunted by the notion that we were holding back. And the thought was intolerable.

Why should it have been? Why the imperative *not* to hold back now? I could not, in all my history, account for the roots of this thought; when I tried to trace it back, the road was all torn up. How could I, a woman who had been in the thrall of disembodiment, of desirelessness and restraint, now hunger for proof of corporeality, for a violent test of somatic limits?

One day, at home just after sparring, I caught sight of myself in a mirror and thought, My mascara's run. I licked my finger and rubbed at the mark beneath my eye, and it didn't come off, and I thought, idly, Funny, I don't actually remember putting on mascara. I frowned at my reflection, genuinely perplexed, rubbing harder at the smudge along the top of the cheekbone, which was tender to the touch, and then I thought, Oh! and in this manner discovered my first black eye. (Later Raphi would tell me she made the same mistake in the locker room after her first fight, rubbing furiously at the "makeup" that had "smeared." Her coach had laughed and laughed at her before letting her in on the joke.)

The feeling that washed over me upon this discovery was one of victory and thanks. I was grateful for the sign of confirmation: We were not constraining ourselves unduly in the ring. This thing was real.

My children were two, four, and five. Boy, girl, boy. As a single mother, I sometimes wound up bringing them to the gym, although I would not let them watch me spar. They adored Raphi and the girls. If Richie was there, they climbed up his body like a ladder. If Desi was there, he pretended to be a monster and chased them and they shrieked. My daughter loved getting in the ring with Raphi, who'd let her hit the mitts. My youngest would rummage through Raphi's gym bag, find a pair of hand wraps, and march over to me, stomach protruding, eyes dancing: "Strap my hands!" My older son was slightly circumspect, as if he alone sensed the complexities of the place. But at the supper table, he'd hold up his palms like mitts for his younger brother to hit. "I'm Nikki and you're Raphi," the little one would agree, just as another time he might say "I'm Robin Hood and you're Little John."

The first time I came home from the gym with a black eye, I worried about scaring the children. But they were amused! They saw that I was fine, the same mother as always. "Who gave it to you?" my daughter wanted to know. I told her. "Really?" She considered this. A smile tip-toed across her face. My older son let out a hoot. The smallest asked for some orange juice and seltzer. They found my bruise interesting, but only a little, and not for long.

Still, I incubated worries about mixing motherhood with boxing. Even if the sight of me bruised caused them no immediate distress, might there be subtler ways I was letting my children down? They needed me to be in a healthy body. This would be true with children of any age. Mine were young enough to underscore the message with concrete de-mands; mothering young children was nothing if not physical. My most basic obligation was to keep strong and well and present for them.

Boxing, like nothing else, had made me desire these things: to be strong and well and present. Motherhood made me want those things so that I could provide for my children. But boxing made me want those things for myself. Really, for the first time I was aware of, I felt willing to count among the aspects of myself *my body*. But was boxing simply beneficent? Wasn't it a dubious good if it sent me home bruised and sore, invited blows to the head, flirted with bodily injury? Then there was the scarier question of the blows I threw. What of my newly discov-ered appetite to inflict damage?

There was a third question, scarier still. It was there beneath the fact that I didn't mind getting hit, that I relished my own lack of fear. Might I be playing out, in a more graphic variation, the awful old story of relin-quishing my body, of proving how little I cared for it, needed it? The thug in the alley turned around once, revealing the face of an angel: So far boxing had given me both the means and the desire to claim my body, to renounce self-abnegation. But was the angel a mirage, masking an-other face, familiar and hopeless? Was I being seduced by abnegation in a different guise?

I thought I knew a place where I could find answers to these questions. It was a place of some precision, being no less than sixteen nor more than twenty feet square, not more than four feet above the floor, bounded on all sides by at least four ropes, these not less than one inch in diameter, the lower rope being eighteen inches above the ring floor, the second rope thirty inches, the third rope forty-two, and the fourth fifty-four; the floor being padded and the padding covered with canvas, tightly stretched and laced securely in place under the apron. It contained within its form possibilities without limit.

In Book Six of his *Confessions,* Saint Augustine writes of his young friend Alypius, who one day in Rome meets up with a group of fellow law students on their way to the gladiatorial games. They basically force him to come along with them, in spite of his vehement resistance. He says, "Though you hale my body to that place, and there set me, can you force me also to turn my mind or my eyes to those shows? I shall then be absent while present, and so shall overcome both you and them."

Once seated, he indeed refuses to look. But upon hearing a particularly excited cry from the crowd, Alypius cannot help himself, and, "as if prepared to despise and be superior to it whatsoever it were," he opens his eyes. And then, Augustine tells us, a terrible thing happens:

> For so soon as he saw that blood, he therewith gulped down savageness; nor turned away, but fixed his eye, drinking in frenzy, unawares, and was delighted with that guilty fight, and intoxicated with the lust of blood.

It is told here just as the contemporary experts on violence say it is, that witnessing or participating in violent acts or play or games does not provide catharsis, does not safely discharge the aggressive impulse, but instills, normalizes, and perpetuates it. Alypius is suddenly unrecognizable; his bloodlust gathers and swells. Augustine writes that he becomes fixated on the gladiatorial games and even begins to entice other innocents to accompany him.

"Yet thence didst Thou with a most strong and most merciful hand pluck him," writes Augustine, "and taughtest him to have confidence not in himself, but in Thee." By rejecting his own sense of self, Alypius, once sullied, is redeemed. No longer must he suffer the horror of his own bloodlust. Through self-abnegation, by trading in his sense of self, he is relieved of the burden of his desire.

For women even more than for men, appetite—be it for blood, food, or sex—has long been regarded as unbecoming at best, repugnant at worst. In her book *The Hunger Artists: Starving, Writing, and Imprisonment,* Maud Ellmann writes, "Of course, eating was traditionally seen as an unseemly and regrettable necessity for women." She invokes the female saints, "the holy anorectics," withholding food from themselves in order to discipline their sexual desires, purifying their souls by scourging their bodies. With a multiplicity of examples, Ellmann demonstrates how this equation has invaded secular life as well. "Gluttony in women aroused abhorrence because of its suggestions not only of the indecorous but of the cannibalistic." Fasting is linked with penance and cleansing; self-starvation becomes a form of remorse and atonement for imagined acts of destruction.

There is something exalted, virtuous, about the state of emptiness, about hunger steadfastly and permanently denied. The Polish poet Anna Swir wrote about longing as a means of purification, even as a kind of virginity. In "Iron Currycomb" she agonizes over the inescapable culpability that seems to come with possessing a body at all, and envisions the body dismantled, sinfully naked, on trial. The only solution is to scrub it all clean, scrub the flesh from the bone. She writes, "I want to be clean / as nothingness."

These are terrifying words. They are so terrifying we might want to call the poet's position aberrant, pathological. Elsewhere, Swir creates an image of attaining purity through abstinence, through denial of one's animal self. Czeslaw Milosz has said of Anna Swir, who was tortured as a member of the Polish Resistance during the Nazi occupation, that she wrote "about not being identical with one's body, about . . . rebelling against its laws." The idea of rebelling against such laws—laws of nature—could seem arrogant as well as absurd. How dare a human being presume to separate herself from her body? Perhaps only out of desperation, out of necessity. The preposterous notion of distilling self from flesh begins to make sense when the flesh is seen as doomed. And it is nothing new to say that far too many women and girls find their bodies dangerous to inhabit.

When I first came across the story of Alypius, at the part where he de-clares he'll overcome his captors (as well as, apparently, that part of him-self he can't bear to discover) by being absent while present, I thought, Of course. When I read that he succumbs after all of two seconds, I thought scornfully, What's *his* problem?

So adept was I at the trick of being absent while present that when I had my first child, it came as a revelation to find myself living suddenly, intensely, in my body. Not so much during pregnancy, but after his birth, having this little being upon my skin nearly around the clock, I felt my own animal aspects clearly and particularly, almost as if under a magni-fying glass. The steadiness of breath, the shape of a mouth when yawn-ing, the quality of a fist clenched and released, all these things I could feel in my own cells when I witnessed them in him. The feeling was one of submersion, descent, but with no negative connotation and no fear of repercussion.

In my children's bodies I took a pleasure that was unprecedented and greater than any physical pleasure I had known. Moving my nose and lips and throat and fingers against their baby hair and cheeks and brows and backs, I felt unambiguous joy and a kind of peaceful greed, an ap-petite that did not scare me. At last I understood the romance-novel clichés about wanting to drink in, to eat up, to inhale the essence of the loved one—and there was no dark underside to the notion, nothing not to trust, nothing ominous or duplicitous or malevolent.

Why was my physical desire allowed only now—why had I at last al-lowed it to myself? It felt admissible, finally, in the context of mother-hood, where it could be cloaked in goodness, disguised as selflessness. So that I could experience it, act on and take pleasure in it, and all the while remain blameless, safe.

A short time after I began sparring, I noticed that when I became angry at one of my children, I would fantasize violence. One of them might pout and whine, or lash out pettily at a sibling, and an involuntary image of delivering a blow, of my hitting the child, would flash through the unknowable, doubled-up recesses of my brain. Even though I was certain I would never act on these fantasies, I was too ashamed to men-tion it to anyone for nearly a year. When I did confess, to Raphi, she replied immediately that she had experienced the same thing after she started training: Boxing led her to fantasies of violence, too.

.   .   .

I went a few rounds with Sefina.

This was months after our first attempts at sparring. While Raphi was buckling my headgear, I asked if she had any special instructions for me, and we both knew I was talking about Sefina's ruptures and excesses in the ring. She said Sefina was usually okay when it wasn't one of her sisters she was sparring, and she was. The level of concentration was more serious and more sustained this time. At thirteen, Sefina had become a bona fide teenager and grown nearly two inches since I'd met her last fall. We did not pull our punches now, and neither did we brawl. We both still had a lot to learn, but we moved around, trying combinations, trying to control the ring space, slipping punches and coming back to counterpunch. And we connected. She blinked like a cat when I got her in the mouth. She crashed a glove into the bridge of my nose, and for a split second I had the queer thought, It's going to rain.

In the second round, we were both more noticeably tired, and Sefina fell back on her reserve energy, which in her case was the fuel of emotion. "Stop, Sefina! Think!" yelled Raphi when she began to flail her arms, and Sefina did. She controlled herself, thought, and got me hard in the jaw, knocking my mouthguard to the canvas. Raphi, to Sefina: "Beautiful. You see?" To me: "You okay?" I was fine. Raphi stepped into the ring to retrieve my mouthguard, squirted some water on it, and slipped it back in my mouth. "Box."

Now the balance tilted. I was landing the bulk of the blows. "Hands up, Sefina! Don't look at me, look at your opponent!" But she was tired now, or had lost heart. The thirty-second bell sounded. Maria began to clap, and Jacinta and Candi, too. Sefina dropped her hands. "What are you doing? Thirty seconds!" yelled Raphi.

"Oh!" cried Maria, laughing at herself. "I thought that was it."

"Come on, box!" yelled Raphi.

Sefina laughed through her mouthguard and looked back over her shoulder. I waited for her to come back to what we were doing, but she never really did.

"Ten seconds!" yelled Raphi.

We exchanged a couple more blows, but Sefina had revoked her concentration. Three minutes in the ring was a very long time. The bell sounded, we spit out our mouthguards, and grinned and hugged. Now the others were clamoring to spar. Richie gave us water, and Raphi asked me if I was up for a round with Candi. The little one was forever champing at the bit. She'd turned eleven and still had never had a fight, for lack of suitable opponents. Sparring with her sisters was always fraught, and Nikki was so strong and volatile. At eighty-five pounds, Candi was too little to put in the ring with almost anyone at the gym. So she never got enough action. We had not sparred together before, and I felt flattered and challenged by the suggestion. It meant Raphi trusted me to handle the young boxer's onslaught with defensive skills, and without retaliating aggressively.

Only our small group, minus Nikki, was here this morning, a crystalline, warm Saturday. It was too early for the men and boys, who usually arrived for practice just as we were finishing up. The only man here now was Richie. The Rodriguez women had shown up flaunting new piercings, all four of them. They had visited the House of Pain in Everett, on the North Shore, last week and picked up an eyebrow ring (Jacinta) and three nostril studs (Maria, Sefina, and Candi). Sefina had removed her stud in order to spar, but Candi couldn't get hers out. Raphi went all squeamish at the thought of assisting, and no one else wanted to do it, either. You weren't supposed to box with any jewelry on at all, for obvious safety reasons, and a nose stud seemed like a particularly bad idea in the ring. Finally, Raphi said she'd just tape it. She got some athletic tape and went over Candi's nose with it, pretty liberally, and then Candi complained she couldn't see, that the tape was obstructing her vision, so Raphi modified the tape job. Then she pulled me aside and said quietly, "Don't hit her in the face."

Looking at her across the ring from me as we waited for the bell, I felt unsure. I thought of a picture I had of Raphi and the girls, in which they'd all assumed tough poses, but tough in a low-key way: bent at the waist with hands up, chins tucked, eyes looking dead at the lens from under dark brows. The exception was Candi. She was straddling Raphi's back, arms raised, fists cocked, à la Popeye. She was in a tank top, and the muscle definition along her arms and across her pecs was fearsome. But her face was the most impressive: teeth bared and clenched; eyes like black darts; and long, arcing eyebrows cutting down toward the nose exactly the way a child would draw them to illustrate someone who was "mad."

Sparring Candi was a mess. I had the idea that because she was nearly a foot and a half shorter than I was, I ought to crouch down low. This made some sense: Since I was prohibited from aiming at her face, my target was her body, and my only hope of reaching that low was to come down myself. A better strategy would have been to work on defense. Basically: to move the hell out of range. To pivot, to dance back, and hold her off with my jab. My long reach was my best tool, for both defense and offense, but I failed to use it. I was afraid to use the jab in case I got her on the nose, but I at least could have held her off with my much longer arms. In any case, I should have moved, but I did not. It was as though footwork was not in my repertoire. As though I knew how to escape exclusively with my mind and not my body. We boxed the whole round in close, face-to-face, center of the ring. And she hurt me.

To my surprise, she landed no body shots. Because of our respective sizes, I expected her to concentrate on my body. But it was all head she was after. Mostly I responded by trying to cover up. She got a right cross by me, and it was dazzling. Raphi had talked to me about seeing stars when you got hit hard in the head, but it wasn't so much stars as sparkles. It was kind of beautiful, actually, all black, with these utterly silent, rather lovely sparkles appearing and vanishing. As they receded and the gym came back, I was a little sorrowful; I looked after them, but they were gone. Raphi said, "Are you okay?" because I'd raised a glove in the "wait a second" gesture. I answered, "Yeah," quite automatically. I felt okay. It didn't occur to me to answer anything else. We kept boxing, and I kept standing there, almost in servitude, being an easy target, trying to give that hungry Candi a rare fix.

Near the end of the round, she landed another good right, and this one was different from any I had experienced: I could feel the exact shape of the outline of my headgear press into the left side of my face at the edge of my eye. We boxed on for however many more seconds; the bell rang; I rubbed a glove fondly over Candi's dark hair; Jacinta helped Candi with her headgear, and Raphi unbuckled mine. As soon as it came off, a chorus of "Ooooooh, Leah!" went up. I could almost feel what they must have been staring at. I didn't even bother looking in the mirror. I could tell this would make the other little shiners I'd picked up look like nothing; it was hot and throbbing. Raphi sent Richie down to the Lil Peach grocery on the corner to buy ice. I got a dollar out of my bag and went and stuck it in the vending machine out in the office. A can of lemon-lime Gatorade. I hated the stuff, but the cold, cold aluminum felt excellent against the bruise.

I was sitting on a pew by the back door, can on eye. Candi stood near me, looking stricken. "Are you okay?" I asked.

"I feel weird."

"I'm okay."

She stared at me.

I shrugged. "I have a black eye. But I'm okay."

She kept staring. "I don't know . . ."

"Is it because kids aren't supposed to be able to hurt grown-ups?"

She nodded.

"You were working. You were doing exactly what you were supposed to be doing. Okay?"

She nodded, not entirely convinced.

Raphi came over, took the Gatorade out of my hand, and rubbed the can, hard, across the spot, as if she were ironing.

"Ow!"

"I'm trying to spread the blood out so it doesn't pool and swell too much."

"Gimme that!" I took the can back.

Maria was pleased. I didn't take it personally. I knew she was fond of me, but it made her feel so good when one of her kids showed toughness.

Later the radio got tuned to salsa, and Raphi and Richie slipped into a dance. Raphi had Candi read aloud an entry from *The Tao of Sports*. Jacinta went a round on the mitts with Raphi, impressively, and Maria sighed and said it was a shame her oldest daughter wasn't using her gift. Jacinta was showing less interest in boxing, and didn't want to train for the Nationals that summer. Later still, out in the parking lot, Richie poured a bottle of water over my head: Bliss, and I was sorry when the water ran out. The sun felt bright as a hammer. Sefina found a firecracker in the weeds. "Raphi, you got a light?" she asked innocently. Raphi pretended to kick her in the gut. We all hugged goodbye. I went to my car. "Ice!" Raphi reminded me. Maria called merrily, "Go home and put a steak on your eye!"

I had a bad headache for two days and couldn't sleep on that side of my face, which swelled and turned gaudy colors. I didn't tell anybody about the headache, but I took a perverse pleasure in not minding it. And then came a sour realization: that this pleasure was not new, and not safe.

I knew that if this was all boxing could deliver me, then it was no good. I knew this as surely as I was unwilling to quit.

PART 3

7

GOOD TIMES

One Saturday in April, Maria arrived at the boxing club with a bundle of white envelopes, invitations to Jacinta's sweet sixteen, which would be held at the gym in a couple of weeks. Not the gym proper but downstairs, in the basement function hall. We'd been hearing details for months. Jacinta hadn't had a *quinceañera*—the elaborate fifteenth birthday celebrated by many Latina girls—so her sweet sixteen was being planned with all the care and consequence of a mini, groomless wedding. The eight attendants would wear long matching dresses of sheer orange, with silver belts. A couple of the boy boxers, Tonio and Pierre, had agreed to DJ; they knew a guy who had all the equipment. Maria would cook trays and trays of the family's traditional Christmas feast: pulled pork and spicy rice and beans.

The invitations were printed on small white cards, illustrated with a decidedly chaste-looking Anglo young woman—herself decked out like a wedding cake in a four-tiered skirt edged with gold—and printed with a prayer vowing, in part, "I offer You my adolescence." We all oohed and ahhed at Jacinta, and then Raphi said, "Okay, who wants to spar?" The invitations were cast aside.

Raphi and I were the only two already warmed up, so we went a few rounds first. She told Nikki and Jacinta to work my corner, and they took the responsibility to heart, coaching me vociferously from ringside:

"Keep your hands up! Jab! One, two. Follow with your right. Don't let her rest. Block with one hand, keep your other hand up! Hit her hard, Leah. Weave. Body shots. Uppercut. Move!"

Candi and Sefina worked Raphi's corner and managed to squirt lots of water all over her face during the round break.

We actually went pretty hard, controlled but hard, and by the time we finished, the others were all hot to get in the ring. Sefina and Jacinta got in next. From the moment they touched gloves, their behavior suggested they were continuing some spat more than practicing their skills. Sefina was worked up, obviously loaded with baggage; Jacinta was mischievously attuned to her sister's emotional buttons. Raphi was shouting from the first seconds, "Control yourself, Sefina! Control yourself!" and then "Jacinta, no wrestling! No holding! Jacinta, if you do it one more time, it's a point off!" Raphi shrugged at her own threat (who cared about points when no one was keeping score?), but it seemed to work for a little while. Jacinta said, "Okay," and they finished the round decently. The next round ended early, though, with Sefina blubbering and Raphi stepping through the ropes to unbuckle her headgear. "I wasn't hitting hard!" swore Jacinta. "I wasn't!"

Raphi checked Sefina out, then told her to go sit down. Sefina ripped off a glove, threw it at Jacinta, and stomped off to cry on a pew.

Maria snorted. "Crying is for girls."

Candi got in the ring. "Jacinta, be careful with the baby," cautioned Maria. They went nearly a round before Candi got caught with a double jab and a right and began to cry. The moment Jacinta realized it had happened again, she grabbed her little sister and tried to dip her, as if they were ballroom dancing, and to kiss her, through headgear and mouthguards and all, but Candi dislodged herself angrily and went to her neutral corner to sob quietly against the ropes. Raphi went to her and stroked her ponytail. "You're hitting too hard," Maria informed Jacinta. She was supposed to hold back when sparring someone smaller.

"I wasn't!" protested Jacinta, all innocent, all *who, me?* She had gotten a fight the month before, at the Knights of Columbus. She'd won the first round, gotten pushed through the ropes in the second round, and during the round break had told Raphi, "I don't want to fight no more." But Raphi had told her to breathe and wait out the round break, and by the time the bell rang, she seemed okay, so she'd gone back out. She had a stitch in her side, though, and took a body shot there and got knocked down crying. The referee started his count, but Richie preempted him, throwing in the towel, hard and high.

Now Raphi surprised everyone by asking Maria if she wanted to go a round with Jacinta.

Maria had been itching to get in the ring ever since she first set foot in the gym, and over the past few weeks, she had been dropping specific hints about it. Twenty years ago, as a student at Brighton High, she used to sneak into the gym after school, when the boys were working out. They'd make room for her, teach her how to lift weights and hit the heavy bags. She clearly relished the idea of having always been tough, a fighter. If only they'd had girls' boxing when she was a kid! Although even as she would say this, her eyes shining, half in earnest, half in jest, it was easier to picture her as a professional wrestler than as a boxer. The staginess of the former would seem to agree with Maria, whose frolicking humor was palpable, but also pointedly on display, so that one eventually wondered what lay beneath. She was quick to laugh and quick to look daggers, and she did both so frequently that they seemed almost interchangeable.

Only rarely did she show a softer, more vulnerable side. When she spoke of Puerto Rico, where she'd spent her eleventh and twelfth years with her family, farming pigeon peas, pumpkins, peppers, *platanos,* and tea. When she spoke of doing laundry in a creek there, next to her mother, beating the clothes on a rock, loving the sounds that the washing made: cloth and water and stone. When she licked her thumb and leaned over to wipe the sleep from her oldest daughter's face. Or when she stepped on the gym scale and muttered and fretted, because last week it had said 186, and she *knew* she hadn't gained eight pounds since then; she hadn't even been eating anything, just drinking tea, mostly, and "Raphi, do you know is this scale *working?*"

But most of the time what she showed off was the sharp glint of her toughness, whether she was reaching out to cuff a kid, or cracking herself up with one of her own bawdy utterances (or making as if to grab the ass of a passing male), or shocking people with one of her cutting remarks about her husband. Her views on the sanctity of motherhood were formidable. She thought nothing of demonstrating the "respect" she had imbued in her daughters by slapping one of them in the face and then pointing out, with satisfaction, their nonretaliation. The younger two scowled whenever she did this, storms gathering behind their eyes and lips, but they kept the torrents in check, and Maria would chuckle. Jacinta was the scarier for how placidly she accepted it. "You got to respect your mother," Maria would say. "You never talk back to your mother." Sometimes she lectured Nikki on the matter, Nikki's relationship with her mother departing woefully from Maria's standard. Sometimes she delivered impromptu homilies on the subject. "Your father is another story. You never know with the man if he's really your father"— shrug, grin, hey-I'm-just-telling-it-like-it-is—"but your mother is it, she's what you've got."

At practice Maria was often busier than the girls, pumping hand weights, doing leg lifts and squats, making the occasional, quickly abandoned foray into jumping rope and abdominal crunches. "Feel this," she'd say, "feel it," thrusting out her arm, "all muscle." In almost any subject she could find a segue to weight gain and weight loss, muscle cramps and muscle atrophy, the tale of swelling up on the Prednisone she was taking for her rheumatoid arthritis, and how she nearly died, and how they thought she had cancer and AIDS and Lyme disease—and back of all this, there was always the myth of a perfect body, a perfect girl, who was once as strong and clean and tough as they come, if only we'd known her before.

"You want to get in?" Raphi asked her again.

"Sure. What? Really? Okay." Maria rose, round-eyed. She was thirty-six, not much more than five feet, not much less than two hundred pounds.

"Okay? Jacinta. You go a round with your mother?"

Jacinta made a face, her eyes going wide. "Oooo-kay . . ."

A ripple ran through the group.

"Ahhhh, *Mami*'s going to box!"

"Kick her ass, *Mami*!"

Nikki was laughing.

Raphi, businesslike, fitted the headgear, fastened the sparring gloves. Why not, what the hell? There was a way in which Maria was always lording her own much-vaunted strength over the girls. Well, Raphi knew, sparring looked easy until you tried it. Why not grant her a taste of what she'd been itching for, and let her see at the same time how hard it was when you were the one within the ropes? It might have been, in part, mischievous of Raphi to extend such an invitation to Maria. But for months Maria had been so wistful about getting into the ring herself, and if at the same time it put to rest some of the goading braggadocio she was always laying on her daughters, so much the better. Besides, it had already done wonders for the general mood of the girls. Everyone was loving it. Sefina and Candi scrambled back onto the ring apron.

If the male trainers and boxers had been there right then, wouldn't they have been scandalized? At the spectacle, the freak show: a girl and her mother in the ring together. Not that boys didn't get in the ring with their fathers, but then it was different, then it was about two athletes working out together. And anyway, if father-son violence wasn't condoned by society, at least a precedent existed for it—almost an expectation that a son's healthy development must include a challenge to his father's strength—that went at least as far back as Oedipus and Laius. No parallel existed for mothers and daughters. And there was no pretending that this was about two athletes trying their skill. Maria might have been a fighter, but she was no boxer. This was unavoidably about a girl and her mother slugging it out, albeit in a controlled setting whose limits made the confrontation possible.

Raphi put a mouthguard in Maria's mouth. At the bell, Maria and Jacinta touched gloves. They were laughing, a little. They were also each in a terrifying position. Maria had to back up all her matriarchal swagger in an arena that demanded her daughter hit back. Jacinta, far more fit but not much more than half her mother's weight, had to box her mother while managing to remain subordinate. The alternative, should either of them have fumbled, would be to see a balance upset, a fundamental boundary redrawn. But they—and we—were at the same time giddy with the fun—and the funniness—of the event.

It was a game and not a game, *a game and not a game* . . . the words stuck in my head. This was somewhere near the heart of the matter, the idea that something could be at once play and real. *Play* could be a way of sampling the forbidden without committing oneself or being held accountable. It could be a way of investigating possibilities without claiming identification with them. To mingle it with *real* was to jeopardize the safety of that play, to cut off an avenue of escape from what was being played out. But acknowledging that an expression of play might be simultaneously expressing something real also emboldened the act of playing, opened up an avenue of growth.

I thought about the USA Boxing official who had asked me not to use the word *fight* in the book. Of *course* boxing was fighting. I thought about Joyce Carol Oates's famous dictum that boxing was not a metaphor for anything. Of *course* boxing was a metaphor—at the same time that it was wholly and inimitably itself. But it was true that what a boxer was really fighting usually entered the ring only in essence, not in substance. And it was true that boxing did not generally wear its metaphors on its sleeve, so to speak. Yet here were Maria and Jacinta, embodying an act of play, and enacting a very real mother-daughter relationship, with all its subtle power differentials intact.

Nikki was cross-legged on the apron, alert and flushed. She slapped her knees in a staccato burst. "I wish I could box with *my* mother!" It came out so heartfelt that a moment later she gasped and emitted a great seal-bark of laughter.

"Go, *Mami!*" squealed Sefina. "Knock her out!"

Candi was hooting with laughter.

They went two rounds, which itself constituted a kind of victory for Maria. Jacinta, of course, was careful and agile and tireless. We all knew that Maria expected total obedience and respect from her daughters. Because of the way Jacinta absorbed her mother's literal and verbal blows outside the ring, it surprised me to see her land a few untimid punches of her own. And though Candi and Sefina purportedly wanted to see their mother trounce Jacinta, they seemed excited by Jacinta's license to inflict some damage. But Jacinta didn't unchain herself completely. She seemed to hold herself in check with an amalgam of graciousness and uncertainty about her role.

Just after the final bell, Maria got Jacinta into a perfectly illegal head-lock and pounded a final, satisfied blow onto her crown and that, too, went over big with the younger sisters. When the headgear came off, both mother and daughter had that red-misted, hair-mussed, vaguely battered, and deeply sated look. Maria, huffing and puffing, collapsed onto the pew. We all knew she understood something now that she hadn't before. Raphi told her she'd done well, and Maria smiled, still panting, and then laughed. "Oh, my nose really hurts!" Her voice held a mixture of pride and surprise. Someone cranked the music, and the girls started moving their hips around, big.

"Who won?" Maria asked Raphi seriously, a week later.

Raphi pointed silently to Jacinta, standing a foot away. The younger girls were in the locker room. Nikki was lying on a mat at our feet, cranking out abdominals.

"*She* did? She *did*? How come?"

Raphi laughed. "Because afterward you were sitting on the bench saying, 'My nose! My nose!'"

"It was itching. It just itched! I had a cold that week from it." Maria contemplated things. "Anyway," she concluded, "I thought I won, because she was afraid to hit me."

The logic of this was in a way airtight.

Raphi cast a look heavenward. But Jacinta, by her silence and the peculiar quality of her smile, seemed to concur.

Nikki, lolling around now on the floor, groaned. "I wish I could box *my* mother," she reminded everyone.

"Bring her next week," suggested Raphi.

"Okay," answered Nikki. As if Maureen would ever come.

The sweet-sixteen dresses were made out of the thinnest material in the world. All night they would keep ripping, and Maria, in the kitchen, would keep stitching them up with the needle and thread she'd brought from home, telling the girls to stand still so she wouldn't prick them. It turned out to make them late, the whole Rodriguez family, well over an hour to Jacinta's own party, because the birthday girl's dress had ripped just as they were getting in the car to drive over.

Not that many people had been on time. A handful of Jacinta's school friends and I had spent the better part of an hour hanging out in the little foyer between the Masons' part of the church and the boxing club, alternately joking and grumbling. Then Desi had shown up, not in his police uniform but in a dress shirt and slacks, his dozens of cornrows grazing his broad shoulders. He'd taken a seat genially on the stairs beside me, unfazed by the absence of his hosts. He checked his watch from time to time, though: Between his police work, leading Bible study and teaching Sunday school, and training young boxers, he barely had time left over for his wife and children, and wouldn't stay long tonight.

Gene McCarthy had shown up, too, not exactly as a guest but in a sort of custodial capacity, representing the club, as it were. He said he wanted to make sure the kids weren't getting served alcohol, and that "the place isn't left a mess." He strolled around, a big white man, leading with his chest and his broad, toothy smile, helping himself to a beer from the well-stocked cooler in the basement kitchen. I suspected he was also curious to see his boxers Tonio and Pierre in DJ mode. Pierre looked shinily handsome and young with excitement, but Tonio had his hair slicked back and was looking very junior-man, not just because of his sport shirt, with the top three buttons unbuttoned, nor even his wisps of facial hair, but because of something in his bearing, his eyes, and the sense of purpose about him this night.

Last week, when Tonio had gone downstairs with Maria and Candi and Sefina in order to assess the space, it had been a different story: the kids all in gym clothes, Tonio in his ubiquitous orange do-rag, the girls in hoodies and shorts, fellow boxers all. "Hi, killer" was how Tonio greeted Candi, who'd grinned. Maria had cackled loudly. "They have crushes on you," she informed him. He'd had the good grace not to react, while Candi and Sefina died a few deaths over in the corner. When Nikki and Jacinta had shambled downstairs a few minutes later, they'd had eyes not for Tonio but for the foosball table in the rear.

In an instant the two of them had been at work, noisily flipping the handles and knocking the ball around. Nikki wore a tight white T-shirt she'd altered by scissoring out diamond shapes along the rib cage and writing G2G in red marker across the chest. "It stands for 'Girl to Girl,' " she'd confided earlier, showing it off. It was also the name of the CD she and Jacinta planned to make, recordings of all their own songs. Maria had sucked her teeth pointedly at the display, but whether this was a financially strapped homemaker's disgust at the defacing of a perfectly good shirt or something else, I could not tell.

On the night of the celebration, the function room had been transformed. Maria and the girls had come in earlier in the day to set up the tables, fifteen of them, laid with orange and silver paper tablecloths, and a big white wicker chair decorated with ribbons and bows, and the centerpieces, amazing glue-gunned concoctions that Maria had been working on for months: female adolescent figurines stuck to small round mirrors; little glass cups of orange jelly beans; everything adorned with miniature plastic fans and cloth rosebuds and netting and lace and doilies. Tonio and Pierre and a few of their boys already had the music grooving, loud. They had the disco ball revolving, too, and the colored lights beamed modishly around the walls. Everything was ready to go except the party.

When at last the Rodriguezes arrived, they brought Nikki and brittle nerves and all the food in foil-wrapped trays. Hector alone seemed easy, jovial. He had gotten hair implants in honor of the occasion and kept telling people about them, parting the dark thatchy forelocks and pulling at them to demonstrate how the roots really went right in. The Rodriguez women were more on edge, smiling, anticipatory, anxious. Where were all the guests? Jacinta's smile was tremulous. She wore the requisite white ankle-length dress, with curling white chiffon trailing down her back. The other girls glowed in their crayon-bright orange. They wore cloth-flower crowns.

Around nine Raphi and Richie arrived, in casual attire, and then a godmother with kids, and some uncles and aunts and cousins, variously decked out or dressed down, one of them a woman in her twenties wearing low-slung jeans with BOOTYLICIOUS inscribed in sequins over the eponymous part of her anatomy. A blender materialized, and Richie started mixing Mudslides, strong and sweet, in the kitchen, where, as it turned out, nearly everyone was chilling. Maria, in a sheer and silvery dress with a matching jacket, gave up on the needle and thread and took up the glue gun. Some of the boys slipped out to smoke pot in the parking lot, under the full moon. Raphi asked Desi if he'd perform her wedding ceremony. "Oh, *my!*" he said. He wasn't ordained, he told her, but if she and Richie got married before a justice of the peace first, he could officiate at a public ceremony. "*Goodness!*"

Nikki danced with Pierre and gave him her phone number. Later she hid out in the bathroom, Candi standing guard outside the door. Pierre, confused and expectant, wouldn't go away. "She don't want to be your girlfriend," Candi declared, gorgeously fierce with her preadolescent posture, the neat curve of her stomach thrust tight against the flimsy orange gown. "You can go now, leave her alone." Pierre, his skin shiny with hope and sweat and defeat, disappeared. In the bathroom, Nikki paced the tiny floor space like a wild horse in a stall. "I don't want to be left alone," she told Raphi and me. "Are you okay? Did he do anything?" asked Raphi. A sharp breath came through Nikki's nose. She didn't answer the question except to say, "That's it. I'm becoming a lesbian." It was as though she knew we were safe people on whom to try out this declaration. She scrutinized our faces for evidence of our reaction. We nodded, more or less blasé.

Later, in the kitchen, more pulled pork, more Mudslides. Candi popped in, panting from dancing. "This dress is *itchy*," she announced, wriggling. "I'm itchy on the *inside*. And look at this." She displayed her hands with charming indignation. "They keep falling off!" Seven long silver press-on nails remained.

Sefina, across the room, was refilling her paper plate. "Is that one a boxer, too?" Gene McCarthy asked Raphi. He'd seen Sefina many times upstairs in the gym, but didn't recognize her in this context. Raphi called her over. "Tell Gene about your fight," she said, and Sefina, glowing, did not need to be coaxed. "Forty-five seconds in the first round," she rattled off, lowering her lashes and simultaneously spearing salad with a plastic fork. Her mother had brushed orange and silver across her lids.

"And this one," said Raphi, hooking an arm around Candi's neck. "How many leg lifts can you do?"

"A hundred and thirty," the kid informed Gene. "Look at my thighs." She hiked her dress.

Near eleven Tonio took the mike and welcomed everyone in Spanish, then read off one of the orange cocktail napkins the names of the eight "maids," who filed in from the doorway to flank the large rented wicker chair. The theme song from *Chariots of Fire* was playing while Jacinta got walked in by both parents. Then, to the romantic timbre of Julio Iglesias's voice on the next song, the birthday girl slow-danced stiffly with her godfather, who was an uncle, and then with her father, who cut in, in all his hirsute glory, and finally her mother, with whom she was not stiff at all, though they continued to dance with the same formal, swaying shuffle. But their version of it was infused with feeling and was overtly intimate, with much kissing and touching of shoulders and backs, and some tears, and more kisses on foreheads and cheeks. When the music ended, they went hand in hand to the microphone.

The daughter spoke first, thanking everyone for coming in a surprisingly formal register. "For those of you who may not know me, my name is Jacinta Rodriguez." Her amplified voice, unusually high and reedy, reached out to and well beyond the thirty or so relatives and friends gathered in the capacious basement room. The mother went next. "It seems like yesterday she was taking her first steps. It's all gone so fast, and now she is so grown-up and beautiful, and I just love her to death." Maria spoke these words as if she were the first person ever to express the sentiment, gazing adoringly at her daughter, who was equally overcome. Maria radiated joy as she spoke, and an understanding of coming loss. Then she and Jacinta, crying, took each other's hands and drifted from the mike, going back to the table to pick up some orange cocktail napkins and dab at their eyes.

Sefina had already announced her intentions to have a *quinceañera* rather than a sweet sixteen: That was one year fewer to wait. Would she be a young lady then? In a long white dress? Would her mother dance with her like that, gaze at her like that, cry? Would she be as placidly opaque as Jacinta, ungangly, unstormy, *tranquila*?

Throughout the dances and speeches, Candi had been absorbed in, completely consumed by, jabbing at the orange and silver helium balloons tied to the wicker chair. They kept bobbing back up like those old clown punching-bag toys. Who knew what monologue was going on inside the head of that youngest and most purely athletically driven of the four girls, as she tried a left, and a right, and her opponent struggled to his feet again and again, not to be put down by Candida Rodriguez, a mere girl of eleven, but oh! A double jab to the silver balloon on the left and a fast right to the orange, and she was tireless, *la tigrita,* look at those combinations! Nine vertical feet and some flooring were all that separated her from where at this moment she was in her heart.

Candi had been told she finally had a match. The venue was Good Times, which was what everyone called the Good Time Emporium in Somerville, a sprawling, overwrought hullabaloo of a place across from the multiplex in the Assembly Square Mall, behind the heavy, tangled arms of the McGrath/O'Brien Highway and Interstate 93 and their various ramps and connectors. Good Times boasted eighty-three thousand square feet of a quintessentially American brand of fun, with everything from laser tag to batting cages, indoor hoops to kiddie rides, and twenty-seven wall-size television screens, open 365 days a year.

The straggling members of the Somerville Boxing Club board had for months been trying to put together some kind of fund-raiser for the

club. Ideas had included hosting a comedy night or a black-tie dinner;
selling autographs by or an intimate dinner with John Ruiz; holding a
gambling cruise, a silent auction, a bingo night, a night at the races. No
matter how they looked at it, money was a problem. Monthly rent at
their old place had been a grand. The Masons were charging them
$2,750. Since John Ruiz had won the heavyweight title the previous
spring, there was the feeling that they ought to be able to cough up a little more now. It was true to an extent: They *had* been able to use his win
and modest fame to some advantage. But with electricity, telephone,
equipment, insurance, the installation of a shower, and the upgraded
hot water heater, the debits mounted faster than the credits. Dues were
obviously a big problem: Nobody paid them. At the last meeting, John
Curran had done a little figuring and announced that the club was currently out about seven thousand dollars in unpaid dues; of approximately a hundred members, a grand total of four were paid up.

In the end, of course, there was no black-tie dinner, no comedy night,
but what they all knew best: an evening of boxing matches. Or, as the
program cover read, SOMERVILLE AMATEUR FIGHT NIGHT. Given the
club's overall functioning capabilities, or lack thereof, and what I had
come to learn about the culture of boxing, I was reasonably surprised
when the event came off as planned on a fine warm evening in May.
Crossing the parking lot toward Good Times, I had some pangs about
the imminent proceedings, and it wasn't from the sight of the ambulance parked out front, as required by law, a stolid white receptacle all
fresh and ready for potential customers.

It was because of Candi, and how she'd been promised her first fight
at last, and how I knew, as did everyone but Candi, that there would be
no match for her tonight, because there was no one to match her up
with. It hadn't started as a lie. When Ann Marie Francey, the daughter
of Ann Cooper and one of the key organizers of the Good Times event,
had promised Candi only two weeks earlier that she would have an opponent, it had been in good faith. When this had fallen through, everyone simply neglected to tell Candi. The plan now was to call her into the
ring and surprise her with a gold medal; she had, in fact, won the gold
medal in the Junior Olympics girls' division 85-pound weight class
(since no one else had entered the tournament in this class), but
whether she would regard with much pleasure being awarded this honor

when her USA Boxing passbook was still as pristine as the day it had arrived in the mail seemed pretty iffy.

Good Times was massive, and it rocked with the perpetual din of more than two hundred video games. One section had been curtained off for the event. I paid ten bucks and got handed a program, whose inside front cover said, THANKS TO JACINTA RODRIGUEZ FOR SINGING THE NATIONAL ANTHEM. JACINTA IS A SILVER MEDALIST IN THE JUNIOR OLYMPICS DIVISION OF THE FEMALE NATIONAL GOLDEN GLOVES TOURNAMENT AND IS CURRENTLY RANKED #2 IN HER DIVISION. I felt a surge of pride and excitement. At one point Jacinta and Nikki, who'd been members of their school's gospel choir (until it began to interfere with boxing practice) had both been going to sing, but Nikki had ducked out, shy, and until this moment I had half expected Jacinta would do the same.

But the program also triggered the slightest cringe of embarrassment. The write-up made Jacinta-the-boxer sound so impressive. She had a lot of native ability and power. And I knew she had trained hard for the Nationals last summer, and winning her first fight was indisputably an accomplishment. But the fact that the single win translated into her being ranked number two in the country served only to diminish the glory of those standings. Granted, female boxing was still relatively new. The first ever female Nationals had been held only in 1997. The first National Women's Golden Gloves had taken place in 1999. Every year, as more girls and women around the country trained and competed, the contest got tougher. Raphi said that this coming summer, even though it was only one year after Jacinta's and Nikki's first matches, the training and ability of the athletes would be so much better that she wouldn't dare bring a couple of novices.

Once inside Good Times's curtained-off area, with its central ring rented and erected specifically for tonight, I had no trouble finding our gang: Raphi and Richie, wearing staff tags around their necks; Maria, made up for a night on the town; Hector, in a stiff-billed FDNY PDNY baseball cap; and Jacinta and Nikki, the former sucking on a lime she'd plucked from one of the plastic cups of beer on the table, the latter with her arms folded on the table and her forehead down on her arms. I gave her shoulder a shove. "Oh. Hi," she said, lackluster.

Hi's all around. I was still trying to assess the odd climate—"What's up? Where're the other two?"—when Hector's cell phone rang. It was

Maureen, Nikki's mother. She was saying the kid had sneaked out, or left without permission, or lied about having finished a school project, or some combination of these. In any case, Maureen insisted Nikki had to come home, pronto. Apparently this was not the first phone call. Nikki, in a blank fury, tossed the phone on the table and started to slam out. Maria and Hector both yelled at her to sit back down. Maria punched a number into the touch pad, started working her mojo. The parts where Maureen was yelling were evident because Maria held the phone away from her ear and made faces. "Yeah, but . . . The thing is," she said smoothly, "we already paid for her to come in." In fact, they had all slipped in without paying. "Yeah, but . . . Yeah. Bye." Maria hung up. "She says you have to walk home."

Nikki, with a furious scraping of chair legs, left. She appeared near tears. Hector and Jacinta flew after her. Maria, applying hot-pink lip gloss the exact color of her tank top, offered her opinion of any mother who would tell her daughter to walk home alone a couple of miles from Assembly Square to Charlestown at night. "She's going on about if Nikki doesn't get her project in, she has to go to summer school. But they're both already getting F's! They're both going to summer school anyway!" Maria laughed. Sefina and Candi arrived, breathless, from some other wing of Good Times, where they had been busy turning quarters into lavender prize tickets. Candi was wearing cornrows, which I recognized as the established fighting hairdo of this clan, and a gray-and-pink LADY BOXER T-shirt identical to the one Raphi had on.

Eventually Hector and the older girls returned, having completed an-other round of telephone negotiations: Now Maureen was saying her daughter could stay. But Nikki was still wild with emotion, breathing like a racehorse, glaring around the room without letting her eyes meet those of anyone at our table, and a muscle flashed like mad in her jaw. The cell phone rang again. "Oh shit!" cried Jacinta; she was holding the phone in her palm. She answered, "Hello?" But this time Maureen was only checking that Nikki would get a ride home with the Rodriguezes. Jacinta and Nikki drifted away and hid out for a while, decompressing in the semi-privacy of one of the more ergonomically resplendent video booths, while the grown-ups smoked and sipped their beers and waited for the event to begin.

I was touched by the way Maria and Hector had stood up for Nikki, gathered her in, lovingly, it would seem. And I was beguiled by the sight of Raphi and Candi in their matching T-shirts, trainer and boxer, god-mother and goddaughter, flicking drops of beer at each other from Richie's cup. But after all, Maria had lied to Maureen. And everyone was lying to Candi: She still didn't know, still thought she was fighting, kept pestering Raphi to warm her up on the mitts. Putting it plainly: This was a table full of grown-ups drinking and smoking around young athletes. The picture felt complicated. The unmistakably nourishing and the unmistakably toxic hopelessly interwoven. How unfair! came the thought, as I regarded the two younger sisters who graced the table, both of them so plainly hungry and beautiful and growing, how unfair that the good comes to them only bound up with the dubious and the sour. But how like the rest of life.

Raphi and I wandered back to the weigh-in room. Ann Marie Francey was back there looking glum. She was in her mid-thirties, with long, choppily layered brown hair and a look of chronic disappointment. She always talked out of the side of her mouth and could be darkly funny, or just dark. She was a sometime boxer herself, although tonight she was emceeing the event, which wasn't shaping up too promisingly. Only five bouts were scheduled. All the people who had paid ten bucks to get in were going to be pissed. "Shoot me now," said Ann Marie.

Raphi laughed. "Where's my gun?"

"She's always so willing to help, that one," Ann Marie told me.

In a boxing-club show, as in no other sport, children as young as eight could theoretically box one match, followed by a pair of opponents in their forties. Patty Yoffe, the fight doc, examined all the evening's contes-tants, young and old, in the quasi-private space of the weigh-in room. Statuesque, with a blond ponytail and a cool professionalism offset by a warm southern accent, she checked their throats and hearts and hands and eyes and lungs. "Do you smoke?" "No." "Do you drink?" "No." "Any tattoos?" "No." "Would you like to date my daughter?" It never failed to get a smile; they'd blink and then grin and lower their eyes, cross their arms over their chests as though only just realizing that they were bare. Patty had been the ringside physician the night Bobby Tomasello went into a coma. After that she'd drawn back, worked only amateurs for a year or so.

Certainly there was less pressure in the amateurs. The boxers, said

Patty, tended to be matched up more evenly. Besides, headgear was required, the gloves were heavier, and there were fewer rounds. Also, the
amateurs had a blood rule: If a boxer's bleeding couldn't be stanched,
the match could not continue; nor was a boxer's corner allowed to stop
the bleeding with coagulants, as in the pros. However, according to the
American Medical Association (AMA), whose position is that all boxing
should be banned, "ocular injuries occur frequently in both amateur and
professional boxers," and both amateur and professional boxers demonstrate a "lower baseline performance on many [neuropsychological]
tests." The American Academy of Pediatrics also opposes the sport in a
blanket statement, saying that even amateur boxers are at risk for ac-
quiring cognitive abnormalities, ocular injuries, and focal neurologic
deficits. It dryly recommends that pediatricians "encourage young athletes to participate in sports in which head injury is not the primary ob-
jective."

They have a point.

However, in a report on boxing injuries by its Council on Scientific
Affairs, the AMA does allow the possibility that "moderate boxing expo-
sure does not cause significant . . . impairment." In light of this, Raphi's
retirement after five fights suddenly looked like genius. None of her former students had stuck with it for more than a year or two. I'd been used
to thinking of this as sort of a shame, a flaw in the picture—how much
better (for them, for Raphi, for me, for all of us) if they'd persisted—and
I'd wondered at the ease—not breeziness, but an acceptance with
which Raphi acknowledged this pattern of girls immersing themselves
in the sport and then moving on. Now I thought, This must be what she
really wishes for them: to taste this, be changed by it, and depart, intact,
with the taste still in their mouths. To get in and out without serious injury. Maybe all the riches the sport had to offer came up front, in the
first year or two; maybe if you kept drinking from this fountain too long,
it became toxic.

It was time. Patty Yoffe took a ringside seat. The three judges, in their
official whites, positioned themselves on high chairs around the ring.
Hector gave Nikki the video camera as Ann Marie Francey, acting as
ring announcer, introduced Jacinta, butchering the pronunciation as
people were wont to do. Everyone stood, and Nikki tried to figure out
where the record button was, and Jacinta began, a cappella, selecting

for herself a needlessly difficult pitch. When she got to "o'er the ram-
parts," she stopped cold. Nikki giggled. Jacinta thought. The whole
room thought with her. A few men in the crowd sang the next line under
their breaths. She didn't hear them. She had blown her hair out straight
tonight, and it fell like heavy drapes around her face, yet it still didn't
hide the blush that was injecting pink into her golden-brown face.
"They don't teach the national anthem in school anymore?" a man with
a cane wondered aloud. A few coughs, a few titters, and an *ak-ak-ak-ak-
ak* of machine-gun fire from a video game beyond the partition.

Maria to the rescue: Swiveling her hips to fit between tables, she extended through the ropes a piece of paper with the lyrics, printed off the
Internet that afternoon. General clapping. Jacinta launched in from the
beginning, starting on an even higher note this time. Her voice was neither unpleasant nor entirely up to the task. I was surprised by this—her
wickedly smooth lip-synching all those days at the gym had had me
fooled—and by her bravery and her aloneness. When she was boxing,
even when she was losing, as she had the previous month, she appeared
far less vulnerable than she did now, in song. Midway through she slid
into a lower key, groping blindly for the note as a person might for the
next descending rung while backing down a ladder. By the time she had
reached the relative safety of "for the land of the free / And the home of
the brave," she was confident enough to finish with a tiny flourish of
pop-inflected melisma.

A burst of applause. Jacinta poured herself slinkily back through the
ropes. Ann Cooper interrupted her clapping to dab at her eyes. Hector
mopped his brow. Nikki was not sure she ever got the video camera on.
She and Jacinta collapsed into plastic chairs at our group's table, the
blanca pulled up behind the *loca*, her pale cheek laid on Jacinta's back:
giving comfort, taking repose. Maria eyed them and looked away.

Ann Marie announced the first bout, a master's, and two middle-aged
men touched gloves and began their lock-gazed shuffle. Raphi proceeded to wrap Candi's hands. Candi, spellbound, watched the gauze
layers, the cotton wraps, as Raphi wound and wove. Candi had changed
into a blue satin tank top, matching shorts, and her new white boxing
shoes. The second match was a finals for the Junior Olympics. These
boys were fast and slim and muscled, and the crowd liked this better
than the first fight. When it ended, Ann Marie took up the mike. "I want

to introduce you to Candida Rodriguez. She has won the eighty-five-pound weight class in the Junior Olympics."

Candi entered the ring amid applause, got a medal draped around her neck and hugs from Ann Marie and from Raphi, who had come in beside her. All the while she was half looking around for her opponent, even after Raphi whispered in her ear, so that her smile, as she posed for the camera, was bewildered and deflated-looking. As she left the ring again so soon after entering, the second wave of applause swelled like mockery. She walked back to the table, a hurt grin fixed on her face. A winner, beribboned and robbed.

Later Raphi would explain why she hadn't told Candi ahead of time that there was no opponent: She'd wanted Candi to understand empirically the importance of training hard and being prepared for competition. Somewhere out there was a record book with the names of all the winners throughout the years, and Candi's name would be included there forever. Nor was this listing empty, but earned through her dedication and readiness to fight. Once Candi took in Raphi's words, she would come to value her medal, especially for having earned it as an eleven-year-old girl at this still-embryonic moment in women's boxing history. But in those first seconds of her return to the table, she looked blushingly confused.

"I want to fight!" she protested helplessly. Everyone made a fuss over her and asked to see the medal. She kept her hand wraps on for the rest of the night, periodically stroking the gold metal disk on its length of bunting around her neck.

Ann Marie did all she could, short of actually tampering with the time clock, to stretch the evening out. Various announcements between bouts, acknowledgments of luminaries in our midst. "She brought women's boxing into the limelight! Give it up for the first female New England Golden Gloves champion ever—Raphaëlla Johnson!" And later: "Now let's have a moment of silence as we give a ten-count for all my friends who are no longer with us: Ralph Palmacci, Frank Murphy, Bobby Tomasello, Frank Shea, Paul Raymond, Luis Ayala . . ." Heads were bowed; the round bell rang ten times.

Nikki and Jacinta stood behind Maria's chair for a while, taking turns reaching out and pulling single strands of her hair until she reached around to swat them. Candi and Sefina occupied themselves by begging as many dollars as they could from every adult around the table to fund their periodic expeditions to buy nachos, sodas, and ice-cream bars. The men went off to get more beer, and the women slipped into franker speech. When Desi's kid fought, our corner of the room madly cheered him on, Hector videotaping, Maria on her feet, the girls screaming, and Richie booing with gusto when the judges decided in favor of his opponent. As the evening dragged on, Candi wound up in Raphi's lap, Raphi circling the eleven-year-old's waist with an arm.

It was right when we were all leaving that Nikki materialized beside me in the lobby and asked, almost shyly, "D'you wanna spar with me?"

First and foremost, I was flattered. An unsolicited overture of any kind from Nikki felt like a rare gift. It was as though she'd said, "D'you wanna dance with me?" Oh yes! Then I reminded myself that we were talking about sparring, and we were talking about Nikki. I looked at her appraisingly. Her face was in high-pink mode, and she was standing way up on the balls of her feet, a wild electron rush almost palpable in the air as she waited for my response.

"I do," I said truthfully, "but I'm a little afraid you'd kill me."

Nikki got a kind of fake-hurt look and dipped her head.

"*Oh* yeah. She would *kill* you." Maria, a few paces behind, had been listening.

Nikki, grinning, pretended to push her, and Maria stepped up to this, pretending to push her back. I was not sure what had inspired Nikki's invitation, but she had asked for something, which seemed in itself a positive sign. Like a sign of happiness or self-possession. It was mostly in delighted response to this that I heard myself accepting. "Okay. *You* wanna spar?"

"Yeah," she said, and surprised me again with how quietly emphatic she sounded. Then she went tearing out the door, banging through it so hard you'd have thought it would crack, and out into the parking lot with a whoop to catch up with Jacinta.

"I wouldn't do it," advised Maria sincerely.

I shrugged. I'd ask Raphi what she thought.

A fine drizzle punctuated the night air. We all said our goodbyes in the parking lot. Nikki, already in the backseat of the Rodriguezes' car, turned to look at me through the rear window. "You and me," she mouthed, pointing, nodding, mock tough. I laughed and crossed the street to my car, got in, and instantly, before I'd turned the keys in the ignition, there was a flurry of palms slapping all over the glass, beating at the passenger-side window. "Give me a heart attack," I said, lowering it. Somehow Jacinta and Nikki had materialized from the dark bushes alongside where I was parked.

"Which way you going?" asked Jacinta suggestively, playing a role.

I laughed. "Which way *you* going?"

"No, say, 'I'm going to my crib,'" Nikki ordered.

"I'm going to my crib."

"No, don't say it all corny! Like this: 'I'm going to my crib.'"

"I'm going to my crib."

"Nooo!" they wailed simultaneously. "Yo: 'I'm going to my *crib.*'"

"You guys, shut up, that's what I said, 'I'm going to my crib!'"

They liked this one. "A'ight! Lee-*yah*!" Clapped their hands very fast and then *whoosh*, they were gone, my headlights picking them up in the rain as they streaked across the road, laughing, the one pulling the other along.

8

BREAKHEART

"Look at this," Raphi told Desi, who was down on a mat doing crunches. She held out her left hand: two rings, a rock and a band. "We eloped."

The cop fell back, belly-laughing. "You did?"

"I'm sorry."

"Girl, just this morning I was *worrying* about what to say at your wedding."

It was the first Saturday in June, eight days after Raphi and Richie had gotten married at Waltham City Hall, no guests in attendance. For the past month or so, when Raphi hadn't been talking about calling the whole thing off, she'd been talking about planning a late-summer wedding. After making their vows before a justice of the peace, the couple had shown up at the Rodriguezes' apartment to break the news and pose for some pictures before heading off for a night in a Boston hotel. Maria had delivered the information the next morning outside the gym, as we waited for someone to unlock the place. Uncharacteristically inscrutable, she'd worn a smile that might have been philosophical or disparaging. My shock seemed to give her some measure of satisfaction. The girls had had little to add, seeming surprisingly indifferent to the whole thing. I knew Candi had been planning on being a flower girl. For my part, I felt hollow, duped. Maybe I affected indifference, too. No one ever did show up to unlock the gym.

Now, a week later, the day was shaping up to be hot. The back door was tied open with a rope. Desi had brought a couple of boys with him, one of the kids who'd lost a few weeks earlier at Good Times. Nikki and Jacinta were absent, Jacinta to "finish a book report," explained Maria, somewhat unconvincingly. And Nikki? Maria gave a compressed shrug, her shoulders jerking more forward than up; she had stopped counting Nikki among her flock. I was saddened but hardly shocked. Remarks Maria and Hector had made to Richie and Raphi had been passed along to me; the parents' discomfort with Jacinta and Nikki's closeness had been gathering shape for some time. Sefina and Candi were there, but neither had bothered to change or wrap her hands. Also, they were bare-foot. Candi had brought a coloring book and crayons, and she and her mother spent much of practice sitting on the steps by the altar, drawing.

Beyond the door it was a beautiful day, as beautiful as the day two weeks earlier when everyone was there, and Richie and Desi had held the mitts for us, and after practice we'd all found ourselves in the weedy little lot, unwilling to drive away, and Sefina had gathered handfuls of petals from the fat rhododendrons that shoved their beet-colored heads through the chain-link fence, and made purple snow of them over our heads. But everything was different today. Raphi, who always seemed tired lately, went into the ring as if to warm up but wound up only lying on her back. After a while, Candi went to the ring and rolled under the ropes and joined Raphi there. They lay side by side on their backs on the blood- and sweat- and snot- and spit-stained canvas, looking up at all the narrow wooden beams that climbed as if endlessly into the dark, steep pitch of the roof.

Participation in the Women's Nationals at the end of July was begin-ning to seem like a mirage. While Raphi hadn't come out and an-nounced that they wouldn't be going, the way she spoke of it had grown increasingly vague. Almost all year it had looked like the main goal: to go back to the tournament again that summer, with Jacinta and Nikki, maybe Candi, too, and even Sefina if she applied herself. But right now was when they should have intensified training, four or five times a week in the gym, and a few miles of running every other day. Instead the op-posite was occurring, a lethargy, if not an actual malaise, settling in.

Raphi said summertime was always slow at the gym. She said it would pick up in the fall, it always did. And she said some days practice was just like that—sloppy, unfocused, nothing coming together. She said you couldn't read too much into it. But I didn't know.

One reason they train you to throw straight, fast punches in boxing is that you don't want to telegraph your intentions to your opponent. Should you cock your arm in preparation, or swing it out in even the tiniest of roundhouse gestures, you offer your opponent advance information and the chance to react before the blow. In spite of Raphi's reassurances, it felt like a message was being telegraphed pretty clearly that day. It was encoded in her gold band and her aura of wistful preoccupation; in the absence of the two big girls; in Maria's reticence; in Candi's absolute absorption in crayoning—crayoning!—inside the lines of a puppy dog. Even with the mitigating and welcome presence of Desi and his boys doing their thing—if unobtrusively—shadowboxing over by the wall of cracked and stained mirrors, an air of attrition, of entropy, had gathered in the gym.

No one but the bride and groom had known about the elopement, which they had decided on a couple of weeks earlier. In hindsight, Raphi had dropped all kinds of small clues. She had been full of talk about wedding dresses; she'd begun shopping aggressively all of a sudden, and then she had bought one. Still, I knew a lot of brides chose their dresses months before the event. She had told me she was taking that day off work, told me she and Richie had plans brewing for that weekend, told me they were registering at Macy's that week. But the flurry of activity hadn't been easily distinguishable from an average bride's anticipation of a late-summer celebration, and no one had suspected anything different until Raphi and Richie showed up that night as husband and wife. In one of the pictures, he was carrying her over the modest housing-project threshold, Richie towering and dapper in a three-piece suit, Raphi beaming in a short white sleeveless frock. There were pictures of the couple with each of the girls, including Nikki, who had been grounded at home a few blocks away, but had managed to sneak out and offer her congratulations, too.

Nobody did much working out that day. Before leaving, Maria handed Raphi a plastic bag from Sears. "A wedding present," she said. "You got to open it in the locker room, though." So we all pressed into the cramped makeshift room behind the weights, and Raphi opened the gift and held up a white camisole, negligee, and thong, which Sefina and Candi pretended to pose in while Maria and Raphi cracked up.

A few days later I asked Raphi what she needed.

"Knives," she told me. Richie, she said, was forever throwing her butter knives down the disposal. Knives struck me as inauspicious for a wedding present, but I ordered the set for which they had registered, and attempted to bless the gift by copying some lines of Pablo Neruda's onto the card:

> *En el limón cortaron*
> *los cuchillos*
> *una pequeña catedral*

> Cutting the lemon
> the knife
> leaves a little cathedral

The sliver of verse seemed apt. Like a wish, a hope, for all little wanderers who laced on the gloves. The acid sting; the translucently blinding yellow; then a miniature world of astonishing order, a kind of holy formalism, discovered, unharmable, within.

A week earlier, on Raphi's wedding night, I'd attended my first pro fights. Patty Yoffe had invited me to shadow her that night at the Wonderland, where she was working as ringside physician. We'd driven up to Revere together, Patty and her husband and I. I'd been hoping Patty could shed some light on the subject of girls' boxing. Although she herself had never boxed, I was intrigued by the fact that she, as a woman and a professional caregiver, condoned and enabled boxing by serving as ringside physician. Hers was so far removed from the position articulated by other professionals in the medical and public health fields. Yet Patty, highly educated and privileged, was also far removed from the cultures most likely to produce girl boxers. I wondered whether she, in her choices and actions, somehow bridged the gap between those worlds. More important, if she was personally drawn to the sport, even as an observer and not a participant, if it provided a direct feed to something that nourished her and that she could not get elsewhere, wouldn't that speak to the question of what boxing had to offer girls and women specifically?

At the Wonderland, Patty had been received warmly by promoters and officials alike ("Doc! Glad to see you") and installed in the back room, at a table near the bar, where she would conduct her prefight exams. The only female fight doctor in the area, Patty navigated the night with her distinctly measured blend of warmth and professionalism. Her voice was low and full-bodied; she spoke with the brisk tempo of a northerner and the luxurious cadences of a southerner, putting at ease each boxer as she fitted the blood-pressure cuff, peered down his throat, had him squeeze her fingers.

"You've got the classic nose," she told one hopeful with a laugh and a tweak of the flattened feature. "But you can breathe through it?"

"Yep."

"Okay. Good luck. Be careful." To another, cutting him off as he sailed through the eye chart: "All right, show-off. You're younger than me!"

Her table had been set up on a small parquet dance floor beneath a disco ball. One of the walls was mirrored, another painted with zebra stripes and a life-size mural of Frank Sinatra. Small red-shaded hanging lights shone down on all the colored rows of bottles behind the bar.

"Did you get that sparring?" Patty asked a boxer who had shown up with a shiner faded to a moldy shade of gray.

"Yeah, sparring with that guy Mickey Ward a couple weeks ago."

"Well, you've been beaten by a good man."

"Yeah, that's how I look at it."

Noting the yellow calluses on his palms, "These from lifting weights?"

"Yeah."

"Oh, you *guys*."

Within the medical community, many doubt out loud whether serving as ringside physician can be entirely consistent with the Hippocratic oath to do no harm. In the United Kingdom, after two bills to outlaw boxing were defeated in the late nineties, some doctors tried a backdoor method of abolishing the sport. They encouraged a boycott by members of their profession; since law required a physician to be present during a boxing match, this would effectively render boxing illegal. More straightforward attempts to criminalize boxing have been made repeatedly by the American Medical Association. Pediatricians, unsurprisingly, are among the most outspoken opponents of the sport, going before state legislatures and likening youth boxing to pornography and cockfighting. All such attempts have failed.

Doctors who enable boxing by serving as ringside physicians find themselves in an odd position. And if most of them choose the work motivated by a well-worn love of the ring—carried over, in most cases, from childhood (how many of them had repeated to me the phrase "watching the fights on TV with my dad," wearing an identical look of faintly humid nostalgia)—then Patty Yoffe's position was made that much odder by her gender. Membership in the American Association of Professional Ringside Physicians, established in 1997, is voluntary; their membership roster cannot claim to be comprehensive, but just to give an idea, out of the approximately 250 doctors currently listed as AAPRP members, fewer than ten are female.

Unlike most of her ringside colleagues, Patty had not grown up with any interest in, let alone affinity for, boxing. Her husband, Doug, a real estate developer and also Harvard's boxing coach, had introduced her to the sport. But surely, I thought, speaking with her in the hush of their penthouse overlooking the Cambridge Common, there must have been something within her that fueled this activity. She spoke of coming to appreciate, slowly, and under Doug's tutelage, the skill involved in the sport, the almost balletic physical prowess and mental capabilities of its athletes. She spoke of the pleasure, as a doctor, in examining such healthy bodies—most of these young people were in gorgeous, robust shape relative to the patients she treated in her practice as an internist. She spoke of the fact that boxing, however violent, remained legal, and that physicians were necessary to keep it relatively safe by making sure boxers were fit before they fought, and by stopping fights before injuries became fatalities. But even as the reasons she offered glided easily from her mouth, they never felt complete.

A little before fight time, we'd taken our seats ringside. The DJ, behind us, spun his music. "Move, bitch, get out the way!" pounded from the speakers. One of the fight promoters offered a hundred bucks to a young woman at the bar to put on a Budweiser bathing suit and strut the ring during round breaks—one of the girls they'd lined up to do this hadn't shown. "I don't think so," said her boyfriend, who wore a BADA BING! T-shirt and held a cell phone to his ear. The on-air announcers did their camera tests; the fights would be broadcast on cable later in the week. A woman brushed behind us with a five-year-old boy on her hip. "I don't wanna watch!" he said through tears. "You don't *hafta* watch," she said, looking for a seat.

Patty draped her black cardigan over the back of her chair. She wore a sleeveless sundress, black sandals, and small gold-framed glasses. Doug came to sit beside her. Between them, they seemed to know half the people there. Many of the officials, trainers, and boxers not fighting that night stopped by to greet them, often with hugs. Patty's first experience as a fight doc, twelve years earlier, had been at a night of pro fights at the Roseland Ballroom, and the boxers had gone hard, three bouts ending in knockouts. During the very first bout, she'd had to battle the impulse to jump in the ring and stop it; she would have been at a near-total loss if not for Doug speaking in her ear, guiding her with his own finely tuned perceptions. After an awful-looking shot, when he could feel her stiffen beside him: "Don't worry about it, he's all right." Or after an accumulation of blows that didn't register with her: "Watch this guy, now. Keep your eye on him."

That night at the Wonderland, the first bout, which lasted only four rounds, was tough to watch. "Put your hands up!" Patty yelled twice, sounding aggrieved. After the second round, one of the boxers was so disoriented that he retreated to the wrong neutral corner. After the match, Patty came back from her brief exam of each boxer to report that the loser had broken his nose and was upset about it. "It won't be pretty," she said, with a shrug as if to add, *If he cares that much about his looks, what's he doing in the ring in the first place?* But there was a furrow between her eyes.

Ann Marie, who had hosted the Good Times event several weeks earlier, was up next. Her fight was neither pretty nor long. She came on aggressive, and even as she took some hard shots, she moved in to throw some of her own. She did not look afraid. But she was outboxed. This was apparent from the first seconds of the fight. Doug was one of the legion of men who do not like the idea of women boxing; even so, he could not help but admire her opponent. "She's spent a *lot* of hours in the gym," he determined, perhaps the highest praise he'd be willing to allow. The other woman, ten years younger than Ann Marie, only grew stronger as the match wore on, finally getting Ann Marie on the ropes in a boxer's most horrific pose: chin up, arms down, entirely unprotected. The ref stopped the fight a minute and thirty-one seconds into the second round. Ann Marie was a good sport, hugging her opponent, coming out to watch the rest of the fights after she'd changed into a one-shouldered white-sequined top. She held an ice pack to her cut and swollen eye and was as cheerful as I'd ever seen her. "Oh well, you got to move forward," she said. "You win some and you lose some." But she acknowledged it was probably a good thing she hadn't brought her kids, and she would spend the next day at the hospital getting a CAT scan and X rays.

The night kept on. The ring-card girls—young women who came out between rounds, parading large cards displaying the round number—appeared in fewer and fewer clothes. They'd toss promotional items—baseball hats, visors, T-shirts, key chains—to the crowd, and the men clamored and dove wildly. The cigarette smoke churned thicker up against the hot lights on the low ceiling, and the empty beer cups multiplied and tipped and rolled across the floor. The fighters hit and bled. Patty tensed and half stood to see; got called into the ring to determine whether a jaw was broken; shone her light into the pupils of dazed or giddy or calm boxers at the end of their bouts; leaned sharply forward to gauge the amount of blood spilling from a boxer's mouth to the canvas; stuck squashed-up bits of napkin in her ears to mute the blaring hip-hop from the speakers directly behind.

In the car on the way home, I asked Patty and Doug question upon question. Did they like it, really? Did they prefer it to amateur boxing? Did they have a hard time watching when there was a mismatch? Did concern for the boxers' bodies or lives ever get in the way of their pleasure in the sport?

Doug liked it unequivocally.

"Why?" I wondered aloud. "What is it that gets *fed* in you?"

"I guess my basic sadism."

Patty allowed that attending boxing matches could be stressful for her, that while she had grown to appreciate the sport, she didn't particularly relish watching a beating. In fact, she didn't bother to watch boxing when she wasn't the attending physician. And yes, she sometimes got a sick feeling inside when a boxer seemed hurt but not hurt enough to stop the fight.

"So what do you love about it that makes you want to do it anyway?" I asked.

"I don't know, I guess it's kind of fun getting to be queen bee," she said somewhat doubtfully. "With all the characters, you know." I could see it,

I supposed, the rare allure of being the lady doc gliding through this motley sea of almost cartoonishly red-blooded men. But then she said, and it seemed as though it was possible for her to say it only because she was so tired and it was dark and late and we had just spent the evening together ringside witnessing bodies knock other bodies senseless, "Mostly I think it's just a way for me to get to be in Doug's world." When she offered that most obvious answer of all, it was like the key that fit the lock; it sounded right, as none of her other answers had.

I had wanted Patty's involvement in boxing to shed light on how its particular version of power speaks to women, proof that it offers something concrete and vital and transferable to the rest of life. Instead I was left with the sense that boxing was something Patty subjected herself to out of a longing for something else entirely: a connection to an unreachable male world.

Nikki stopped coming to the gym. She hadn't been to a single practice since she asked me to spar with her that night at Good Times, and I teased her, when I saw her, that she was just scared I'd kick her ass. But I barely saw her. She invited me to her science fair at school, but when I got there, I learned she hadn't bothered showing up that day. We went Rollerblading along the Charles River one weekend; it was my first time, and Nikki was in her adorable-obnoxious mode, eagerly anticipating my many wipeouts, literally rubbing her palms together with glee. When I did at last fall, she complained that it wasn't a very *good* fall, and the whole way home she was completely shut down; she might as well have had the word CLOSED scrawled on her T-shirt. Raphi and I worried about her. We both called and called. Once her mother's boyfriend answered and yelled, "Who the fuck's this?" into the receiver. Sometimes we left messages on the machine, but we never knew whether Nikki received them.

We knew a little of what had happened. That Jacinta had become friends with another Puerto Rican girl at school, that Nikki had been edged out. That one day in Spanish, Nikki had drawn a cartoon character with a speech bubble containing a message that could be interpreted as suicidal, and that she had left the drawing behind, and her Spanish teacher showed it to her guidance counselor, who had begun meeting with Nikki daily. That Nikki had made some kind of threat about hurting Jacinta's new friend, and all three girls had been hauled in to talk things out with the guidance counselor. Each new piece of information, revealed by Nikki herself, or Jacinta, or Maria, or one of the girls' teachers, was disheartening less for being extraordinary than for being ordinary. Intense friendships bloomed and combusted among adolescent girls all the time. Which made the quality of this particular loss no less singular or severe and lent it a dismal feeling of inevitability.

Nikki told Raphi she'd start coming to practice again once school was out. Maria told Raphi she didn't think Nikki was coming back, period. Then the Rodriguez sisters told Raphi they were being sent to stay with their grandparents in Puerto Rico for the summer; Maria told Raphi she had no idea what they were talking about; Hector told Raphi he *was* thinking about sending them away for the summer, but he hadn't decided yet; and Raphi, reporting this to me, lifted her eyes to heaven and said, "Isn't summer practically over?" By then we were well into July, the weeks having slipped through our fingers like butter on a hot day. In fact, it had been so liquidy hot that Raphi kept canceling practice anyway. She said it was dangerous to practice when the temperature was over 90 degrees and there was only feeble air-conditioning; Franky and Ralphy used to send her home when the weather got like this. Day after day, the radio gave the temperature as 91 or 94 or 97, and the brothy atmosphere inside the gym heated up to over 100. The two industrial-strength floor fans didn't do much good unless you stood directly in front of them, which was of course all Candi and Sefina were wont to do whenever they showed up these days.

But mostly, whenever Raphi didn't cancel practice, Maria did. It was too hot and they all had headaches, she'd say, or she couldn't wake the girls up. Now that it was summer, the kids were staying out until three, four, five in the morning. When they did come to the gym, it was more often just the younger two. Jacinta was either "at the library," or home with "a stomachache," or "you know, what do you call it, the *melancólica*." Hector was worse and worse. Only in his late thirties, he had a heart attack; nobody knew what had caused it, but naturally everyone had a theory: the pain medication, the smoking, the medicine he'd been taking to help him quit smoking, the hair tonic. He came home; his heart was okay, no big deal, said Maria, but his back was worse; he was walking with a cane.

Sometimes it was just Raphi and me, and KISS 108 or Jammin' 94.5 on the boom box, and the periodic voice of the time clock. One day we wrote our names on the sign-in sheet between the office and the gym, and the piece of paper was nearly bare, only three names above ours in the entire last week, just a few of the regulars we almost never saw anymore. The DUES IS DUE NOW! sign was on the floor. The vending machine was faintly aglow with little amber sold-out lights.

In the past, when I had voiced concerns about the gym's ability to remain open, Raphi had always reassured me, but that day she told me she was worried about the gym closing. Always previously, for twenty years, even when it had flatlined, the gym had proved revivable. But now, with Franky gone, Ralphy gone, Vinny Busa gone, and Team Ruiz concentrating its attention on Vegas, not to mention being months behind in rent and no one paying any dues, she wondered whether it could revive once more. Maybe it was the right moment to open her own gym. That was her and Richie's dream, she confided languidly, in the dim, rank, intensified heat of the locker room: R&R Gym. But she said it with some futility, as though relating a dream she already knew would never become anything else. Or maybe it was just that she had barely slept the night before, again.

We worked out. We were damp before we even began, cloaked in sweat from the simple exertions of changing into gym clothes and wrapping our hands. We jumped rope, but only one round. On the radio they kept announcing that the air quality was bad; young children, pregnant women, and the elderly were supposed to stay indoors and keep physical activity to a minimum. We lifted weights, stretched. We couldn't hear over the radio and fans to know whether a car had pulled into the lot, so we took turns checking out the back door to see if Maria and the girls had arrived. Eventually Raphi called them from the office, and the phone rang and rang. "They're sitting there saying, 'Don't pick it up,'" said Raphi. A highly plausible scenario. "Did I ever do any counterpunching with you?" Raphi asked.

"No."

"Want to learn?"

"Yeah."

We got in the ring, and she showed me the technique. I practiced mirroring her as we moved around, throwing whatever she threw. She jabbed, I jabbed back. She hooked, I threw a hook.

"That's it?" I asked after a bit.

"Basically."

It seemed like a theater game. I was restless. Still no Rodriguezes.

She looked at the clock. "Want to spar?"

"Yes."

We got our mouthguards. We'd been sparring with some regularity, never going hard, never going more than two or three rounds. We put on our headgear and gloves. There was a minute and a half on the time clock. "Want to just go?" she said, her speech all distorted around the hunk of molded plastic. I understood her more by context than diction: Did I just want to start midround instead of waiting for the clock to begin a new round?

" 'Kay."

Immediately she threw a great right cross that knocked my mouthguard out, and it was a grand comic routine trying to pick it up with gloves on. I'd have done better to prostrate myself and pick it up between my teeth. Giving up, I stuck my glove between my knees, yanked my arm free, scooped up the mouthguard, doused it with water from the sport bottle, shoved it back in, and got the glove back on only to have the round bell blast. Raphi jumped out of the ring and restarted the clock so we wouldn't have to wait around. It was as though the idleness of the summer weeks had caught up to us in a mad dash, and we couldn't stand to waste another moment. She climbed back through the ropes; we touched gloves, boxed. I knocked her headgear crooked with a right. She jabbed me smack in the nose, which felt like it glowed and expanded, a foolish, clownish feeling.

"Y'kay?"

"Yeah!" It gave me the resolve to land a combination, backing her up at the same time. She was in the corner now, and I moved away to give her some room. "Never do that!" she chided me later. "When you get someone against the ropes, keep going." She came at me now, jabbing and weaving, the look in her eye that was all business, but not scary, never scary, no matter how she stepped in and jabbed, twice, snapping my head back, and followed with a right, which I slipped—elation! I was still lame enough at defense that when I did elude a punch, I felt immeasurably pleased with myself, as though I'd gotten away with something sneaky and slick. Bobbing back up, I was in perfect position to throw a hook that knocked her sideways.

We quit at the bell, and I experienced no relief as I removed the head-gear. No matter how strong the urge to go inside the ring, I always had some butterflies in the moments before sparring, and always in the past had felt relief upon finishing, some pleasure and release at having gotten through it. Today, for the first time, my desire to go another round was untempered and unambivalent. I was not done. But Raphi could feel her asthma lurking in the corridor, and she was, as she had been remarking increasingly, out of shape. She wasn't sleeping well, and her weight was down to 103. She'd been having dizziness, she said, and I understood.

That summer I had come into a strength I'd never guessed at. But all my guides, my shepherds and stars, Raphi and the girls and the gym, were ailing, hurting and waning. I had thought the girls would be training like crazy for the Nationals, and instead they were barely making it to the gym. Outside, the rhododendrons and yellow roses and purple rose of Sharon were all running rampant, pressing insistently through the fence and the weeds and the cracked cement around the church. Inside, it was dim and hushed, and less and less inhabited, as everyone fell away, and no one came. I wanted them back, Raphi and the girls—selfishly, because I wanted to box them, and also because I didn't want them to grow small.

A few days later I got a note from Raphi. "You have a beautiful and invisible straight right hand. Really, I admire that you seem to breathe so easily and nothing really seems to scare you. You are moving well, too, becoming a harder target, and much more scary." And then the bitter-sweet words: "I know pretty soon you will be too good that we can't spar anymore."

> Doesn't really matter what you're thinking
> Doesn't really matter what you say
> Doesn't really matter where I'm going
> 'Cause you ain't coming with me anyway.
>
> —from "Doesn't Really Matter," a song by
> Nikki Silvano and Jacinta Rodriguez,
> written in spring 2002

Recently I coached an athlete to compete in an amateur boxing tournament. I was excited for this show because . . . this athlete was the best one on the team—she had beaten everyone at the gym and seemed to possess all the qualities of a winner: strength, perseverance, heart, and dedication.

Furthermore she came from a severely dysfunctional background, a so-called broken home . . . and [exhibited] symptoms of trauma. Given her athletic skills, this edge of anger could potentially translate itself into success in the boxing ring. She was, after all, used to fighting.

So it was somewhat of a shock for me to see her winning her bout and then suddenly quitting, giving the win to her opponent, someone she should have easily beaten. The entire round seemed to take place in slow motion, and I noticed that her face changed at the point when she chose to give up. She looked away, looked down, and dropped her hands. At that moment I knew that she was not a fighter but a quitter.

—from Raphi's final graduate school paper, "Resilience and Lack of Resilience in Urban Adolescents"

August had come, and Nikki had ventured back to the gym after what turned out to be a nearly two-month hiatus. Although she'd pledged, over the phone, her intention to resume boxing after the school year ended, her rift with the Rodriguezes had made Raphi and me wonder whether she'd make good on the promise. The fact that she really had come back seemed to say more about her strength than all of her famous left hooks and right crosses. She had also begun bringing two friends along, more for companionship than because they were seriously interested in the sport. Crystal and Tori were both overweight, one a little, one a lot. They would come to the gym bulky with layers of clothes, denims and hoodies, turtlenecks and flannel work shirts, alarming choices for summer, and what skin was showing was very white. They looked uncomfortably warm as they worked out, but oddly game.

Nikki had begun wearing large black Chinese characters penned the length of her forearm; she was careful to re-ink the decoration in indelible marker each time it threatened to fade, so that it persisted for weeks. She was mysterious about what it meant, first claiming not to know, later pulling me aside to whisper that it was the name of another friend who was away for the summer. I could well imagine that it helped to come in with these friends and this ink. When the Rodriguezes were there, too, there was some effort to work out as a unified group. Raphi would command us all into the ring and tell someone, Candi or Sefina, to lead us in warm-ups. We'd stretch and do our drills, moving around the ring and throwing combinations.

I was heartened to see Nikki and Jacinta still come together as team-mates occasionally, in little ways. Jacinta held the heavy bag for Nikki, or did leg throws with her, hands locked around Nikki's ankles while the *blanca* pushed the *loca*'s feet repeatedly back toward earth. But while Nikki's desire to mend their friendship was palpable, Jacinta's seemed strained, perhaps even half hidden.

One day near the end of the summer, Nikki and her friends showed up bright and early. It was a special day; I had promised to drive them to Breakheart after practice. Breakheart was Nikki's favorite place on earth. I had seen pictures of her as a little girl, and when she talked about Breakheart she looked like herself in those pictures. Breakheart Reservation, about a half hour north of Boston, was a seven-hundred-acre pine-oak forest, with a lake for swimming and another for fishing and seven high rocky hills to climb. Its name was supposed to have come from the Civil War era, when soldiers training there found it achingly lonely and remote. All through the spring, Nikki had spoken ex-citedly about our going there in the summer—she had meant to show it to Jacinta, of course, and also to Raphi and me. But when the day we had picked for the trip arrived, Raphi begged off in order to go home to Richie, and none of the Rodriguezes showed up.

Still, the rest of us would go as planned. After practice. First, there was another promise I had to fulfill: This was also the day we had desig-nated for Nikki and me to spar.

Now, it was true that Desi had advised me not to spar with Nikki. Maria had advised against it. So had Richie. Raphi alone had said she thought it would be okay; she thought Nikki had matured and that she would control herself in the ring. But the night before sparring, she e-mailed me: "See you bright and early, ready to rumble with Nikki? Try to eat well tonight and sleep well too and make sure you eat breakfast!" She had never done anything like this in the past, never felt the need to remind me to get a good night's sleep or eat when I was planning to spar with anyone else, and as a result, I did not get a good night's sleep and was nervous all morning.

After warming up, Nikki and I got our headgear. Raphi greased my face with Vaseline first, which would help the blows slide off, something else she had never done before—it was usually only the men, who threw heavier punches, dipping into the communal pot of petroleum jelly that sat open by the ring.

After all of this, I was surprised by how it went once we began. It was hard to land a blow on Nikki, she moved with such agility. But that only made me concentrate harder on landing something, so I was lost in a peaceful haze of aggressive behavior. When I say *peaceful,* I mean engaged wholly in a single directive, and therefore emotionally unimpeded by fear or franticness, confusion or doubt. I might as well have been working on a difficult math problem or trying to balance an egg on its end; all my energies, all my resources, were channeled that narrowly. It *is* a kind of peace.

So I was further surprised at the round break when I retreated to my neutral corner with Raphi (Crystal and Tori were working Nikki's), and she said, giving me water, "Did she hurt you?"

"No."

"Are you sure?"

"Yeah." She really hadn't. I drank. Then I gulped some air; I was panting more than usual, and my nose was running, that was all. I thought maybe I had allergies that day—it was August: could it be ragweed time already?—and it was just a bit extra awkward to breathe when I had the mouthguard in.

"Okay," said Raphi with a certain sobriety, "there's something I have to tell you. You have another black eye."

Was that all? I shrugged.

She tore off a piece of paper towel, wet it, pressed it beneath my eye, and held it up for me to see, displaying it as if we were in a Bounty commercial. There was a little blood on it, whatever. It seemed remarkably trivial.

"You want to do another?"

"Yeah."

She gave me more water and helped me get my mouthguard back in. The bell went off, and we began round two.

"Move, Leah!" Raphi called. "Move! Stop!"

We stopped.

"You're standing right in front of her. You have to move. Every time you throw something, move. Okay, box."

I knew this was my problem. This was what had happened with Candi, when we stood there head to head and traded blows, except that time I hadn't been able to hit her back. Now, with Nikki, I was doing the same thing. I either wanted to back her up or stand my ground. The thing I was unprepared to do was get away. Even thinking about it rattled me. I was thinking, Step left? Step right? Never did I think, Take a step back. I didn't want to run. The thought of trying to get away was the only thing that put fear in me.

"Move, Leah!"

Nikki never rushed me, never lost control. The few times I connected nicely, I wondered whether I would trigger that famous anger, but she didn't brawl, she only boxed, with measured grace and power. I came forward, jabbed, jabbed, stepped right. She slipped it, blocked it, took it on the temple. It didn't rock her hard, nor did she rock me hard. I knew she wasn't hitting as hard as she could. We circled and danced till the bell.

"Why am I so out of breath?" I panted to Raphi, back in the corner.

"You're being really aggressive. Both of you are. You're keeping busy the whole time. You want to go one more?"

I nodded, grinning at myself because I was so winded I could barely speak.

In the third round I noticed Nikki doing this thing when I threw my jab, a neat darting lift backward that put her out of range. Earlier I was just plain frustrated at my own inability to land a blow, but now I took note of how she was outwitting me. It was a tiny, deft movement that made me think of Hermes with his winged shoes. And she looked, through the partial mask of her headgear, when she did it—was it my imagination?—faintly gleeful, as if she were having fun. I thought, Oh! I want to try that. Moments later, here she came lunging forward, and I tried her move, and it worked. I felt a buoyant lift—not the simple satisfaction of having slipped her punch, but the real, small victory of having tried something fresh in the ring, of having experimented, playfully, and been thereby delivered to a fuller apprehension of what was possible within the space. It was one thing to face off against an opponent and hold my own. It was quite another to imagine the possibility of ad-libbing, inventing, in such a circumstance. To imagine the possibility of *playing*.

When Nikki and I had finished, and finished hugging, Raphi told us we both did really well, by which I supposed she meant Nikki controlled herself and I went all out. I didn't care, I'd take the compliment; it felt good today. By *good* I mean *just*.

An hour later, we were en route to Breakheart, slogging up through the giant strip mall that was Route 1 North, Nikki and her friends futzing with my car radio and cheerfully informing one another at regular intervals that they were evil and psycho. We saw the exit, and just as I pulled into the right lane to turn off, Nikki, whose excitement had been mounting, wanted me to know that around this curve was her favorite mountain. "Where?" I said, because we were midway around the curve and I didn't see any mountain. "Right there." She pointed. I followed her finger. It was the sheer wall of rock they'd blasted out to make way for the exit ramp. No taller than a house, no longer than a dozen car lengths. I checked her face for signs of irony, a glimmer of humor. Nothing. Only soft, inward rapture and a rising anticipation as we got closer.

She hadn't been to Breakheart in years, not since her grandparents had been in better health; it was they who always used to take her here, every summer, for day trips, a picnic and a swim, a frog hunt and a climb. Still, she promised me that she would remember the way once we were off the highway, and she did. She'd gone quiet and straight-backed, and Crystal and Tori, sensing it, grew quiet, too. After all the rhapsodizing, I had thought we'd be someplace hinting of wilderness by now, but instead we drove along wide suburban streets with low, matching houses and trees too youthful to offer much shade. "Go right," said Nikki. We turned in to the parking lot of the Northeast Met Regional Vocational School. "Park here."

"This is it?"

"This is it."

We'd each packed a lunch but hadn't bothered with towels or anything like that. We "hiked" in down an asphalt path, to the beach at Pearce Lake, and Nikki commented unenthusiastically on the new diversity of the beachgoers ("There didn't used to be so many Spanish people. Not that that's bad"). We threaded our way to the far end of the beach and into the water, Crystal and Tori in virtually all of their clothes, Nikki, in first a furtive and then a purposefully brazen gesture, stripping to a bikini before heading to join them. The look of pride and shame with which she conducted herself across the sand recalled to me my first impression of her, almost a year earlier, when, after sparring, she'd seemed to resurface anxiously from a wild state. I recalled Raphi's role in the matter—it had been among my first impressions of her, too—the way the coach had had to guide her back gently, with praise and reassurance about how brave Nikki had been to descend to that wild state. For a girl, wielding power was as terrifying as it was exhilarating.

In the paper on resilience, which she had based on Nikki, Raphi had written:

> What surprised me about the girl who quit in the boxing show should not have surprised me at all. I have seen numerous athletes who seem to possess every advantage in a situation but for lack of mental strength will sabotage the situation and lose. I have also seen situations that seem hopeless for an athlete, and then watched that athlete turn the situation around to win. What is it that made the first athlete purposely lose, and the second one intentionally save himself?
>
> When I asked my boxer what happened in the ring, things became a little more clear. She said she loved the beginning when the first bell rang, when she forgot about the crowd and her training and everything else, and just focused on her boxing. But . . . when in her performance she was reminded of her mother . . . of her own lack of confidence . . . [she] quit."

When Raphi wrote this, and the line about Nikki's being a quitter, she had been zeroing in on one specific instance of quitting, but she had not meant it prophetically. Indeed, in talking about it with Nikki afterward, she had continued the work of coaching, helping the girl unravel the meaning of what had happened so that in the future a different choice might not elude her. As it happened, Nikki never boxed in competition again. After that August day with me, she never even sparred again, not with fists, not in a ring. But she was by no reckoning a quitter. Her loss in the ring, if anything, had made her more determined not to repeat the old pattern of giving up.

In the fall, things would get worse for her. The demise of her relationship with Jacinta would become intolerable; there would be efforts to speak truth met by subterfuge and lies; there would be efforts to reconcile met by demurral and indifference; and Nikki would find herself going to her high school advisers' office, up in the fourth-floor haven of the Visual Arts Department, where she felt most safe, most able to admit her true self, and telling them, red-faced, glitter-eyed, simultaneously breathless and clenching her teeth, that she could not be in class right now, that she was on the verge of exploding. Then she would go into the teachers' bathroom and wash her face and emerge . . . okay. Her teachers would comment later on her shift, her leap in maturity. It seemed a cruelly peculiar twist that the test of her growth would come in this form: being abandoned by the one with whom she was practicing to be strong. But given the rigor and heartbreak of the test, the fact of her passing with such flying colors—winning the pleased (and surprised) admiration of her teachers, solidifying other friendships, being named best defensive player on the school's softball team, and having her best academic year ever—would be a marvel.

The fact of Nikki's power had not been in question since her earliest memory, that of slamming the little boy's head into the Dumpster until he bled. But whether her power would be cause for only fear and shame or something different; whether she should reject it, trade it in for something else, claim it as it was, or coax it into a more palatable form—these questions had bedeviled her, as they have so many girls. If boxing gave Nikki the license and means to hash out some of these questions free from fear and shame, then she had emerged from the experience with some important answers. The choices she would make in the coming year would stand as a testament to her will to fight. She would give every indication of intentionally beginning to save herself.

That day at Breakheart I was the first to climb out of the water, removing myself to a rock littered with cigarette butts and the sharp green and brown remnants of broken beer bottles, to dry in the sun and watch Nikki and her friends play. They were such children—these three girls with their women's bodies, and their women's burdens weighing in their skeptical eyes—playing games underwater like fish: Who could hold her breath the longest, swim the fastest, dive the deepest? Nikki, Nikki, and Nikki, of course. She rose through the water, which was glossy and black, almost obsidian under the bright sun. Then she jackknifed and vanished again, safe like a mermaid, all her power locked fast within her body.

9

THE RING

In the mid-nineties, a friend sent me an enormous, sweat-stained T-shirt from Gleason's, the famous Brooklyn boxing gym. She had taken up cardio boxing, mixed in with light sparring, at the Wall Street Gym in Manhattan, and had managed to coax/steal the Gleason's shirt away from one of the guys she'd met there. Today, married, with a baby, and working as a psychiatrist at a busy downtown hospital, she still keeps her old boxing gloves hanging from a hook on a bookshelf in her bedroom. I still don't know exactly why she gave the T-shirt to me. She must have known I'd love it. It comes to my knees, is incredibly soft, and on the back bears Virgil's lines:

> Now, whoever has courage and a strong
> and collected spirit in his breast,
> let him come forward, lace on the
> gloves, and put up his hands.

I wore this shirt to labor in when I gave birth to each of my children. I don't remember ever thinking about it or deciding on it. It just seemed right, that in the act of becoming a mother, I would align myself with fighters. That in this most quintessentially corporeal event, an anguished split between *body* and *goodness* would have to be mended, and a fighting spirit would be required to do so. I recall the unexpected peace of labor as being like the unexpected peace inside the ring: the intense focus, the giving of one's body to work, the giving of one's mind to the body. In a way, I think the day my first child was born—five years before I ever dreamed of walking into a gym—was the day I found out I could box.

"Female physical frailty is not a reality," writes Colette Dowling in *The Frailty Myth,* "but a myth with an agenda." She dissects the ways in which athletic prowess can be evaluated, and shows that buried within the broad claim for men's physiological superiority lies a more complicated tale. On average, men have more lean muscle mass, carry and use more oxygen, and are heavier and taller. On average, women are more flexible, sweat better, adjust to environmental changes better, can endure longer exercise sessions, and are better protected against microtears in muscle tissue. Dowling cites examples from archery, fishing, shooting, fencing, cliff diving, tennis, golf, swimming, jumping, and running to demonstrate that the ability gap between men and women is closing.

"Female strength is, even yet, seditious," writes Natalie Angier in *Woman: An Intimate Geography.* "It can make men squirm." It can make women squirm, too. Angier doesn't try to make the case that women are approaching equality with men in physical strength, but she does point out that among primates, the size and strength difference between the sexes is relatively slight. She shows how context (historical, cultural, political, economic) as much as biology has determined what we think we know about women's strength or lack thereof.

I went to talk with Dr. Sumru Erkut, a research scientist and the associate director of Wellesley College's Center for Research on Women. I went with the purpose of asking about her project on the effects of sports on girls' development, but it was a rather by-the-by remark she made about natural selection that caught my attention. "Women have been selected over the millennium under tremendous pressure," she told me. "There's far greater variability for men, in terms of how they were selected."

I squinted at her. "But isn't it—didn't we learn in school that men were selected mostly for strength? I thought the requirements for male selection were the more extreme, and with women it really was mostly for—wide pelvises? And, like, docility?"

Dr. Erkut allowed that a certain hip structure was important. But she pointed out something I'd never considered before: that relatively weak as well as relatively strong men stood at least a chance at getting their sperm out there. Given the unsanitary conditions under which women gave birth for most of human history, and the consequent high rate of maternal death in childbirth, a woman's progeny would not survive unless she herself was built to withstand what Dr. Erkut calmly referred to as the "assault on the body" of pregnancy, the "trauma" of childbirth, and the long-term "drain" of lactation.

But wasn't a woman's whole reproductive cycle supposed to be natural, and wasn't *natural* supposed to imply gentle, harmless, sort of goddessy and serene? Wasn't that paradigm the key to wresting prenatal and childbirth care back from the male medical profession and into the more holistic hands of midwives and doulas and birthing centers? At the same time, I felt oddly great, hearing those words, aglow with self-worth and pride. Hadn't I been through this "assault" and "trauma" and "drain" repeatedly in recent years? Hadn't I proven myself strong? I was delighted—with the novelty of this notion as much as anything—and also slightly sheepish, as though if I looked deep enough, I would see it wasn't a novelty but something I had known all along.

Raphi stopped coaching that fall, by degrees. She felt bad about it, bad about letting down the girls, but she said she really wanted to spend more time on her marriage. The girls' interest had seemed to be waning over the past few months anyway. It was true that many times she had driven over to Somerville in order to hold practice and then waited around for an hour or more, only to have the girls show up without their gym clothes or not at all. She told me she'd still be going to the gym herself, and said if I wanted to meet her there, she'd work with me, but the offer felt lackluster. Even the way she became reflective about her boxing experience seemed to carry the unmistakable whiff of goodbye.

"I think boxing transformed my life," she wrote to me in October, a year after we'd met. "Just for the outlet it gives me to hit things, mainly."

I had to laugh when I read that. From the lofty to the profane in one short step. That's something I always loved about the gym: the way no one ever tried to gloss the activity that took place within as anything other than what it was.

"I am glad I am not obsessed with [boxing] as I used to be," she went on. "I was putting too much pressure on myself to perform and succeed and do it all for myself and everyone else too. I think through that, in a strange way, it taught me that that is not possible and to let go, of my expectations for myself and others . . . That 'in love' feeling is always temporary and obsessive but eventually you have to ground yourself and remember the rest of your life too."

I read her words, this e-mailed ersatz eulogy for her years in boxing, and cast a desperate eye about for other possible meanings. What expectations did she mean? Her plans for the year had been so grand: lots of bouts for everyone, culminating in a trip to the Nationals. Did she feel a sense of personal responsibility for the fact that it hadn't turned out this way? Or had the dissolution of Nikki and Jacinta's friendship soured her on the idea of the girls' team? Over the course of the year we'd gone ice-skating at Frog Pond and gathered for pizza nights and cookouts and birthday parties; the strength of the group had seemed located as much in the personal connections with one another as in the improvement of our athletic abilities. Did she feel a sense of failure or bitterness at having been unable to hold our group together? Had we, in relying too much on her as our nucleus, overburdened her and thereby let *her* down? Or was Raphi's shift brought on more by the pull of her marriage and its struggles, of which she'd begun to confide to me?

In naming the loss of that "in-love feeling," her message, however rational and optimistic it tried to be, seemed laden with regret—although whether this was an accurate reading of her feelings or simply a projection of mine, I couldn't be sure. A year after meeting her, I was still looking for her to articulate something true about me, and however right a retirement felt for her at this point, for me it was sad if unsurprising news. My own desires railed against it.

We sparred one more time, Raphi and me. Mid-autumn, chilly out, a light rain falling. Inside the gym, Raphi pushed the heat up to 75, but the cavernous room refused to warm very much. By November, we'd learn, the place wouldn't warm up at all, because no one had been paying the oil bill, and the tank was empty.

That day the gym was empty but for the pair of us, and desolate with the scarce natural light coming in through the transom windows, all watery and dim, and the boom box turned up absurdly loud. We kept having to say, "What?" "What?" during our conversation fragments as we jumped rope and stretched. Raphi and I hit the bags for a while, then we got inside the ring and did a round of jabbing and blocking, then a round of sparring, and then we quit. When she took off her headgear, I was gratified to see a plump little strawberry of a bruise next to her right eye. As for me, the inside of my lip felt raw where my mouthguard had slipped and my teeth dug in, and my nose was all sore and wide-feeling from when she'd smashed her fist into the cartilage. No one else showed up, not even any of the guys, so Raphi went around closing everything, shutting everything off, punching in the code to turn on the alarm as we left the place, locking the door behind us.

A day later she wrote me, "Wasn't that fun? I had almost forgotten what it feels like to have my arms and face banged up, to sweat and breathe like that, to be scared and mean at the same time." I thought, Oh, no *way* is she ready to hang up the gloves, no way is she ready to be done with this in her life. But a month later her body took over the task of communicating the curtain speech she'd been issuing in fits and starts all fall. She called Christmas morning with the news that she was pregnant.

Though I knew better, it was hard not to feel bereft, and not to confuse her departure with mine. Raphi insisted otherwise, said there was no reason I couldn't continue boxing, even in competition if I wanted. This seemed far-fetched. Having turned thirty-five, I was now officially excluded from the eighteen-to-thirty-four-year-old bracket. If I were ever to compete, it would have to be in the Masters Division, and how many female boxers over thirty-four could there possibly be in my weight class? Even to continue training and gym sparring would be hard. Raphi approached a few of the Somerville trainers on my behalf, and they demurred politely, on the grounds that they were too busy coaching the boys. I couldn't fault them; the boys were prospects, were potentially going places, the Golden Gloves and beyond. She racked her brain to think of other trainers, at other gyms, whom she would trust to work with a woman. There was one. I left him a couple of messages. He didn't call back.

I tried out the boxing class at the rather spiffy women's health club nearby; this class was semi-famous locally, having been written up on various occasions for being sort of cutting-edge and legitimately tough. I went with as open a mind as I could muster. But the hand wraps were pink and kept in an attractive wicker basket, and although the cardio workout was rigorous, the whole class seemed more about attitude than boxing. When it came time to shadowbox before the mirror, the instructor, who herself had never had a real bout, kept exhorting us to "look mean" and "look meaner." She also reassured us that if we eventually sparred, no one would get hurt. Neither the exhortation nor the reassurance held any value for me.

Oh well, I thought. Really, wasn't it all a bit silly anyway? Here I was, mother of three small children, periodically unnerving people by showing up with a purpled eye. Middle-class white woman, physically wispy by nature and practice, solitary by circumstance and disposition, scrambling to arrange babysitting once or twice a week in order to go *spar*. Wasn't the whole thing, if not unseemly, at least absurd? The thing to do now, I told myself, was be thankful for my taste of pugilism and throw in, so to speak, the towel.

What are the causes to which we enlist our bodies? We employ them for love, for work, for battle. From the earliest days of our kind, this essential trio: sex, toil, combat. And the subaltern uses, among them art and sport, beauty and play. I have danced with my body, unfettered and happy. I have labored with it, washed and cooked, dug and carried, and I have surrendered it to the endeavor of birth and triumphed in what it could bring forth: babies, for whom it then provided milk and solace. But always, even so, my body has felt beside the point, almost literally a thing adjacent to, apart from, *me*. I have tried to lose it, to leave it behind in train and bus stations, as it were, and short of that, to hide it, to disavow it, to deny knowledge of it, responsibility for it, pleasure in it.

Until I got in the ring.

The literature on aggression, even as it focuses on the problems aggression generates, nevertheless is full of the recognition that it cannot be linked exclusively to its most famous offspring: hostility, violence, destruction. Biologists, psychologists, philosophers, and anthropologists have all acknowledged, at various times, its positive aspects. Aggression is implicit in the very act of survival. It is a crucial component of creativity and productivity, of exercising free will and expression, and of developing both the self and positive connection with others. This last is perhaps the least obvious claim: that aggression, rather than subverting relationships, is a necessary part of building and maintaining them. The ethologist Irenäus Eibl-Eibesfeldt calls aggression "a precondition of love and friendship."

One day I found myself confessing to a friend something I had suspected for a while but had been loath to articulate: that all of this boxing stuff might have something to do with sex.

She got a funny sort of smile. "I hadn't realized . . . You mean when you spar, you can feel your juices flowing?"

"No." I was horrified that she misunderstood me this way. "I don't mean I think boxing is *sexy*. I mean I think it has something to do with— Oh, never mind." I meant that coupling and sparring were both about two people expressing and receiving with their bodies. Ideally, both people had power. They were intensely, intimately alone together within the limited confines of a particular series of actions. They committed their bodies to a kind of wordless dialogue. And it didn't seem any real puzzle to figure out which of the two was the more potentially treacherous, and which of the two, by flying its colors clear and high from the outset, was the more innocent.

Sharon Lamb, in *The Secret Lives of Girls*, says the two most important prohibitions for girls, entering the twenty-first century, are against sex and aggression. For women, exhibiting either kind of behavior—sexual or aggressive—is a potentially dangerous transgression. It can be seen as reneging on the promise that, according to Dana Crowley Jack in *Behind the Mask*, extends chivalric protections to women in exchange for their agreeing to be gentle, nurturing, and submissive. To be caught desiring either is to be caught eating forbidden fruit. And the repercussion is to be not only cast out but recast, positioned as something other than purely feminine, at once deprived of and liberated from a certain social compact.

What is sparring if not a kind of coupling? Or turn it around: What is coupling if not a kind of sparring? We come to them both for pleasure and knowledge. We come in the hope of finding ourselves well matched. It is not the same wordless conversation that gets carried out in the ring as in bed, but there are many terms in common, and some of the identical questions lie, inarticulate and urgent, beneath the paired movement and contact of each.

The psychoanalyst Melanie Klein writes of the fusion of erotic and aggressive impulses. She calls this fusion a sign of health. They are intrinsic, these two impulses, to the intangible prescription that keeps us alive. Eros is libido and eros is love, but eros is also the impulse toward life, and without aggression, without that ability to *step toward, with desire,* eros loses, as they say in boxing, its legs. The fusion of eros and aggression is crucial, is perhaps the very quiddity of life.

D. W. Winnicott calls the act of growing up in itself "aggressive." The process requires us repeatedly to test ourselves, pit our energies, with a kind of joy, full force against the world—and, crucially, to have the world survive. If the world seems unable to withstand our aggression—the impression so many girls receive—we learn quickly to tamp it down, stash it away. But without aggression, no less than one's personhood is compromised. The Nobel Laureate in medicine and physiology Konrad Lorenz writes: "If you are devoid of aggressivity, you are not actually an individual."

If we are not fully individuals, how can we possibly connect? We cannot meet, we cannot grow, we cannot love, without aggression.

In January, John Hazard called. He was the trainer Raphi had recommended, the one I'd tried to contact earlier. He owned City Gym in Boston, next to Fenway Park, and during part of the Somerville Boxing Club's homeless period, he had let Raphi train the girls there for free. City Gym isn't a straight-up boxing club; it's more of an all-around gym, with a full battery of weight machines, yoga classes, the works, and because of its location, its clientele is composed largely of college students and young professionals. But there's nothing upscale or sleek about it. Signs posted along the three flights of stairs leading up to the gym tout its affordable membership fee above all: BEST PRICE IN BOSTON.

John had coached, most famously, Joy Liu, who in 2001 won the Women's Nationals, the Women's Continentals, and the Women's National Golden Gloves. Raphi had worked Joy's corner with John at the Women's Nationals in Scranton the same summer Jacinta and Nikki competed. I knew he had a good reputation for training women as well as men. Still, I found myself nervous as we set up an appointment for my first lesson. Some of this had to do with his gender. Some of it had to do with it being private instruction. And some of it had to do with my own initiative. The first time around, I'd been swept up into boxing, and my involvement could be at least partly explained away as research. Now here I was recommitting myself, at some expense (its self-proclaimed cheapness notwithstanding, City Gym doesn't comp its boxing instruction as Somerville inadvertently did). In other words, this time around I was coming as a private person, no strings attached. I showed up for that first lesson exposed, unmasked by any rationale for this pursuit other than my own desire.

John Hazard began boxing more than four decades ago, when he was five. He wore kid-size gloves, and his father would get down on his knees and teach him the punches. At age eight he began boxing in a church basement, where the coach was a priest. He was a Silver Mittens champion and later a U.S. Armed Forces champion. He is compact and muscular, with dark coloring and watchful eyes. His last name and some of his blood are Native American; mostly he's Italian. He loves to talk and he loves to listen. He studied psychology for a while in college, and worked in a hospital for the mentally ill. He once commented that being a boxing coach is a little like being a bartender, for all the tales of hurt he hears.

Before my first lesson, in the boxing room at the back of the gym, I wrapped my hands. There were two heavy bags, a double-end bag, two speed bags, a hook for jump ropes. A boom box and a time clock. A wall of frosted windows and a wall of mirrors. Boxing photos and poster-size boxing sketches on the remaining walls. No ring, the room being much too small. I warmed up: some stretches, a couple rounds of jump rope. It had been months since I practiced in Somerville, and I was a bit winded by the time John came in. The first thing he had me do was shadowbox in front of the mirror while he watched. The worst thing he could have asked.

I never shadowboxed in Somerville. Sometimes Raphi would tell us to, but then she'd be busy in the ring holding the mitts for someone else, and we'd all drift away from our reflections well before the round bell. I always felt at my most ridiculous shadowboxing before the mirror.

Once Raphi handed me some snapshots of myself sparring with Sefina, and I was nearly paralyzed with disbelief. "Is this me?" I had to ask her, really in fact not knowing, needing her to confirm it before I could believe. The face in the photo was obscured by headgear and mouthguard and the fact that the chin was tucked, but I thought I could recognize my hair hanging down in back. The left arm, however, frozen in full extension, did not look familiar to me; it was the picture of authority, powerful and crisply defined. "Yeah," said Raphi. "I know, I love those jab pictures; everybody looks great throwing a jab." So I was slightly deflated, but only very slightly, because it was true: *Damn* if I didn't look good throwing a jab! "I know how you feel," she added kindly. "I fell in love with my first boxing pictures, too."

But standing before the mirrors in John Hazard's little boxing room, with him leaning up against the radiator, arms folded across his chest, watching, I was so nervous I wanted to go home. I wanted to unwrap my hands and apologize for my mistake in coming. "Just . . . throw combinations?" I asked stupidly.

"Yeah. What's the matter?"

"Nothing, I just . . . sorry . . . I hate shadowboxing."

He was not surprised. Women, he said, almost always hate practicing before the mirror. "I don't know why that is. Guys love it," he added cheerfully. "Go."

So I went, and he watched and narrated softly. "Nice straight jab . . . look at that reach . . . you're not turning the hip . . . do that again, right cross . . . yeah, you're not turning the hip . . . try that again . . . turn the hip over . . . see that?" Over and over I threw the four basic punches, and then just the first two, and then just my right, over and over, and then that in slow motion, until I was turning the hip properly each time. Then I did another round, and another. "I can't hear, are you breathing?" he asked at one point. He meant breathing in the boxerly sense, the sharp exhale through the mouth that's supposed to accompany each punch; I had not been, quite. The art of audible breath was as much a struggle for me as watching myself throw punches in the mirror. Frustrated with myself, I answered him by making myself do it. The thirty-second bell sounded, and I gathered up my reserves for a final half-minute barrage, scowling eye-to-eye with myself: truly, facing my real opponent.

I trained with him more or less weekly after that. I surprised him with how hard I hit the mitts. My footwork was terrible, and he was patient and smart about deciphering the causes: my stance a little wide; my pivot not tight enough; my tendency to initiate movement with my back leg instead of pushing off with my front. For every weakness, he taught me a drill. I'd go a half hour early to work out on my own; lessons with John meant a full hour of individual attention, with no downtime for hand weights, speed bag, jump rope, the like. I missed the camaraderie of Somerville, the dramas and antics of Raphi and Maria and the girls, missed the feeling of working out with a team. But I was training much harder than I had during the previous year. Slowly I was improving.

I began to be able to shadowbox round after round without really caring what I looked like—well, caring about whether I was dropping my hand a fraction before I threw my jab, or whether I was turning the foot as well as the hip when I threw a left hook, but no longer concerned with the total picture, the visual representation of the *idea* of it. I began to be able to jump rope round after round without getting a stitch in my side or wondering how many more seconds until the bell would ring and release me from the lung-burning monotony. When John, holding the mitts, would rattle off a combination—"One two duck two three four three"—I didn't need time to process it but could produce it instantly, my body knowing the language.

He taught me to watch his eyes while he held the mitts, not his hands. Raphi had a different style. She made it a rule never to look into her opponents' eyes; she felt it gave them a kind of power over her, a power to rattle her, to psych her out. But John said you could read the most valuable information by looking nowhere else than the eyes, and so his eyes became a kind of resting place for my eyes as we moved about the room. I learned to anticipate when he would change direction or suddenly hold the mitts up, giving me an opening to throw my combination. On occasion he would say something mildly flirtatious, in the manner of men to women, and I would begin to flee the scene, to vacate my body and gaze on from above. But inevitably I would return; he was too good a teacher, and I was too hungry for learning, to whisk myself away for long. It was a comfort to me that he was married, and that from what I could witness, he engaged fully and equally with all his students; his interest seemed solidly in teaching. I began to really trust him. The physical self I brought to him for instruction grew less inhibited, more driven. In this way, over time, I was able to eke out a relationship with a man that was more unabashedly physical than anything else, yet safe and clear, clear and free. Perhaps it was like what Raphi had experienced with her old coaches, Franky and Ralphy. A revelation.

John was surprised that I didn't have my own gloves. "At Somerville we always just used whatever we could find," I explained. Raphi had a few pairs she let us take turns with, and there was a big pile of variously ripped and duct-taped gloves over in the corner near the door. He said that was like sharing shoes, that boxing gloves eventually mold themselves to the shape of your own hands, and they fit best when you don't trade them around. Besides, he said, didn't I find it kind of disgusting, ramming my hand into the dank recesses of a communally sweaty glove? He sold me a pair of black-and-white sixteen-ounce Ringside bag gloves that smelled like a new car. I was secretly thrilled to shell out the thirty-five bucks. I had trouble sometimes with jamming my wrists and hurting my knuckles, so he made me a little present of a pair of Mexican hand wraps—sixty inches longer than the kind I'd been using, with some stretchy stuff blended into the cotton for a better fit. He started taping my hands, too, to hold the wraps in place. After enough badgering from John, I went out and bought my own jump rope so I could keep up my wind at home in between practices. He would laugh at me for stuffing all my gear into the old diaper bag I'd been toting around forever; finally I chucked the ratty thing and got a real gym bag. Carrying it to practice for the first time, I felt like such a total jock.

All this time I was going crazy, wondering when he'd put me up against a real opponent. John would mention, from time to time, the other women he trained. He'd tell me a story about a sparring session they all had. Or I'd meet one of them at the beginning or end of a lesson. I'd notice how we sized each other up, even as we smiled and shook hands; we'd be checking out each other's height and build. It was March before John asked me one day, "Do you know how much you weigh?"

My heart leaped, because I knew what he meant. "On your scale, today, a hundred and three."

"I train someone who's about your size, a few inches shorter, a hundred and five, a hundred and ten, somewhere in there."

"Does she spar?"

"*Oh* yeah. She can't get enough. She hasn't been training all that long, but pound for pound, she's the most aggressive fighter I have right now."

Kimber Brown was a college freshman with a long straw-colored ponytail, wide, almond-shaped blue eyes, and biceps like river rocks. She worked at the gym part-time, behind the desk. I met her once before we sparred, just to say hello. She was neither friendly nor unfriendly.

It took a few weeks to find a Saturday when we could both come in. It was April by then, a good seven months since I'd last sparred, under entirely different circumstances. As Kimber and I warmed up, jumping rope and shadowboxing in the slant of early-spring sunlight, I tried not to watch her. She threw tight, sharp combinations in the air, emitting whiplike breaths through her teeth. I decided to focus on the absence of a ring. At City Gym, boxers sparred in the large exercise room where yoga and aerobics classes were held. In Somerville, Raphi wouldn't let us spar outside of the ring. One time when Nikki and I had planned on sparring and it was clear the men were going to be monopolizing the ring for some time, we suggested doing it on the floor, but Raphi said no, it wasn't a good idea to spar in an open space, without the frame. At the time, she indicated that it wasn't a realistic way to prepare for competition; plus, she didn't want us tripping over the edge of the rubber exercise mats, but I wonder if it wasn't the metaphor of the ring she felt uneasy letting us box without. I wonder, too, whether my preoccupation with the absence of a ring at City Gym wasn't in some way a worry about the absence of frame in this metaphorical sense. If part of boxing's appeal is its directness and clarity about what it entails, then erasing the absolute demarcations of the ring, the famous squared circle made manifest with ropes, is disorienting.

John was there, of course. He had once instructed me, unnecessarily, never to spar when he wasn't present. In the weeks leading up to this, he had told me, too, that sparring was for learning, and that he would always stop a sparring session if it looked like it was getting dangerous, physically or psychologically. He told me that if he saw me covering up and turning away from the fight, he would stop it. He told me that Kimber was a scrappy fighter who liked to charge her opponent. He repeated that he wouldn't let a sparring session get out of control. He was driving me bananas; obviously he was worried.

The other person there that afternoon was Joy Liu, the national champion herself. There were pictures of her, laminated newspaper and magazine clippings, posted behind the front desk, and John talked about her in such a way that I almost felt I knew her, though I had not yet met her in person. I liked her immediately. Joy is one of those boxing oddities, a graduate of Harvard and Columbia Law, currently working as a corporate attorney in Boston. She's tall and rangy, a junior welterweight at five-feet-ten; she carries herself large. Irreverent, funny, she begins every other sentence with "dude." She talked about the hot-dog festival at Suffolk Downs that she was planning to attend the next day. "They're going to have fifty different kinds of hot dogs," she announced. "Dude, I love hot dogs."

In 2001, Joy had made it as far as the first Women's Internationals, where she lost to a Swedish woman after both of her contact lenses fell out in the first round. ("In the event of a boxer's glove or dress becoming undone during boxing, the referee shall stop the contest to have it attended to," says the rule book, but no such provision extends to contacts.) She no longer boxed in competition; since getting mired in the grueling hours of a rookie lawyer in a big corporation, she was no longer boxing at all, so I was surprised to see her there that morning. John was delighted; obviously, he'd missed her. They dogged each other verbally back and forth, in a way that was light and funny and helped me relax, until John, fastening the strap of my headgear under my chin, peered in at me with some concern and said, "Are you nervous?" I wanted to slug him.

"A little." I shrugged. "I don't like this headgear, though." It covered more of the face than the kind we used in Somerville, with extra wings of leather that curved out under the eye, nearly meeting at the nose. "I can *see* it."

He adjusted it slightly on my head. "Is that better? This is the good kind of headgear, really. Can you see now?"

"Yeah." Whatever, I just wanted to start. He put on my gloves, laced and tied them, taped over the ends. Then he had to rag on Joy for taking so long to lace on Kimber's, and she had to counterquip, and then John said, "Ready?," and Kimber and I got our mouthguards in and moved over to the center of the floor space, and John started the clock.

We touched gloves and immediately began to circle. I watched her eyes watching me, blue and wide and serious. We were not friends. We were not enemies. We were strangers, mostly, who'd made a pact. I didn't know her reasons for being there; she didn't know mine. Nor did it matter. We began to trade blows. She hit hard; there was something more concentrated and unrelenting in her blows than I had experienced before. I used my jab. My reach was longer. She was squaring off as she rushed me, offering me her face full on. She knocked my head back, and my headgear twisted sideways and up. She waited, watchful, for a second while I shoved it back on, hard. "Are you okay?" John asked. "Yeah." We traded more blows. She got in several punches to my body. My knowledge of the awfulness of body shots was worse than the actual feeling of these; I didn't mind them, somehow. I felt dull regret at having left myself open to them, and that was all. We got out of the clinch, and again John asked, "Are you all right?" "Yeah."

Midway through the round, I saw blood coming from her nose. I had never seen blood on my opponents before. She must have felt it, because I saw her glance at the wall of mirrors as we danced past. I was almost certain that it made her angry, the sight of her own blood, because she seemed to return to the fight with a more acute fury. "Getting wild," cautioned John a moment later. We both backed off for a moment, resumed circling. The thirty-second bell. Our eyes were locked. I could see her timing me even as I was timing her. Another exchange; we got into it just as the bell sounded, and neither of us wanted to break then. We did, though, reluctantly.

With no sense of favoritism, Joy worked my corner, and John, Kimber's. The next time we sparred, it could easily be the other way around. But as he lowered his voice to talk to her, it was a little odd knowing that he was giving her tips on how to get the better of me. I wondered whether he'd come before the bell and offer me any advice. It was an odd room to box in, so different from Somerville. Instead of being at our neutral corners, the towels and bucket and water had all been laid out neatly on the square platform used by, I supposed, yoga and aerobic instructors. A large disco ball hung overhead. People using the exercise machines out in the next room could, and did, view us through a long rectangular window. Because it wasn't exclusively a boxing gym, there was the sense that our sparring was exotic to some of the men and women using the treadmills and weights in the next room. And because we were women before a small audience, I wanted that much more to box well, to make it impossible for spectators to regard us as an amusing curiosity.

John worked on Kimber's nose, tipping her head back and pressing the towel against her nostrils. Joy gave me water and tried to get me to take deep breaths. "Breathe in for a count of three," she ordered, counting out loud for me. I panted in and out about eight times. "All right," she said. She was great, all business. I stopped minding that John was with Kimber. "You're throwing the jab like this, and you're leaving your face wide open. Keep your chin tucked behind your shoulder, because she's getting you back every time. And keep throwing the jab. Two jabs and a right. Just keep firing it. One, one, two."

We went out and did two more hard rounds. Joy and John coached us from the sides. When we finished, Kimber and I hugged and thanked each other, and she apologized for getting her blood on me—it was on my T-shirt and arms—and I told her she was the hardest sparring partner I'd had. Later John would tell me that she was the hardest sparring partner I'd be likely to have, or even to face in competition. Various planes and patches of my body would hurt the next day.

There were things I wasn't happy about—in practice, John had been working with me on counterpunches and reaction punches, and I hadn't managed to use them at all in sparring. Also, my wind wasn't as good as I'd like, and my movement, I knew, still stank. Yet I also knew that Kimber hadn't pulled her punches with me. Her energy and focus were fierce. Every second in the ring with her had been a test of bravery, of heart. I slept well that night.

When John and I went over the session, he said he couldn't believe how hard we'd both sparred. A few times, after a particularly hard shot, he'd been tensed, ready to step in and stop us, and he said he was impressed that we both kept going. But, he added, we both had the same problem. Neither of us liked to move. We stood and traded blows, made ourselves easy targets, and didn't bob and weave and pivot enough. He said he wanted to work with me on the ring style Joy Liu had used so successfully.

The one time I saw Joy spar, I was inspired. She went five rounds with two different opponents, a man and a woman, and in spite of the fact that she hadn't been training regularly since becoming a lawyer, she boxed circles around them, almost literally, for her style in the ring was all about movement. John had told me she hated to get hit like a cat hates to get wet, which struck me as funny, what with her being a boxer.

But when I saw her spar one day, right after Kimber and I had gone three rounds and were sitting on the platform under the disco ball, sweaty and bruised, I saw what he meant. Joy seemed to float and glide out of reach of her sparring partners, almost like a skimmer bug on the surface of a pond, holding them off with her commanding jab, hardly ever firing a right, never throwing a hook or uppercut; she was never in close enough to do so.

John got me working in a similar vein. My physique suggested it. With a low weight relative to my height, I would, like Joy, tend to be taller than my opponents, with a longer reach and a naturally long stride. It made sense to take advantage of these factors, use them to hold my opponents at bay, to move around and make them try to get past my jab. The problem was, when I tried it in the ring, it was disastrous. My mental game crumbled. I felt I was trying to escape an attacker, only I never would. True enough, Kimber charged in relentlessly, repeatedly, and I got tangled in my feet, was afraid, almost panicky, and wandered away in my mind.

It was near the end of the third round. She threw a beautiful right into my solar plexus, and I felt a metal-tinged torquing sensation all through the right side of my body. That was it. We stopped before the bell; John stepped in and asked me if I wanted to keep going, and I shook my head, then fought back tears for the rest of the morning, furious with myself for my weakness.

John and I reassessed the situation after that, agreed that in spite of my build, my mental disposition dictated a more aggressive ring style. As soon as we'd come to that understanding, I settled much more comfortably into training and successive sparring sessions. The odd thing is that my instinct in the ring is the opposite of that in the rest of my life. In the ring I feel no compulsion to slip away, to elide, to turn myself into a mirror trick. I am impelled rather to plant myself, to remain, and represent myself through my oldest, most intimate adversary: my body.

I face myself in the mirror and slip the blows of my own reflection. Nikki knocks her coach out cold and then turns into a little girl, thin-voiced and sorry, balancing her weight on one foot. Jacinta and Nikki pen a notebook full of love songs and then stop speaking to each other.

Candi says she wants to hit a boy and then asks Raphi if she still loves her. Sefina threatens to step on a moth and then gets down on all fours, picks it up by a single wing, carries it out the back door, and blows it from her palm into the black velvet sky.

To and fro. Back and forth. This is a constant motion for me, like the rhythm of the sea. I run to the edge of the water, and when the foam laps close to my feet, I run away. I play this game with my body in the world, only it's more real than a game. I know this by the constricting of my throat, the quick hollow sensation beneath my ribs. There is a need to evacuate, to hurtle headlong backward and away. And there is a desire, guarded but tough, to stay. To come forward.

I visit Raphi and her baby boy, just home from the hospital. There are milk and flowers everywhere. Richie is not around. Raphi is very tender with her baby. He suckles and spits up, suckles and spits up, and everything smells sweet. The Rodriguezes had gone to visit her in the hospital. She shows me a funny picture of Candi in the hospital room, wearing a surgical mask and looking fierce. Raphi doesn't see their family often these days, so it was a rare treat for them all to be gathered together.

When I tell her about sparring with Kimber, she allows that sparring is something she misses, but says it feels very far away, and her voice itself sounds distant when she says this, mild and without immediate hunger, as though even imagining sparring is incompatible with her life these days.

I miss her. From the moment I first laid eyes on her, standing on the ring apron, built slight as my twin but carrying herself with defiant solidity, her presence had constituted a personal challenge. And in all the months that followed, she had extended that challenge to me with complete generosity.

She seems smaller now, more fragile, within her domestic boundaries, her increasingly troubled marriage. I wish she were fighting still, coaching at least. I look at her and think of myself several years back, tethered within a similar framework, vanishing into a kind of compliance, almost literally disappearing before my own eyes. I know it's natural for people to move in and out of periods of strength and weakness in their lives. I know Raphi's toughness and her will have not deserted her. She tells me she dreams of going back to boxing, that she still hopes to open her own gym someday. I am hopeful for her.

As for the girls, none of them boxes anymore. A couple of weeks ago I took Nikki swimming at Walden Pond. We were with my children and a friend of hers. She asked me if she was allowed to go out beyond the ropes, and I said she was. Her seal head, wet and sleek, bobbed in and out of sight for a while. Then she came back to us. She showed my children how to do handstands underwater, and we made drip castles and ate melon and sandwiches on the beach while the sun lowered heavily behind the fringe of trees.

She credits boxing, in part, with getting her through a difficult season relatively intact. She says it helped her to grow up and feel at peace. The difference between Nikki when I met her and Nikki now is that once she seemed at the mercy of her aggressive impulses, and now she seems to control them so that they nourish her strength. Even Nikki's posture has changed; she no longer appears to be shrinking away from her full height and breadth. There's a poignancy about Raphi's diminution, her choosing to step back just as Nikki is coming into sharper focus, forging a clear and hungry path ahead. There's a timeless feeling about it, too: the idealized image of the teacher shifting into something more complex as the student steps closer to embodying her own ideal.

The Rodriguez sisters' paths look a little ambiguous, lined alternately with victories and defeats, good grades and bad grades, minor run-ins with local law enforcement and narrow escapes from shady neighborhood characters. I wonder how much a year and a half in a boxing gym can do to arm them against the threats they will face en route from girlhood to womanhood. But both Nikki and the Rodriguez sisters, although they do not speak anymore, remain unanimous on this point: that before boxing they got into fights constantly—at school, on the street, in playgrounds, back lots, anywhere—and that since boxing they don't, a fact they report with pride and relief. When asked why they think this is, they dutifully prattle off rote sound bites about discipline and self-control.

It is something Jacinta happened to say months earlier, in a different conversation, that provides real insight. "In the ring," she told me, "I feel safe, very safe—I feel as if I won't hurt people that much because of the rules and boundaries of boxing." What is so extraordinary to me about this statement is the fact that she chooses to define safety as feeling *safe from hurting others*. This is a girl who lives in a neighborhood where rape, assault, and gun violence are reported in the news more or less routinely. But she is clear. The safety she craves most is the safety to let go, to unleash all her body's power without fear of it being too much. The freedom to bring forth every aspect of herself and hold nothing back. In delivering this, boxing offers something invaluable to girls.

With these words, Jacinta shows me our common ground. The girls, Raphi, Maria, and me. We are from vastly different backgrounds. Our past relationships to our own aggression could not be more dissimilar. But there was one thing none of us could find until we got inside the ring. Having tasted it there, we may recognize it forever and seek to find it in other places—or to bring it other places, since it is something we carry within us: namely, our whole selves, with no apology.

How odd that I'm the only one of us still boxing! I suppose it means I'm still listening for what it has to tell me. Its promise about what a woman can be is not yet something I can retain without the physical reminder. When I have to miss a few weeks at the gym, I feel an aspect of myself begin to fade, like a mirage, like something that was never real to begin with. I lose a few pounds; even my voice seems less substantial. I sleep fitfully, and in my dreams I waft like smoke. Each time I return to the gym, it's as though I recover substance, ferocity, vigor.

Kimber and I keep sparring when we can. The last time I gave her another bloody nose and she gave me a black eye, and we stood side by side in the bathroom afterward, washing the Vaseline and sweat and blood off our faces. She offered me some of her apricot facial scrub. She wants to train hard this fall, to get ready for the Golden Gloves. I asked John if he'd let me work her corner with him, and he said yes. He said nobody at the gym spars as hard as the two of us together, because neither of us likes to back down. "You know how they say 'Styles make fights'? That's you and Kimber." He shakes his head, grinning. "You battle. You both like to stand in the pocket and fight."

Today, after saying goodbye to Raphi and her baby, I go to the gym. It is a fine day, rare, a tang of autumn in the air. I have no appointment for a lesson; the gym is all but empty. I wrap my hands, put my water bottle on the windowsill, turn on the time clock, do three rounds of jump rope. The nylon rope smacks the floor like a firecracker. I stretch, shadowbox three rounds in front of the mirror, my breath singing finely through my lips on every punch. I make a little story out of each round, not a story but a game plan, an imagined opponent and the footwork and weaving and punches I would employ. *Work tight, work small.* John's voice in my head. *Throw it out straight, don't drop the arm. Turn the foot.* The time clock keeps sounding, pulling me out of the story, the physical narrative, setting me up for the next one. A drink of water, warm and sweet. The front of my shirt darkly speckled with sweat. Walk around, walk around. My hands like glowing embers in their gloves. Wait for the bell. Bell. I work the double-end bag, moving in, moving out, circling it, circling back. Bob and weave. *Keep your chin down. Double jab. Stick it!* Stretching out between rounds. The spun gold streaming in the open windows, the promise of coming apples, coming wood smoke. I strike the heavy bag. Two jabs and a right, push off out of range and then fast back in for another one, two, step in, three. Two years ago at this time I dreamed of leaving my body forever. Bell. Two more rounds on the heavy bag. I set it swinging, court and dodge it, pound and pummel it, face it and pivot away. I work on the double hook John showed me: one to the body, one to the head. One, two, hook low, hook high. *Get in close! Commit!* Bell. My arms ache. I pull off my gloves, toss them toward my gym bag. I swig more water. I am wet all over and bathed in heat, in saffron and yellow and rose. *Finish with the speed bag.* John's routine. I go over to the tear-shaped bag, wait for the bell, work up a rhythm. *Chuddica chuddica chuddica.* The bag and my fists go to and fro, they meet and part, meet and part. The bag is a blur I cannot see. It's as though all of myself has converged in my body. I might almost trust it to be true.

ACKNOWLEDGMENTS

I will forever be grateful to Anne Rearick for leading me into the Somerville Boxing Club.

From the bottom of my heart I thank Raphaëlla Cruz and the four girls she trained between the autumns of 2001 and 2002. What they and their families offered me as a reporter and a person is a gift I will always treasure.

I thank everyone affiliated with the Somerville Boxing Club who welcomed me and helped with this project, especially Ann Cooper and all the kids whose names I do not use here, and also John Curran, Richardson Cruz, Jerry Lee Johnson, Tommy Mari, Moses Matovu, Gene McCarthy, Mark Nolan, Ralph Palmacci, Sr., John Ruiz, Sahara Ruiz, Marshall Simpson, Linda Stone, Norman Stone, Ann Marie Toland-Francey, Desmond Tyler, Doug Yoffe, and Dr. Patty Yoffe. Thanks to Beth Bolero, Barrington Edwards, Kathleen Marsh, Sunny Pai, and Abigail Parrilla of the Boston Arts Academy; Arthur Romalho, Dave Romalho, and the completely lovely Dan Perreault of the Lowell Golden Gloves; Irene Postma and Julie Goldsticker of USA Boxing; Melanie Ley of amateurboxing.com; the Center for Documentary Studies at Duke University; Katie Wheeler of Girls' Coalition; Christina Matheson and Rachel Goldstein of CityPlays; Alison Amoroso of Teen Voices; Alecia Humphrey of the Girl Scouts; Shruti Desai of the EdLaw Project;

Dr. Sumru Erkut of the Center for Research on Women; Dr. Deborah Prothrow-Stith and Marci Feldman of Harvard's Youth Violence Prevention Center; Dr. Robert Sege of the Harvard Injury Control Research Center; Ronald Slaby of the Center for Violence Prevention and Control; and Dr. Peter Stringham of East Boston Neighborhood Health Center. My great thanks to John Hazard.

I am grateful to—and for—my editor, Ileene "TKO" Smith; her assistant, Robin Rolewicz; my agent and friend of over a dozen years, Barney Karpfinger; his colleague, the beautifully unflappable Laurie Marcus; Idé O'Carroll, Tina Rathbone, and Annie Rogers; my family; and Lori Lyn Taylor, to whom this book is lovingly and rightfully dedicated.

Finally I thank everyone who has sparred with me, in or out of the ring. Mike.

ABOUT THE AUTHOR

LEAH HAGER COHEN is the author of the nonfiction works *Train Go Sorry: Inside a Deaf World; Glass, Paper, Beans: Revelations on the Nature and Value of Ordinary Things;* and *The Stuff of Dreams: Behind the Scenes of an American Community Theater,* as well as two novels, *Heat Lightning* and *Heart, You Bully, You Punk.* She lives near Boston with her three children.

A NOTE ON THE TYPE

This book was set in Fairfield, the first typeface from the hand of the distinguished American artist and engraver Rudolph Ruzicka (1881–1978). In its structure Fairfield displays the sober and sane qualities of the master craftsman whose talent has long been dedicated to clarity. It is this trait that accounts for the trim grace and vigor, the spirited design and sensitive balance, of this original typeface.

Rudolph Ruzicka was born in Bohemia and came to America in 1894. He set up his own shop, devoted to wood engraving and printing, in New York in 1913 after a varied career working as a wood engraver, in photoengraving and banknote printing plants, and as an art director and freelance artist. He designed and illustrated many books, and was the creator of a considerable list of individual prints—wood engravings, line engravings on copper, and aquatints.